World University Library

The World University Library is an international series
of books, each of which has been specially commissioned.
The authors are leading scientists and scholars from all over
the world who, in an age of increasing specialization, see the
need for a broad, up-to-date presentation of their subject.
The aim is to provide authoritative introductory books for
university students which will be of interest also to the general
reader. Publication of the series takes place in Britain,
France, Germany, Holland, Italy, Spain, Sweden and
the United States.

Frontispiece Knocker of the door of the Royal Chapel at
Aix-la-Chapelle. Lion's head in bronze. Ninth century.

Jacques Boussard

The Civilization of Charlemagne

translated from the French
by Frances Partridge

World University Library

McGraw-Hill Book Company
New York Toronto

© Jacques Boussard 1968
Translation © George Weidenfeld and Nicolson Limited 1968
Library of Congress Catalog Card Number 67-26357
Phototypeset by BAS Printers Limited, Wallop, Hampshire. England
Printed by Officine Grafiche Arnoldo Mondadori, Verona. Italy

Contents

List of maps

1 Origins

Europe at the end of the seventh century

The reign of the Carolingian dynasty over western Europe began officially in 754, but its origins can be more accurately dated from 714, when its leaders initiated the task of organisation which was to change the structure of society and lead to the birth of a new civilisation. The Frankish princes of this dynasty left their mark on the whole of Europe, and in many respects on the whole world. The ground was prepared for this transformation during the first quarter of the eighth century.

The unification of the Frankish kingdoms, begun in 717 by Charles Martel, was not an isolated phenomenon. At the beginning of the eighth century we find the same desires for organisation, the same aspirations to order and unity, all over Europe. It was in 717 that the Moorish peril first declared itself, when the Moslems, after driving the Byzantine Greeks out of Africa, reached the Pyrenees and threatened to cross them. In the East, an outstanding leader, Leo the Isaurian, acceded to the Empire and re-established the State. In Great Britain, Aethelbald was gathering Angles, Jutes and Saxons under his rule. In Italy, Liutprand undertook the task of subduing the Lombard duchies in 712, and formed them into a single kingdom under his hegemony. Gregory II had been head of the Church since 715, and had followed up his successful conversion of England in the previous century by launching a great missionary movement to take Christianity to Frisia and Germany.

But threatened and divided though it might be, Europe was full of youthful vitality, and there were latent defensive impulses everywhere, needing only brave leaders to direct them, not of course in order to recreate the organisation of the Roman Empire, but to create a new form of society based upon it.

Almost nothing now remained of the Roman civilisation that had once moulded Europe. In the course of three centuries it had completely crumbled. Since 275, Gaul and Italy had been subjected to repeated invasions, and anarchy reigned in both. Faced with the impossibility of keeping the barbarians from crossing their frontiers, the emperors had adopted the expedient of making allies of them, integrating them within the Empire, and entrusting them with its defence. In 334 this task was given to the Sarmatians and Vandals. In 350 the Salian Franks, an obscure Germanic tribe, had occupied Toxandria, the region north of the mouths of the rivers Scheldt, Meuse and Rhine, and in 358 Julian acknowledged their possession of this territory. Vandals, Suevi, Visigoths, Burgundians, Huns, Ostragoths and Heruli had each in turn invaded the West during the fifth century. The Roman army no longer existed. Emperors were created and deposed by the barbarians. In 476, Odoacer, chief of the Heruli, had made himself master of Italy, assassinated the Emperor Orestes and proclaimed and afterwards deposed his son Romulus Augustulus. The Western Empire ceased to exist even as a fiction after this date. The Roman world was divided among tribes occupying regions of varying size: the only race that seems to have possessed a kingdom with some semblance of organisation as a State was that of the Visigoths, who had been ruled over since 466 by a remarkable man called Euric. Ruler of southern Gaul, he conquered the provinces of Berry, Limousin, Velay and Auvergne, and governed them in a more or less orderly manner, thus preparing the way for the province of Aquitaine, which was to preserve its almost national status in the heart of the Carolingian realm until the tenth century.

All that now remained of the Empire was a little kingdom situated between the Loire and the Somme, where the authority of a 'Roman' was still recognised; here, at Soissons, Syagrius, son of Count Aegidius, took the titles of king, duke and head of the army in turn, and retained his independence though surrounded by barbarian kingdoms. This territory was the headquarters of Clovis and his descendants, and later at the beginning of the tenth century it became the 'Duchy of France' and the nucleus of the kingdom of the Capets. Finding themselves barred to the south-east by the impenetrable barrier of the forest of Charbonnière and the Ardennes, the Salian Franks infiltrated unnoticed towards the south, until the day came when their forceful leader Clovis led them in a prodigious campaign of expansion across the Rhine and as far as the Alps and the Pyrenees.

Frankish royalty and nobility

The unity of Gaul and its dependencies had now been re-established and was to last for two centuries: although it was a theoretical unity, under the domination of the most powerful of its peoples, the *regnum Francorum* was universally accepted as a reality. There was no question of political unity, nor of its constitution as a State. The conquered territories were administered as the inherited property or patrimony of the reigning house, the dynasty descended from Meroveus. Each heir had a right to a share, and this became his kingdom. The concept of the State had so completely given way to that of patrimony that whenever a partition took place, the sole consideration was that the shares should bring in equal revenues, without thought for the population, their wishes or ethnic relationships, or for geography and communications.

Not only had the idea of the State been abolished, but a radical change took place in the very concept of government. The Roman emperor had been a magistrate, to whom, in the interests of the public good as expressed in the maintenance of the law, the Romans had entrusted *auctoritas*, or absolute authority, as well as *potestas*, or effective power. In place of this philosophical and judicial notion of power, a Germanic concept was now adopted, according to which the king exercised actual power, and his subjects owed him the same obedience as soldiers do to their general; this was the idea of *Gefolgschaft*, or fidelity to the leader. It was an idea which was at one with the notion that the king was also essentially a judge and that, as leader, he could set up an administration. He was also the richest of the Franks and he shared his riches with his men. The decadence and collapse of the Merovingian dynasty coincided with the impoverishment of its leaders, for their estates had dwindled and they could no longer win loyalty with gifts of land. There was no suggestion that any superior jurisdiction could exist: the king's power was absolute; he disposed of the lives and possessions of his subjects and was their incarnation and representative. However this primitive concept of monarchy began to be modified during the seventh century: it was very slowly absorbing Christian ideas. The Franks, who had been Christians since the reign of Clovis (481–511), admitted that the king could not act on pure caprice, but held that God had entrusted him with power to be used for the common good; they were beginning to have a glimmering of the idea that followed logically from this theory – that charism, or special grace of God, was one of the foundations of the king's power. But this Christian view of power was still extremely vague, and was first applied to the kings of the Carolingian dynasty. During the whole of the preceding period, right up to the middle of the seventh century, we find the Germanic notion of *Gefolgschaft* (or actual power combined with the personal obligation of subjects) existing among the ruins of the old theories of power, now remembered only by the popes. The germ of a rudimentary State existed in the king's 'palace', that is to say the somewhat chaotic organisation which helped him administer his treasury and see that justice was done and the laws enforced, while the religious life of his court was centred in the Royal Chapel, where 'St Martin's cape' was preserved – a famous relic believed to protect the Frankish royal family, and which had become the nucleus of worship.

All the kingdoms of the *regnum Francorum* ruled over by these omnipotent monarchs shared the same form of social structure. It was the result of repeated invasions, and the subjection of a population with an ancient but extremely decadent civilisation to uncouth barbarians. When they first reached the West, the Germans found the Gallo-Roman nobility firmly established in often vast domains populated by simple peasants, under the control of the local authorities who had gradually taken over from the officers of the Empire the task of making them pay taxes and carry out military service. The master of a large domain, the *potens*, lived in his *villa* and maintained a tight control over his peasants or *coloni*, who were bound to the land they were cultivating by a law

Binding of Theodolinda's Evangeliary, end of the sixth century. Monza, Basilica of San Giovanni Battista. Cloisonné encrusted with antique cameos. The book was probably offered to Queen Theodolinda of Lombardy by Pope Gregory the Great at the time of the conversion of her son, Adaloald.

emanating from the central government of the Byzantine Empire. The onerous task of administering the towns fell to the urban nobility. The Church had at first established itself in the towns only, but later, as a result of the rural missions of St Martin and his followers, in country places too where paganism still had deep roots.

The Germans had to some extent respected the existing order, but local authority and a large proportion of the revenues from the land had fallen into their hands as a result of a system of 'hospitality', by which land was divided between its original owners and the newcomers. Fusion of the two took place extremely rapidly, since the Germans did not go in for racial or social segregation in any form, and official duties – even in the king's house or personal guard – could therefore be entrusted impartially to Romans or barbarians, freemen or former slaves. At the end of the seventh century, no social difference between the descendants of conquerors and conquered existed in the West; the aristocracy were hardly aware of their own origins, nor could it be said that a hereditary nobility really existed: social rank depended solely on wealth, official duties, individual merit and the king's goodwill. The inferior social classes, who were indifferent to change of master and had no political influence, had no reason to feel repugnance for the new régime, and easily took to German customs and manners; it is impossible for the historian to be sure whether the owner of a Germanic name came of German or Gallo-Roman stock.

In legal matters, however, there were signs of discrimination. The essential principles of Germanic legislation were national legal status and pecuniary compensation: everyone had to be judged according to the law of his race rather than that of the country where he lived. And again, everyone except a slave was let off the penalty for his misdemeanour or crime in return for payment of a sum of money (*wergeld*) proportionate to the offence or its results; this served both as a pecuniary compensation to the victim or his relations, and as a means of stopping private vengeance (*faida*),

which to the Germanic way of thinking was definitely owed to the
victim and must be exacted by his tribe. Just as the Franks, Burgundians, Visigoths and Lombards lived according to their national
laws, so did the Romans live according to Roman law, which was
considered as a part of their national customs and was an adapta-
tion of the Theodosian code; yet a Frank's *wergeld* was higher than
a Roman's. Was this a sign of discrimination between conqueror
and conquered? Was it a result of the fact that *wergeld* was not a
Roman custom? It is an arguable point. But in spite of these
differences between the laws of different countries and the treatment
of their nationals, it is clear that the fusion of races was complete
by the end of the sixth or during the seventh century.

Religious unity

An important factor conducive to unity was that the Christian
faith was adopted by almost everyone. As a faith, it was more
formal than real however, since social customs at every level were
still primitive and very far from the Christian ideal. But the
organisation of the Church had been preserved and was developing. Although at first the more important clergy in the barbarian
kingdoms were all Romans, by the seventh century they were being
recruited among Romans and Germans alike. At first, freedom of
worship had been assured. Some of the bishops gained advance-
ment through their personal qualities, and the Church was gradually
acquiring land; that was all. But when the power of the monarchy
began to decline and the influence of the mayors of the palace
increased, in fact at the moment before the change of dynasty, the
Church started playing an extremely important part. A bishopric,
which was formerly a purely religious dignity, now became an
official one as well. At this time rural parishes were being created,
and gradually separating from the mother church of each *civitas*
(where the devout had assembled to worship in the previous
period); but the bishop still had authority and jurisdiction over
these country churches, in spite of the increase in the number of

Below The archangels Michael and Gabriel. Miniature from the Echternach Evangeliary, about 730. Treves, Domschatz, ms. 61 (134), fol. 9. *Right* The lion, symbol of St Mark the Evangelist. Miniature from the *Codex Millenarius*, about 800. Stift Kremsmünster, Cim. 1, fol. 110. These two miniatures show the technical and artistic progress made in the central regions of the *regnum Francorum* during the eighth century. The Echternach Evangeliary was illuminated by two artists, one an Anglo-Saxon, the other a Frank; the archangels are clearly inspired by paleo-Christian models. The *Codex Millenarius* was produced in Austria about seventy years later. Here the Evangelists and their symbols face each other on opposite pages, beneath arches decorated with sober entrelac motifs, the artist drawing on various sources to give life to the figures. Text and illuminations remind one of Cuthbert's Evangeliary, both manuscripts deriving from a late fifth-century Italian model. The *Codex Millenarius* is one of the most richly decorated manuscripts to have come from the ecclesiastical province of Salzburg, which stood at the centre of varied artistic currents.

St Augustine, *Quaestiones in Heptateuchon*, northern France, middle of the eighth century. Decorative art dating from before the Carolingian Renaissance, much influenced by the styles of illumination which spread from the Columban monasteries of Britain. Paris, Bibliothèque Nationale, ms. lat. 12168, frontispiece.

local clergy. In fact the bishops' role became so important that after Clovis's reign the Frankish kings adopted a custom that even the Roman emperors had never allowed themselves: they nominated bishops themselves, instead of allowing them to be freely chosen by the clergy, the people and the other bishops. This intervention of the civil power in the nomination of bishops was a radical innovation made by the barbarian kings in opposition to Roman custom. In 614, Chlothar II issued an edict making royal assent to the nomination of bishops obligatory; this was the first legislative document regulating a practice which was to persist for over a thousand years throughout the west.

While the official position of the Church was being recognised, monasticism was a growing movement. Since earliest times laymen who wanted to lead a blameless Christian life had abandoned the world and lived in communities of various sorts dedicated to poverty and charity. Besides oriental forms of monasticism, St Caesarius, Bishop of Arles, had founded in the sixth century an order based on the earlier customs of the monastery of Lérins; the rule of St Benedict had spread through the south of Italy and was to control the lives of thousands of monks for centuries to come; while in Ireland a Celtic form of monasticism had developed, involving less contemplation and more missionary activity. These three streams of monasticism had spread through the western world. In the seventh century, the preaching of St Columba, and the monasteries he founded, led to the Celtic form of monasticism becoming the chief inspiration for the religious life. Pious foundations and endowments abounded, and monasteries of every order acquired more and more property; sometimes their domains were vast, and much better managed than privately owned land. By the beginning of the seventh century, monasticism had become an institution, an essential element in the spiritual and material organisation of country life.

The Church had also become the sole guardian of intellectual culture. During the Merovingian period there had been a decline in scholarship, speculation and the arts. Whereas in the early part

of the sixth century Roman culture and thought still persisted, at least in certain regions where the Latin language was still in use, like Italy and southern Gaul, by the beginning of the seventh century it had entirely vanished. Of course the nobility had adopted Latin as the language of culture, and also of written documents, which were unknown to the Germans; but what was left in the way of scholarship? There were no longer any schools. Only in the close circle surrounding a bishop, or in monasteries, was a new culture gradually being evolved, nourished less on the great writers of antiquity than on the works of the Fathers of the Church. From about the year 650, classical culture was generally abandoned. Latin gradually became deformed and simplified, and finally gave place to a new and extremely rough and uncivilised language – Vulgar Latin. The fusion of races emphasised this development. Laymen were almost uneducated, and except in the king's palace, where some form of elementary instruction still went on, the only educated men were to be found among the clergy. Even in the Church there were illiterates, and the end of the seventh century saw the general disappearance of literacy. In this domain, as in every other, everything had to be rediscovered and created afresh.

The economy was at an elementary stage. The only true form of wealth was ownership of land, which was divided into vast domains, exploited for their seigneur or some ecclesiastical community by a population of rude, half-pagan peasants. Agriculture was the basis of the economy. Some trading was however carried on, mostly between colonies of Jewish or Syrian merchants, concentrated in the towns and occasionally having connections abroad, for instance with the Mediterranean or Anglo-Saxon countries. But the means of exchange were rudimentary. Roman money had remained sound until the end of the Empire; it was taken over by the barbarians (who ceased minting it in the fifth century), and deteriorated rapidly under the Frankish kings. It became more and more mediocre in weight and composition, and the kings handed over the right to mint it to a host of coiners, with the result that coins were struck in hundreds of different workshops, without any

Gregory of Tours, *Historia Francorum*, page of a manuscript
executed at Luxeuil, early eighth century. Paris, Bibliothèque
Nationale, ms. lat. 17655, fol. 41. Gregory's history is a basic
source for the Merovingian period and an example of the
semi-barbarous Latin used at that time. The decoration
is primitive, consisting merely of zoomorphic initials.

concern for preserving their uniformity of value. Silver gradually began to compete with gold. Here, as everywhere else, anarchy was on the increase.

The rise of the Arnulfians

In 714 Pepin of Heristal died. He was a famous mayor of the palace of Austrasia and one of the founders of a new dynasty, the Pippinides or Arnulfians, so called because of a marriage which had united the powerful family of Pepin of Landen with that of St Arnulf, Bishop of Metz. Anarchy in the *regnum Francorum* was then at its height. Not only were Neustria and Austrasia separate kingdoms and enemies by their own choice, but Aquitaine had regained her independence as long ago as 675; in 700 the Alemanni had proclaimed their freedom under their Duke Gotefrid; Provence had escaped from Frankish rule, and Frisia was in a state of slumbering rebellion. Royalty was now of little account, though the fiction was still maintained. At this moment a remarkable man came to the fore: Charles Martel. All the circumstances were favourable for authority to be placed in his hands: he was an important figure, one of the famous line of mayors of the palace of Austrasia, and related to the richest and most powerful families of that kingdom; there was no one in a position to form a coherent opposition to him; he represented a dynasty that had long since sunk into oblivion, but which nobody dared say was extinct; and finally, there was imminent danger of the *regnum* collapsing altogether and being

Merovingian coin, probably of the reign of Clovis III (691–5). Paris, Bibliothèque Nationale, Cabinet des Médailles, catalogue M. Prou, No. 71. The coin is gold-plated, an example of the debased coinage of the late Merovingian kings. It weighs 1·28 grams. Its nominal value – a third of a gold *solidus* – was quite considerable, that of one gold *solidus* of the Later Roman Empire. The inscription on the obverse is EBORINO MON. – the name of the coiner; on the reverse, CHLODOVIO RIX (*Chlodoveus Rex*).

invaded by foreign tribes, particularly the Moors, who had conquered Spain and were advancing north of the Pyrenees. All this combined to make him the man needed at that moment. He triumphed over all opposition, particularly that of his own family who denied the legitimacy of his birth, and imposed his rights and authority as leader over the mayors of the palaces of Neustria and Burgundy by force. In 717 he began the enormous task of unifying the *regnum Francorum*, by joining Austrasia and Neustria, subduing Aquitaine, Frisia and Thuringia, and forming a powerful, united army with which he conquered the Berbers near Poitiers in 732 or 733, so acquiring glory as the undisputed leader who had delivered the Franks from imminent danger. After this victory the Franks became champions of Christianity, and gave their support to the missions sent to convert the Germans of the north and east. With the papacy under threat from the barbarian conquerors of Italy, the Church concluded a firm alliance with the only power that could be counted on – the reorganised Frankish government. One can already see the ideals of the Carolingians and the house of Capet beginning to take shape.

Charles Martel was virtually King, particularly after the last Merovingian prince, Theodoric IV, died in 737 leaving no successor. When Charles died in his turn in 741, the throne was officially vacant, and his kingdom was divided between his two sons Pepin and Carloman, both of whom had the title of mayor of the palace.

But the old legitimist notions were not completely dead. In 743, the mayors of the palace had to take shelter behind a phantom monarch who at least belonged to the Merovingian dynasty: Childeric III was crowned King. Now began a period of reform in the *regnum Francorum*. Religious reforms, inspired by St Boniface and approved by Carloman, re-established synodic assemblies of bishops, and the hierarchy of the ecclesiastical provinces. Control was regained over the rebellious duchies after a merciless struggle against Hunald, Duke of the Aquitainians, Odilo, Duke of the Bavarians, and Theutbald, Duke of the Alemanni. After Carloman's

Coronation of a Frankish prince,
illustrating the belief in divine intervention
which gave kingship its sacred character.
Sacramentary of the latter half of the
ninth century. Paris, Bibliothèque
Nationale, ms. lat. 1141, fol. 2v.

abdication in 747, Pepin went on with this programme as sole mayor of the palace, and added to it some administrative and monetary reforms which made it possible for him to restore regalian rights; he also reconquered southern Gaul, and recaptured Narbonne and Elne from the Moors. Before this task was even finished, Pepin took the decisive step which removed the line of Clovis from the throne and substituted his own: after making sure of the consent of the nobles and support of the Church, he deposed Childeric III in 751, was acclaimed by the nobles at Soissons, and consecrated by St Boniface and several bishops. On 28 July 754, Pope Stephen II, who had come to France in search of a protector, renewed Pepin's consecration at St Denis, and afterwards anointed his sons Charles and Carloman, at the same time confirming the new dynasty and forbidding the Franks to choose their king from any other line henceforth.

Thus was formed, in the middle of the eighth century, a single monarchy with dominion over the whole of the *regnum Francorum* and even Italy. The alliance between the new dynasty and the papacy led to the constitution of the States of the Church, and also to the intervention of Pepin against the Lombards. A new era was beginning for western Europe.

2 The reconstruction of western Europe

Restoration of power – the administrative framework

Pepin the Short and his son Charlemagne between them laid the foundations of the new Western Empire. On the death of his father in 768, Charlemagne had to share the kingdom with his brother Carloman: this had been the wish of Pepin, who, in spite of his breadth of vision and the task left so nearly completed at the end of his eighteen years' reign, could not bring himself to abandon the old Frankish custom which had weakened the Merovingian dynasty, of dividing the realm among the late king's sons. Three years later, in 771, Carloman died, leaving Charlemagne sole master of an immense territory stretching from the mouth of the Weser to the Pyrenees, and from the Danube to Brittany. He was to rule over it for more than forty years. It was he who would finish the task outlined by Charles Martel and carried on by Pepin, and leave on it the original and individual imprint of his political genius; it was he who would revive the idea of a Roman Empire of the West, forgotten since 476.

The administrative reforms of Pepin and Charlemagne were aimed at re-establishing the king's authority. Although no one at this time disputed the impressive character of the king's power, his authority was not always respected. It had passed into the hands of the mayors of the palace; but they in their turn had been obliged to come to terms with local officials. The measures taken by the two first sovereigns of the dynasty were aimed at controlling the establishments of the counts who governed the towns, and at recovering regalian rights, such as those over the coinage. At the same time the central government was reorganised. Organs and methods of government were created whose effectiveness was proved by the real authority now exercised by the sovereign, and this prevailed throughout his vast territory for the whole forty years of his reign, in spite of occasional opposition. The theory of monarchy now taking shape was to last for several centuries.

This administrative framework helps us to understand the civilisation of the period. It was also one of its essential features.

Ever since the Merovingian epoch, when some Roman organisations were preserved, local administration had been in the hands of the counts who governed the provinces derived from the old Roman *civitates*. Under the Merovingians, a count was a potentate exempt from inspection or control, and the only brake on his tyranny, or even brigandage, was that in cases of notorious excess the complaints of the inhabitants could be supported and laid before the king by the bishop. The counts united the functions of the Roman *comes* and the German *grafio*, an officer whose duty it was to collect fines imposed by tribunals. They formed the rudimentary personnel of the king's administration, and were dependants of the mayors of the palace. Since Pepin and Charlemagne both wanted to create a strong and stable government, it was clear that they must begin their reforms by imposing their authority on the counts.

Under the preceding dynasty the counts had been of very various origins, and might include Franks, Gauls, Romans, noblemen, freemen and former slaves; but the choice of the two first Carolingian kings fell almost exclusively upon members of the Frankish aristocracy. To break the independent spirit of the Aquitanians, some Frankish nobles, who were regarded as foreigners by the inhabitants, were put in command of the counties of that region by Pepin. Pepin and Charlemagne also put an end to a custom which had gradually been adopted by their predecessors, by refusing to allow this office to be inherited; however, this practice reappeared under their successors.

Until the middle of the ninth century a count derived all his power from the king, and represented him in every way; as under the Merovingians, his office was conceived of as an emanation of the royal power, and because of this he was entitled to *wergeld* three times as great as that of a free man. He was responsible to the king alone, and the inhabitants of the *civitas* he administered had no control over him. His authority was administrative, judicial, fiscal and military. It was he who exercised the *bannus*, or authority enforcing obedience on the king's subjects; he prosecuted criminals, arrested malefactors, saw that distraints and punishments were carried out, and that its beneficiaries profited by the *mundium*, or royal protection. As head of the judiciary, he presided over a tribunal that was at first the only one in the *civitas*; but at the end of the eighth century Charlemagne introduced an important reform: in each district under the count's authority there were to be two forms of jurisdiction – the count's tribunal and that of his auxiliaries, the *centenarii*. More important still, the count's tribunal, or *mallus*, was reorganised: when a count was prosecuting, he was also sole judge; when he had to hear a suit involving a number of pleas, he had advisers to help him. At first these were the *rachimburgi* or *boni viri*, chosen from among important citizens; but they were afterwards replaced by the *scabini* – seven professional judges, trained in law and chosen to advise the count.

In the fiscal department, a count had to collect fines and transfer them to the treasury; he also collected taxes, such as customs duty, market dues and tolls, which were the only taxes payable to the king – the land-tax had disappeared during the anarchy that prevailed under the last Merovingian kings. It was also the count who conscripted men for military service in the royal army, and was responsible for the defence of his county when threatened by an enemy. In common with all other government officials before the later Middle Ages, the count received no fixed salary; he had a right to a third of the fines he collected, and the property attached to the countship and certain revenues were at his disposal; he also often profited personally from the sovereign's generosity in making over land or an abbey to him. A count was a personage of high rank, and his office was invested with a dignity suitable to the responsibilities it entailed; at the same time it was a very lucrative one.

A count could not perform such diverse and extensive duties single-handed; he was assisted by centurions, the *missi comitis* (who acted both as deputies and agents), the *vicarii* (subordinate officers chosen by him subject to ratification by the populace) and above all the viscount, to whom all his powers could be delegated.

The territory administered by him was the county, an innovation

A Carolingian King, said to be Charlemagne. Paris, Musée du Louvre. Bronze figure formerly in the treasure of Metz cathedral, probably dating from the latter half of the ninth century. An admirable illustration of the ideal of the monarch as judge and soldier held by the most illustrious members of the dynasty.

belonging to the Frankish period and often corresponding to the *civitas* of the Gauls, though sometimes smaller. It usually contained the seat of a bishopric, so that many counties coincided with dioceses. Counties were often juxtaposed and shared a common boundary, but this was not an invariable rule, for in quite a few cases they were separated by forests and desert regions under no count's administration; also the division of the land into counties had sometimes been belatedly carried out or even omitted altogether, as in the regions inhabited by the Slavs in the south-eastern part of the Empire.

Wherever Roman traditions persisted, the county was a well-established subdivision; elsewhere it was an artificial one. There were over 300 counties in the Empire in Charlemagne's day.

Taken as a whole, the countship was a useful instrument of government, but it was also an imperfect one, which presented the Carolingians with a dilemma. Should the administration be adapted to the region, with counts chosen from the local nobility, who might collect too large a following and become dangerously powerful? Or should purely artificial divisions be created, unrelated to the land and under the control of counts who might seem like foreigners or even enemies to the inhabitants, though in close touch with the central power? Some counties were subdivided into hundreds, or more often into *vicariae*. These first appeared in Charlemagne's reign; they were more practically acceptable to the inhabitants, and so lasted for a long time, even after other administrative categories had disappeared.

A difficult problem was raised by the marches, or regions on the frontiers of the realm. Their administration must be primarily a military one, and the man placed in command must be first and foremost a soldier – that is to say a duke or marquis. Under the Roman Empire, a duke had been the head of a vast frontier territory; under the Merovingians this title borrowed from the Byzantine Empire was given to a purely military leader; since the seventh century and under the Carolingians, dukes had carried out the same functions as counts, with the difference that they did not govern a single city but a group of cities, temporarily united when the king needed to create a high command to oppose invasion or rebellion. Sometimes a duke was also the prince of some ethnically defined group: this happened in Bavaria, Thuringia and Alemannia. He then became as it were a superior vassal of the king; he exercised regalian rights over his people, and was only linked to the king or emperor by a somewhat vague agreement. During the first part of his reign, Charlemagne undertook the task of submitting these national dukes to his authority, and unifying his kingdom by putting an end to the particularism they personified.

The king's authority was stronger and more stable in marches governed by marquises. These were usually regions that had been recently conquered, where colonies of inhabitants and Christian missions had been established. Over them was placed a man with the rank of count, the *comes marcae* or *marchio*, who had authority over the other counts and was always a distinguished soldier. In Charlemagne's reign there were seven marches: those of Spain, Brittany, Bavaria, Pannonia, Friuli, Nordgau and Swabia. Royal authority was permanently delegated to these military leaders, who shouldered heavy responsibilities and had to take immediate action in difficult situations. Charlemagne made use of the dukes and marquises to control the counts and other officials at the nerve centres of the *regnum Francorum*. And the same purpose was realised by the institution of *missi dominici*, to transmit decisions made by the central government to every quarter of the realm.

The *missi dominici* were inspectors sent out by the government to represent the sovereign and supervise the counts. The very essence of their function was that they acted without intermediary, and took the place of king or emperor wherever they went, just as if he had been present in person. They had existed before Charlemagne's time in the form of *missi discurrentes*, who were personal assistants to the mayors of the palace as well as envoys extraordinary; they took the authority of their master wherever they went, their activities were confined to no special region and, although their mission was precisely defined, they enjoyed extremely extensive powers and high rank. The inhabitants of the kingdom gradually got used to applying to them for the enforcement of their rights and using them as intermediaries in their dealings with the central government. Charlemagne regularised this institution right at the beginning of his reign: the *missi* became permanent organs of government, acting in direct contact with the central authority; their role was particularly important in cases where the administrative functions of count or bishop had been entrusted to members of the local nobility, whom they could oppose officially on the king's behalf; thus they helped the development of the notion of a single central government, superior to all local authorities. Their duties were more general than those of the *missi discurrentes*, and they were instructed to suppress abuses of every sort. The first mention of these officials dates from 779, in the capitulary of Heristal, which declared that their mission was above all to pronounce the law. At the same time groups of counties, or *missitica*, were defined every year, each under a *missus*. From 802 onwards this function underwent a further transformation: certain special *missi* were chosen to carry out the same duties, but only for a limited period and with the authority and prestige due to their important social position.

There were also changes in the method of recruiting the *missi*: whereas at the end of the eighth century they had generally been chosen from among the direct vassals of the king (*vassi dominici*) – bishops, abbots and counts – in 802 Charlemagne started entrusting this office to members of the highest ranks of the nobility. One gets the impression that he felt the need of an intermediate class between himself and the regional administration, and thus one more rung was created in the ladder of the imperial hierarchy. Thenceforth the *missi* were given the task of supervising the highest officers, both ecclesiastics and laymen, as well as the counts. There were defects in this system which led to its downfall within two or three generations: for one thing these missions entailed a crushing amount of hard work for men who had other occupations as well; then the number of official circuits was always increasing; finally, under the feeble kings of the end of the dynasty, the *missi* had to be given power over regions where they were already fulfilling other duties, so that the administration and the inspection of the same region was left in the hands of the same individuals, a confused state of affairs which inevitably contributed to make these areas practically independent, and create the upper strata of feudal society. However, in Charlemagne's day such abuses and inconsistencies were carefully avoided, the organisation was working well; it was not without defects but its basis was logical, and it was an undoubtedly useful means of ensuring that local officials were controlled by the central government.

Regalian rights

The finances of the new monarchy had also to be reorganised. The mayors of the palace had appropriated the landed property of the Merovingian kings, and added them to their own inherited possessions which were already immense. It was mainly from these that the Carolingian kings obtained their revenues. Some of these domains could also be used to endow those whose support the king wanted to gain, and these gifts secured him faithful vassals, obliged to serve in the army. Apart from Crown lands, the chief income of all States came from taxation. The Romans had made considerable use of direct taxation of land and poll-tax. The Merovingian kings did not understand this system in the least, and saw no difference between the principle of taxation and exaction justified by custom; during the anarchy of the seventh century, direct taxation finally disappeared altogether. It was impossible for the Carolingian kings to re-establish it, besides which their ignorance of Roman ways, and their Germanic notions of power, prevented them from conceiving of such a system. Pepin the Short and Charlemagne therefore confined themselves to regaining control of the two sources of revenue that were universally accepted: indirect taxation and the profits from minting money. Customs dues and tolls were therefore subjected to a very close inspection.

The proceeds of market dues (*teloneum*), of *portaticum*, *rotaticum* and *pulveraticum*, falling upon merchandise in transit either at the ports or on the main roads, and collected at the tollbooth or turnpike, made up the chief indirect resources of the monarchy. Those already in existence were preserved, and in case of need new ones were created, such as trading rights. Besides this, freemen who came to the assembly every year had to bring the king a 'gift'; this was voluntary in theory, but had become an obligatory custom.

As to the rights of minting money, the decline of royal power and the Merovingian kings' indifference to the whole question, led to its completely escaping from royal hands. And the weight and composition of coins was left to the whim of coiners and therefore extremely variable; in any case such an enormous amount of alloy was added that gold was no longer the true monetary standard. The currency was in a complete state of anarchy and all confidence had been lost in the exchange value of Frankish money; payments had to be made in the remarkably stable Byzantine *nomisma*, or else by melting down coins and weighing the pure metal. Silver was no better guaranteed than gold. The reforms carried out by the Carolingian kings consisted in improving the quality of money, and introducing a silver standard without altogether renouncing the gold standard. The weight and composition of coins was tested and guaranteed, and silver money was equated with a certain weight of gold.

Pepin the Short began by insisting that the name and monogram of the king should once more appear on coins, thus restoring the idea that money was publicly guaranteed, instead of leaving it in the hands of coiners, which had been one of the chief causes of trouble. Then he set himself to fix the weight and composition of coins. Later he and Charlemagne gradually introduced silver currency into the whole of Gaul. There was nothing experimental about these reforms: on the contrary they were systematic and authoritative, and were imposed by a series of capitularies. Before 755 Pepin had fixed the relationship between the denier and the pound, as well as the remuneration for coiners, now reduced to less than five

Silver denier with the head of Charlemagne,
after 804, minted at Frankfurt. Berlin,
Münzkabinett der Staatlichen Museen.
Charlemagne introduced sound silver currency
throughout most of the Empire which was to become
the official instrument of exchange.

per cent. Next, silver deniers were struck, passed into current use,
and their weight increased; in about 781 Charlemagne adopted
491 grammes as the standard weight of a pound, instead of the 327
of the Roman pound which had been used hitherto. Now that the
relative value of gold and silver was guaranteed, this money could
be used even for transactions outside the *regnum Francorum*. This
sound currency was to endure for a century, though there were a
few regions at least, Bavaria for example, where the old ways died
hard and payments continued to be made for some time in weight
of metal. Nor did gold currency entirely disappear from the Empire:
in Italy it persisted for a long time. None the less, Pepin the Short,
Charlemagne and their successors were responsible for effective
monetary reforms: they re-established a sound currency, which
was guaranteed by the State and provided them with an appreciable
source of revenue, and they did their best to keep it under control.
At times they took measures which turned out to be inappropriate,
such as Charlemagne's decision to keep only a single mint at

Aix-la-Chapelle for the whole Empire. But although they handed over the management of some workshops to ecclesiastical establishments, they had the responsibility of being sole guarantors of the currency so long as they remained in power, and the Edict of Pîtres, issued by Charles the Bald in 864, was designed to safeguard the uniformity and quality of the currency. But later on, when the monarchy became impotent and the nobility all-powerful, the counts – whose job it was to supervise the workshops – appropriated both minting and the revenues derived from it, as well as other property belonging to the *comitatus*, and treated it as their own instead of as a trust held on behalf of the king. This was a belated development however, and, like their assumption of judicial functions, had its roots in the political and social changes of the end of the ninth century.

In Charlemagne's day justice was done in the name of the king, and for a very long time it had been accepted that the king was its fount. But the old Germanic tradition of popular participation in the exercise of justice had given rise to the creation of a council to assist the king or his representatives in making their judgments. During the Carolingian period the judiciary consisted essentially of the king's tribunal and the count's tribunal. The count's tribunal, or *mallus*, was at first held in the open air, but under cover after 809; the count gave judgment assisted by the *rachimburgi*, or later the *scabini*. Court service, or attendance at the *mallus*, was originally strictly obligatory for all freemen; Charlemagne limited this when he replaced the *rachimburgi* by the *scabini*. The latter had to pronounce judgment, but only the count could enforce the sentence, and he could also amend the *scabini's* verdict. An important feature of the development of justice under Charlemagne was that offences began to be classified, and the influence of Roman law was again apparent in the distinction between *causae majores* and *causae minores*, criminal and civil cases. On the other hand the national laws were still enforced, and old Germanic customs dominated legal procedure. Thus there was no official prosecution, and an action could only be brought on the plea of an individual, even in criminal cases; the onus of proof lay with the defendant, a fact that shocks our present-day Romanist practice, though it was consistent in that the accuser (without whom the case could never have been brought) ran the risk of suffering the same punishment as the accused was threatened with, should the latter succeed in proving his innocence. Proof could be in writing, by witness, by ordeal or judgment of God; and the accused might or might not be the only one to take the oath. The importance of all this judicial organisation was that it owed its existence to delegation of royal authority. Justice was the highest prerogative of the central power.

The central government

This was embodied in the person of the sovereign, surrounded by the group of close supporters who made up the 'palace'. The palace included all those who helped the sovereign administer his kingdom, and the services they provided were gradually organised into offices, or as it were embryo ministries. The highest official at court was the count of the palace, who had already existed under the preceding dynasty, but had seen his function eclipsed by the growing importance of the mayor of the palace. With the change of dynasty and the disappearance of the mayors of the palace, he once more regained the supreme position at court. At first entrusted with bringing actions and presiding over the palace tribunal in the king's absence, under Charlemagne he had at his disposal a regular department for the drafting of judgments, an activity no longer carried out by the chancellory. Henceforth there existed a sort of judicial chancellory as well as the royal chancellory, where favours were officially granted. The count of the palace now always represented the king as president of the tribunal, took action in his absence, and judged all cases himself, except those of very important persons, which were reserved for the king. Thus a permanent tribunal under the count of the palace existed alongside that of the king, and the count had become the chief official in charge of temporal affairs.

Spiritual affairs were taken care of by the Royal Chapel. This was another extension of a Merovingian institution, but Charlemagne changed and adapted it. It had begun as the royal oratory, where a group of clergy ministered to the king's spiritual needs and were in charge of St Martin's cape (*cappa, capella*). Both the relic and the chapel were taken over by the mayors of the palace and afterwards the Carolingian kings. In Charlemagne's day the chief clerics of the Royal Chapel were chosen from the highest aristocracy (Fulrad, who held office under Pepin the Short and Charlemagne, was a close relation of the royal family), and were therefore the most important ecclesiastics in the kingdom, the most influential spiritual advisors, and the men really responsible for the nomination of bishops and the direction of the Frankish church. The clergy who made up the personnel of the chancellory were dependent on them.

The chancellory no longer enforced the judgments of the royal tribunal as it had done in the preceding period. But it formulated the decrees issued by the king, whether the granting of favours or legal acts. The referendaries – high lay officials of the Merovingian court charged with expediting and ratifying such acts – had now disappeared. This duty fell to the chancellor, who directed the work of scribes and notaries, was responsible for the seal and in charge of the royal archives. After the time of Charlemagne's son Louis the Pious (813–40), the head of the Royal Chapel and the head of the chancellory were honoured with the titles of arch-chaplain and arch-chancellor.

Management of finances was the business of the king's chamber. The chamberlain collected the king's revenues, whether from his domains or fines, gifts from vassals, tribute-money or spoils of war. He also controlled the king's private expenses, which were not at this time kept separate from those of the State, any more than they were in the Middle Ages and up to the sixteenth century.

The seneschal, the chief caterer, the marshal, the master of the royal stables, the cup-bearer, the sword-bearer, and the head librarian completed the senior officials of the court, and gave orders to the hordes of huntsmen, falconers, cooks, porters, couriers, doctors and clerks who made up the king's household and without whom he could not have played his part.

The higher positions were as a rule specialised. But it would be a mistake to suppose that the men who filled them were chosen for their technical ability. There was no rigid system of seniority, and men were selected to be at the head of these specialised departments principally for their faithful service to the king, and might be employed on missions of the most diverse sorts: a count of the palace, whose duty was to administer justice, might be nominated ambassador or general of an army; an arch-chaplain or arch-chancellor might carry out an extremely important diplomatic mission. Government was still almost patrimonial in character, and the fidelity, energy and judgment of these important and distinguished men was made use of as seemed best. In a world where educated and able men were very rare, a good character inspired more confidence than technical skill.

The same spirit presided over the selection of the king's council. In the Middle Ages men never made judgments or decisions without the help of advisers. The king needed faithful supporters to help him govern, and he discussed questions of policy with a few experienced men. The role of counsellor was not given to those holding some definite office, but to men whom the king liked to consult freely on various matters, to his friends, companions, relations, and any dignitaries or faithful followers who happened to be at court.

A council of the nobility was also held at the time of the annual assembly, which took place each spring before the season of military campaigns; this was an old Germanic custom, handed down from the days when the king was first and foremost head of the army, and used to gather his soldiers together to hear their advice and give them his orders. There were also two smaller assemblies, one made up of important laymen, the other of ecclesiastics, bishops and abbots. These two councils met separately, and then advised the king as to the political measures to be taken,

or decrees to be issued. The latter were then read to the general
assembly, and given approval, which amounted to no more than
agreement to conform.

The existence of these political and administrative organs shows
that the idea of the State was beginning to take the place of the
patrimonial government practised by the Germans and Merovingians. And the theory of monarchy itself had undergone profound
changes since the events of 751–4.

In 751, Pepin the Short had profited from the decline of the
Merovingian dynasty to have himself proclaimed king and, as we
saw earlier (page 23), consecrated first by St Boniface and the
bishops at the assembly of Soissons, and then by Pope Stephen II.
To the old Germanic notion that only a man of the royal family,
elected by the nobles, could accede to the throne and be invested
with the *mundium* and the *bannus*, there was now added a religious
element: the belief in the divine nature of monarchy, and the
notion of charism. Pepin and his descendants thus based their
authority on a new foundation: the king was not elected by free
choice of the nobles, they simply owed him obedience; consecration and heredity combined to give royalty the character of
magistrature representing the divine will. Charlemagne made a
further change by insisting on an oath of personal fidelity from his
subjects, and later, in 800, by reviving the Roman idea of *auctoritas*.
Of course few men of the eighth century were greatly concerned
with judicial theory, but these practical steps taken by the king to
assert his authority led insensibly to a concept of royalty made up
of diverse, and to our eyes contradictory elements, which nevertheless lasted for ten centuries. It was the prelude to feudal royalty.
On three separate occasions when his authority was in danger, in
789, 793 and 802, Charlemagne insisted on the oath of fidelity:
he hoped to bind his subjects to his person by this solemn and
religious covenant. However, by so doing he introduced a new
concept of power as a contract, in place of the idea that obedience
depended on the transcendant notion of law – a theory familiar to
the Romans, developed and fed by philosophical and judicial

thought, but impossible for the Franks to understand. From this moment the king's power no longer depended either on Roman *Auctoritas* or German *Gefolgschaft*, but on a religious imperative and a covenant between man and man. One also sees the dawn of the Augustinian theory of a magistrature conferred by God, and its consequences: that royalty must be judged and controlled by the true delegates of God – the heads of the Church. After Charlemagne this step followed quickly: Louis the Pious was deposed and reinstated by the bishops, and Charles the Bald openly declared at the council of Savonnières that a king could be judged by the bishops and must submit to their judgment. Charlemagne was a long way from such theories, and even if he read St Augustine any infringement of his power would have seemed intolerable to him. But it is plain that he was incapable of a general theory of the State and that he thought of royalty as a trust conferred by God, and even more as an inherited possession. The titles Charlemagne assumed and the measures he took to assure the succession, show that, whether as King or Emperor, he never really conceived of a united Frankish State, but had his mind fixed on the function of the king ruling over a part or the whole of the *regnum Francorum*. With its emphasis on inheritance rather than territory, the Frankish view of the new Roman Empire was very different from that of the Romans. The emperor was merely the guide or governor of the Empire; the Empire was not a territory, it was a power, a dignity and a collection of Christian peoples governed by the man God had chosen for the task. Charlemagne was a king-priest in the biblical tradition. His model was David. There was no distinction between civil and religious power. God's people – who were identified with the Empire, for only Christians existed in the Empire – were ruled over by him in the interests of peace, and the propagation of the faith. Even after the bishops had returned to the forefront of the scene in the reign of Louis the Pious, even after Hincmar's essay on the theory of monarchy, even after the revival of Roman law in the eleventh and twelfth centuries, this tradition of the king-priest survived and was to be handed on to the house of

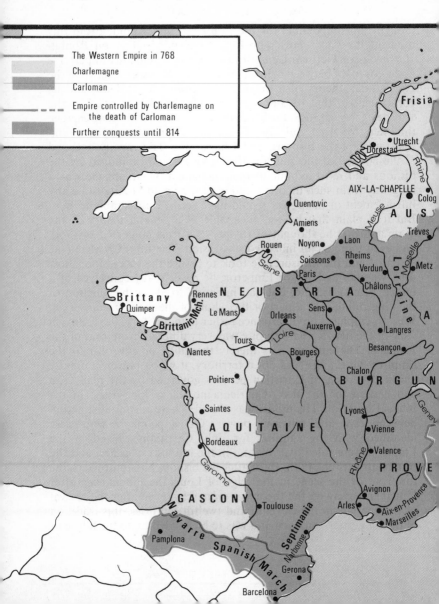

The Empire, 768–814. During this period a united *regnum Francorum* was formed by the unification of Carloman's territories with those of Charlemagne. It was enlarged by the annexation of vassal States such as the duchies of Alemannia and Bavaria, and the conquest of the kingdoms of Lombardy and Saxony. When Charlemagne died he left an immense Empire, which included three vassal States: the kingdoms of Italy and Aquitaine and the Papal States.

The Western Empire in 768

Charlemagne

Carloman

Empire controlled by Charlemagne on the death of Carloman

Further conquests until 814

Frisia

Utrecht
Dorestad

AIX-LA-CHAPELLE
Colog
AUS
Trèves
Metz
Lorraine
Châlons
Verdun
Rheims
Laon
Noyon
Soissons
Amiens
Quentovic
Rouen
Paris
NEUSTRIA
Rennes
Brittany
Quimper
Brittanic Mch.
Le Mans
Sens
Orleans
Auxerre
Langres
Besançon
Tours
Nantes
Bourges
Chalon
BURGUN
Poitiers
Lyons
L. Genev
Saintes
Vienne
AQUITAINE
Valence
Bordeaux
PROVE
Garonne
Avignon
Aix-en-Provence
GASCONY
Toulouse
Arles
Marseilles
Navarre
Septimania
Pamplona
Spanish March
Narbonne
Gerona
Barcelona

Capet and strengthened by the custom of anointing and consecrating the king.

This was the innovation, incalculable in its results, that signalised the beginning of the Carolingian dynasty and was to lead to feudal monarchy and its two definite characteristics: first, absolute power, limited only by the advice of the nobles and of the Church, guardian of Christian morals; secondly, power based on a contract, and depending on an oath of allegiance from the subjects. In a strong monarchy such as Charlemagne's this reinforced the prince's authority; in a weak one, it was the germ of destruction of that authority and the obedience due to it. When, later on, the practice of *beneficium* became widespread (bestowing property in exchange for fidelity), the oath to the sovereign was inevitably confused with the personal pledge to the seigneur, and the beginning of feudalism put an end to notions both of State and of sovereignty. It was the sacred or priestly character of the king's power which alone gave a new orientation to royalty, and in the end saved it by gradually restoring Roman ideas of sovereignty.

But during the ninth century, organised authority had to contend with economic and social upheavals due to the rapid transformation of an evolving society and the regrouping of the aristocratic families who wished to play a part in it.

3 The social structure

The aristocracy

During the latter part of the eighth, and the whole of the ninth century, the concept of royalty dominated society and determined its structure. For the kings came from the family of the Austrasian mayors of the palace and therefore belonged to that Frankish nobility which formed the upper stratum of society; those who a hundred years earlier had been the equals of the Arnulfians now took an oath of allegiance to their sovereign very similar to that exacted from vassals.

Under the Merovingians no real nobility had existed in the usual sense of noble birth. The aristocracy was above all an aristocracy of function. The king need not entrust the highest positions, such as those of counts, bishops and palace officials, to Franks only; they could be given to other races, Germans or Gallo-Romans, or even the descendants of slaves. Gregory of Tours tells us that Count Leudaste was the son of a slave; this may have been an insult due to personal enmity, but it may also quite well be true. At this period titles and functions do not seem to have been inherited. In any case there was no trace of that class-consciousness which insists that nobility is a matter of lineage and social status is transmitted by blood relationship. Marc Bloch has rightly stressed this phenomenon. He shows that a dominant class does not necessarily constitute a nobility. He emphasises the late appearance of a true nobility in the West, and dates it, broadly speaking, from the beginning of the twelfth century. This is probably too extreme a view, for German and French studies published in the last thirty years go to show that since the beginning of the eighth century aristocratic families had been firmly entrenched in such regions as Austrasia, and that they often possessed vast landed property, handed down from generation to generation like their high government positions. Moreover those belonging to this class formed a hereditary aristocracy; families intermarried and became powerful clans; they were very conscious of the importance of their lineage. When, in the middle of the ninth century, Heberne, Archbishop of Tours, was confirming the foundation of the abbey of Villeloin, he described the founder, Mainard, as a man 'descended from a famous line', and Thegan, biographer of Louis the Pious, declared that the Welfs came from the noblest family in Bavaria. Noble birth must therefore have already been recognised at this date, and probably long before.

It seems likely that even before Charles Martel there were already some families that could be described as noble. The best known was the one from which the mayors of the palace of Austrasia were descended.

In the ninth century this aristocracy began to play a part in society and in the State. The reigns of Charlemagne and Louis the Pious favoured its ascendancy. The families and family clans, and the landed estates on which their influence depended, became essential elements in the structure of society.

Although the sources of our information are obscure and confused, we have records of a certain number of these families; but relationships are not often clearly indicated in chronicles and diplomatic documents, and genealogies have to be reconstructed bit by bit. This is reasonably easy when the inheritance of an *allodium* can be traced; otherwise one must have recourse to guesses founded on similarity of names, for it is well known that each family had traditional names, and passed them on to another family by marriage. After the marriage of the Goth Acfred, Count of Carcassonne, to Adalinde, daughter of Bernard Plantevelue, the names William and Bernard crop up among their descendants, both being traditional in the family of St William, from which Adalinde was descended. This is just one example; one could quote many others, among which the most famous is the name Philip, introduced into the house of Capet as a result of the marriage of Henry I and Anne of Kiev.

Research, comparison and critical study of this sort has made it possible to establish that most of the aristocratic families throughout the Carolingian Empire had Frankish names; also that most of the great Frankish families came from Austrasia. As a result of the many high positions occupied by its members, the Austrasian nobility swarmed all over the Empire. It must not be assumed, however, that they were the only privileged ones. We often find that the counts of a certain region were scions of a very ancient local and autochthonous nobility. Thus in Italy under Frankish rule, the names Adalgis, Pandolf and Siconolf are found among the dukes of Benevento and the *gastalds* of Bari; in the Spanish march, Counts Suniar, Sunifred, Wicfred and Acfred were clearly Visigoths, although they are found alternating with indubitably Frankish Bernards and Williams. But during the ninth century, counts throughout the Empire generally had Frankish names, and relationships can be traced by their persistence.

It is therefore clear that in Charlemagne's time administrative posts all over the Empire were mainly held by Franks belonging to the highest ranks of the aristocracy, who settled and founded families in the regions where they carried out their functions. They married and multiplied, and so founded the majority of the noble families of the eleventh century. And most of them came from Austrasia, the region enclosed by the Seine and the Rhine, which was also the native land of the new dynasty.

The Carolingian dynasty seems to have begun as the most illustrious of these noble Austrasian families. Before they came to the throne they were established in the Ardennes, where they made brilliant marriages at the end of the seventh century and afterwards. As was mentioned earlier, Pepin of Landen's family gained lustre by marriage with that of St Arnulf, and this was increased by the ability of its members and the positions they occupied.

But in the same region we come across other clans, not at first inferior to Pepin's, whose descendants formed the nobility of the Carolingian period. The family of Etich had been established in Alsace since Merovingian times; in the ninth century it became the rootstock of several families of counts of Lorraine, and the most important figures of the reign of Louis the Pious were descended from it. This line can be traced back to an Adalric or Etich living in the seventh century, who owned great possessions in Burgundy, played an important part in the struggle between the mayors of the palace, and made a bid for power in the time of Ebroin, mayor of the palace of Neustria; as a result, his possessions were confiscated by Ebroin, but restored by Pepin of Heristal whose supporter he became a few years later. Between 664 and 666, we come across an Adalric-Etich established in Alsace, as the duke entrusted with the defence of the country against the Alemanni. Evidently this was either the same man or his son. After 682, a son of this Etich called Adalbert and his son Liutfrid became dukes of Alsace. It was Liutfrid who conquered the region to the east of the Rhine for Charles Martel between 709 and 746. Pepin the Short seems to have been reluctant to maintain a dukedom in Alsace. Possibly he suppressed it. In any case, Etich's descendants were loaded with gifts by Charlemagne, but disappeared almost completely from the political scene. At this time their power in terms of land-ownership was colossal, and it is difficult to realise what vast domains, divided into regions as large as some modern French *départements*, made up their inheritance. They also held administrative posts. One of them, Hugh, was Count of Tours under Charlemagne and Louis the Pious. One of his daughters married the Emperor Lothar; another, Count Conrad of the Welf family, brother of the Empress Judith; the third, Gerard, Count of Paris and later of Vienne, and regent of the kingdom of Provence. Hugh's son Liutfrid held an important post in Alsace and Italy. Perhaps Matfrid, Count of Orleans, was also a descendant of Etich; he founded the family of the counts of Eifelgau, and his daughter married Boso, one of the outstanding figures of the second half of the ninth century. This family of Etich is a good example of a line that was well-known by the ninth century and which can be traced back to the beginning of the seventh century; it took the lead by reason of its ancient origins, its vast domains and the important marriages it contracted.

We find another example in the house of Welf, a Bavarian family whose nobility is vouched for by Thegan. Duke Welf, a contemporary of Charlemagne's, was the father of several well known personages: the Empress Judith, second wife of Louis the Pious; Count Rudolf, Abbot of St Riquier and Jumièges; and Count Conrad, father of the famous Abbot Hugh. The property of the Welfs was centred in Ammergau; afterwards we find several of its members established in Alemannia, Argengau and Rheingau. Abbot Hugh finally amassed property and responsibilities which made him the most important man in the kingdom at the end of Charles the Bald's reign. In the twelfth century the Welfs were outstanding figures in the duchy of Saxony, and were to accede to the Empire.

Yet another example: the Guy and Lambert families held power both in the west of France and part of Italy. They came from Trèves. Pepin the Short entrusted one of their members, Garin, with an important mission to Alemannia. In 787 we come across an individual with the same name; he was son-in-law to the Lombard Duke of Spoleto, Hildebrand, and almost certainly the brother of the Count of Florence, as well as being related to the Lamberts, counts of the march of Brittany under Charlemagne. A Lambert who was a contemporary of Louis the Pious compromised himself on behalf of Lothar, and lost office when the latter was disgraced. He took refuge at Spoleto, while another Lambert succeeded in carving a sort of principality for himself between Nantes and Angers, in the reign of Charles the Bald. He was killed fighting against the King and his representative, Robert the Strong, while his brother Garnier was executed by order of Charles the Bald. However, one branch of this family was still established in Touraine, where Garnier of Loches possessed vast domains. A marriage between his daughter and Fulk the Red, founder of the house of Anjou, gave Fulk's line the means of an astonishing rise in importance at the end of the ninth century, whereas Guy of Spoleto, who had not forgotten his relations in the West, was King Odo's competitor at the time of the first eviction of the Carolingians.

The Unroch family was no less noble and important: Berengar of Friuli, King and Emperor in 888, was descended from it. Unroch, one of Charlemagne's most famous vassals and a native of

Alemannia, was one of the five Frankish counts who, with six Saxon counts, were given the mission of concluding a truce with the Danes by the river Eider in 811. His brother Autchar was Count of Alemannia, and Autchar's son Albgar, after going as ambassador to Byzantium, was made Duke of Carinthia. Of Unroch's sons, Everard was Marquis of Friuli and married Gisela, daughter of Louis the Pious and Judith; the other, Berengar, was Count of Toulouse. During the ninth century the house of Unroch inter-

Charter dated 3 June 799. Paris, Archives Nationales, K.7, no. 14. Charlemagne's sister Gisela, Abbess of Chelles, grants a domain in Artois to the Abbey of St Denis. The charter is signed by Charlemagne's three sons, Charles, Pepin and Louis, and is thus a deed executed by a private individual requiring the presence of witnesses, unlike royal deeds, which, from Merovingian times, needed only the signatures of the King and a member of the chancery.

married with that of Etich. Their domains formed enormous territories scattered in various parts of the country – Alemannia, Friuli, Toulouse and Flanders. This was therefore another family with origins in the Rhineland that became powerful throughout the Empire.

Many more family groups could be mentioned, such as that of Boso, ancestor of the kings of Provence, the counts of Périgord and the marquises of Tuscany; or Roric, descended from a count of Maine who was either the husband or lover of Charlemagne's daughter Rotrud (this line disappeared towards the end of the ninth century, but the same stock is found in the eleventh, in the viscounts of Châteaudun and therefore in all the nobility of the river Loire); or Hilduin, a relation of the royal family, whose name was still preserved in the twelfth century, in the form 'Audouin' by their descendants, the counts of Angoulême.

It will be seen that all these families were interconnected, and made up a nobility of Austrasian origin which was as ancient as the royal family itself. Moreover it was among the members of this nobility that kings and emperors looked for wives for their sons. Under the descendants of Charlemagne, the thrones of several kingdoms were occupied by brothers or close relations, and there were canon laws preventing consanguineous marriages. Royal brides must therefore be chosen from among the nobility. Everard of Friuli married Gisela, daughter of the Emperor; Conrad, son of Duke Welf, became the Emperor's brother-in-law and the uncle of Charles the Bald; Lothar married the daughter of Hugh of Tours; his son, Lothar II, King of Lorraine, married Theutberga, of Boso's line; Charles the Bald married Ermentrude, daughter of Odo of Orleans and niece of the seneschal Adalard. We know of these ninth-century marriages because this period is relatively well documented; but we have every reason to believe that long before this time alliances were being contracted between Austrasian families and the Arnulfians. The flourishing clan spirit of the period certainly explains the fact that the highest positions in the realm were almost exclusively entrusted to the aristocracy.

Ownership of land as the basis of social importance

These families possessed considerable wealth in the form of inherited property, or abbeys given to some of their members, who
had handed them on to their descendants with their other estates.
The habit of making such enormously valuable gifts as abbeys dated
at least from the reign of Charles Martel.

We know what landed property was owned by a few of these
families. This is the case with a very important figure, Fulrad,
Abbot of St Denis, head of the Royal Chapel, confidential adviser
to Pepin the Short and Charlemagne. He belonged to an Alsatian
family connected with that of St Chrodegang, bishop of Metz,
and so probably with the Carolingians. In 768 he bequeathed his
fortune to St Denis, and his will gives us evidence that he owned
extensive lands in three regions: six places in Alsace, in the
neighbourhood of Strasbourg, Selestat, Haguenau and Colmar;
eight in Lorraine, in the valley of the Seille, near Metz, Château-
Salins, Nancy, Sarrebourg and Dieuze; and six in the Sarre, near
Sarreguemines in the valley of the Blies. All this represented an
immense fortune in real estate on both sides of the Vosges, without
counting some isolated villages on the right bank of the Rhine and
as far as the upper valley of the Danube. Of course these lands
were not all contiguous, but they made up regions of vast extent;
it must also be remembered that Fulrad belonged to the Church,
was the younger son of a noble family, and that his inheritance
seems to have been the least valuable part of his parents' possessions.

We also know what property was owned by the Welfs. This
consisted in a group of domains in the valley of the Schüssen, north
of Lake Constance, around Weingart and Altdorf. If we remember
that each domain may have had an area of from 1,000 to 12,000
acres, we shall realise how immense was the landed wealth of the
aristocracy of the ninth century. The lands we know most about
are those that belonged to the Carolingians before they came to the
throne. They stretched from both sides of the Meuse between
Revin and Maastricht across a huge region bordered on the west

by Nivelles and Frasnes, and on the east by Malmédy and Bastogne. As well as the royal residences of Estinnes and Heristal, there were a great many domains in the diocese of Tongres, some of considerable size, like Fosses which included five communes, and also several abbeys, such as Nivelles, founded about 640 by Itta, widow of Pepin of Landen, on family property. One of Charlemagne's charters tells us that Pepin of Heristal had presented to the church of Chèvremont property in Toxandria, Brabant and Hainault, between the old Roman road and the Sambre. One of his relations may have given five domains to the abbey of Floreffe. In 691, his mother founded the monastery of Andenne and endowed it with all the surrounding villages. Yet all these gifts evidently only represented a fragment of the family inheritance, which seems to have swallowed up the whole region of more than 2,000 square miles and included the land from two Roman *civitates*. The Arnulfians certainly must have disposed of the revenues of several bishoprics and counties, besides this land, and also the tolls payable on that part of the road from Cologne to Bavai lying within its boundaries. If as seems probable Fulrad belonged to this family, it is clear that, as a result of the penetration of the Franks into Alemannia, the huge territories owned by the Arnulfians extended into many other regions besides the neighbourhood of Tongres.

These family estates only formed a part of their wealth however. After the end of the eighth century not merely one, but several abbeys might pass into their possession. The family of Tassilo, Duke of Bavaria, owned those of Jumièges, Chelles and Laon. Laymen abbots were frequent, and officially recognised by the kings from Pepin the Short to Charles the Bald, who distributed monasteries as gifts to their faithful supporters. And before Pepin the Short's day, the nobles used to seize them for themselves if they were powerful enough. Often too, in the eighth and ninth centuries, the abbeys were given to a neighbouring count to provide him with revenues; this happened to St Maixent and Brioude. Often too, they were given to a bishop: the Bishop of Trèves owned the abbey of Mettlach, the Bishop of Le Mans the abbey of St Calais, the

Bishop of Saintes the abbey of Noirmoutier, the Bishop of Sens the abbey of Echternach. People of importance regularly acquired abbeys; Charlemagne's friend and mentor Alcuin, an enlightened and devout man, possessed at least four abbeys, possibly five or six; Ansegis, later Abbot of St Wandrille and Luxeuil, was given St Sixte at Rheims and St Memmius at Châlons by Charlemagne.

Counts and bishops belonged to the Frankish aristocracy and were chosen from noble families, for it was among this nobility that men could be found with the education and class-consciousness to carry out the official functions of the realm. It was natural therefore, that, since the bishoprics were almost as rich as the monasteries, any family that had furnished the same see with several bishops began to think of the bishopric as a family inheritance. Two generations later, when the descendants of counts were established in towns where their ancestors had held temporary and terminable office, they often appropriated the bishopric as well as the title and office of count. This happened at Bourges, Angers and Chartres, for example. In this way they built up a fortune for themselves.

The people

Ownership of land was in fact the only real form of wealth, and the only means of acquiring power and social importance. Classes that possessed none were treated as of humble rank, and carried no weight in the kingdom. Very little is known about the town-dwellers of the period, but something is coming to light about the peasant classes, the people who lived on the domains of laymen or ecclesiastics, and developed the land – whose labour in fact supported the whole population.

It is often said that the peasantry was a numerous class living in great poverty. This is very probably true, but we cannot treat it as certain, for we have few facts bearing on the population and their standard of living. The most probable hypothesis is that there were regional differences, and that as a whole the peasants had to work very hard with primitive methods for little reward.

The only facts we know for certain about them are: first, that from the legal point of view peasants were of two distinct categories, those who were free and those who were not, and secondly, that economically speaking this made very little difference.

Free peasants, or *pagenses*, were entirely free; there was no question for them of slavery or semi-liberty; they could be smallholders or tenants, but in either case their status as freemen was respected, and involved all the usual obligations: military and judiciary service, and an oath of fidelity to the sovereign. The fact that they did the same work began to diminish the difference between those who were free and those who were not, but even after this the legal distinction remained: in law, a *pagensis*, unlike a serf, was always free to abandon his holding. However, among these freemen, some were attached to the soil; these were the tenant-farmers, whose status was ill-defined, but they reaped the profits from the land they cultivated and were attached to its owner. In their case military service was confined to providing transport for the royal army. But they kept their status as freemen, as is proved by the fact that their personal obligations were their own responsibility, instead of their master's as in the case of *servi*.

Although the *servi* or *mancipia* took their names from Roman slavery, their conditions were very different from those of the slaves of antiquity. Of course true slaves did exist and would continue to do so until the tenth century, but they were relatively few. The ancient idea that a slave was not a man but a thing had already been attacked in pagan times by the Stoics, and later on by the Christian belief that slaves had the same fundamental rights as men who were legally free. The Church had not insisted on the abolition of slavery, but had been content to proclaim that a slave was a man, that his master had no right to kill or ill-treat him, and – particularly important – that any contract entered into by a slave, such as marriage, was as valid as in the case of freemen. Also, the economy of the early Middle Ages was very different from that of antiquity, and the old means of recruiting slaves no longer existed, nor did the organisation for dealing with hordes of them, as in ancient Rome. These two reasons, one moral, the other economic, gradually changed the conditions of this stratum of society. Although slave trading was still widespread in the seventh century, as the laws of the barbarians prove, and although it still existed in the Carolingian epoch, especially before the end of the Saxon wars, it was only with Moslem countries. In the Christian West slavery took the new form of serfdom. In the Carolingian Empire there were still numerous serfs, most of them 'villeins', that is to say they led independent lives with their families on holdings given them in exchange for working without wage. As a general rule the *servi* and *mancipia* mentioned in documents, or the polyptyches of the large abbeys, belonged to this class of villeins.

Already some of the characteristics of eleventh- and twelfth-century serfdom were beginning to develop. Serfs had to pay 'chevage' and marriage dues, and their legal relationship with their seigneur was based on his help and protection and regulated by custom. As Benjamin Guérard and Marc Bloch have explained, a serf was not a thing, as a slave used to be; he was as it were an inferior vassal, but – unlike a freeman – his vassalage was automatically passed on to his descendants. If *mancipia* who were not villeins still existed, and if villeins seem to us the aristocracy of slavery, the fact that both of them had to pay chevage distinguished them from the slaves of antiquity. They were not at the mercy of their master's caprice.

The position of serfs was changing all the time. The category known as *lidi* or *liti*, who figured in barbarian law and were entitled to a *wergeld* between a freeman's and a slave's, were gradually disappearing; except that they seem to have been a superior rank of serf, we have very little information about them. But our information about those who were not freemen is on the whole vague. It seems that in certain parts of the Empire, particularly in Bavaria, there were three chief categories: journeymen serfs, living with their master or his officers and employed as domestics or on the land; villeins, under contract to do a great deal of hard work, but living on their holdings; and *ministeriales*, carrying out various trades indispensable to society. All these classes overlapped, and journeymen serfs and *ministeriales* could be recruited from among the younger sons of villeins, bastards, delinquents or bankrupts, and might one day be granted a holding of their own.

It is therefore clear that a class of men existed who were not slaves, nor yet free in the eyes of the law, who were closely bound to their seigneur, yet remained within certain limits masters of their own persons and possessions, and who might very often be villeins, a condition which put them almost on an equality with the free peasantry from a legal point of view, and finally who owed no allegiance to the king, but everything to their seigneur.

But social developments in the Carolingian period were not confined to serfdom; the whole of society was moving towards a seigneurial regime, that is to say towards the creation of bonds of dependence even among freemen, which replaced the king's authority by the real, immediate and present power of the man on whom other men depended. As a result, all the inhabitants of a domain tended to become incorporated among the *servi*. The tenant-farmers, for instance, were freemen who had to swear allegiance to the king, were subject to the count's tribunal, and could act as assessors at the immunity tribunals. Yet there were limits to their liberty, for they were attached to a piece of land which they were not allowed to leave; they were subjects of a master who held them under his *mithium*, and thus in almost the same position as tenants of servile origin. In the middle of the ninth century, Charles the Bald extended to these tenant-farmers the corporal punishment used for slaves; and instructions given to a *missus* have been perserved, ordering him to apply the same rules to the marriage of tenant-farmers as to those of *servi*, 'for there are only two categories of men, freemen and *servi*'.

All these factors resulted in some confusion. Irminon's Polyptych (a record of the possessions and revenue of the abbey of St Germain-des-Prés at the beginning of the ninth century) records that a man's status as a tenant-farmer, a *litus*, *servus*, or free-man was a matter of minor importance. Two things really counted: first, that service was owed by the land not the man, and tenure took the place of legal status; secondly, whether the man in question belonged to St Germain-des-Prés. Henceforth, the bond of personal dependence, with its counterpart – tenure – was far more important than legal status. These changes were taking place in Charlemagne's reign, the period when the Polyptych was drawn up, and continued until the end of the ninth century. The seigneurial regime had begun, and was rapidly developing.

It is not surprising that society was becoming organised as a hierarchy of dependence. In the end the king had lost all control over freemen, except through the agency of men known to them, living near them, and on whom they directly depended. A whole series of intermediate rungs of the ladder were being constructed between subject and sovereign, until, by the end of the ninth century, the hierarchy was complete. By that time the king was merely the supreme overlord, surrounded by a few faithful followers, while the administration, not merely of separate counties, but of vast groups of counties, was in the hands of the nobility.

This new structure was gradually forming throughout the Carolingian era. From the top to the bottom of the social ladder, men were being regrouped as a result of marriage or kinship, or the accumulation in the hands of influential families of the true source of power – wealth, and especially land.

4 The economy and the sources of wealth

Domanial economy

Wealth played at least as considerable a part in the Carolingian world as in any other epoch, and was the means to power and honours. It was now that one of the most deceptive currents of medieval mentality originated: high office, even a purely spiritual one, was no longer distinct from high social rank. Counts, abbots and bishops had to demonstrate the importance of their function by outward display; they must be powerful; they must be 'rich men'. This was the reason for the important endowments they received – a *comitatus* (often accompanied by a benefice) for a count, an *episcopatus* for a bishop, and an *abbatia* for an abbot.

These were all forms of landed property. Movable property also existed, but on a smaller scale, and was concentrated mainly in the hands of those occupied in trade, an indispensable branch of the economy. On the whole we know little about Carolingian economy. Only a few scattered and vague references have been preserved, and there is an extreme poverty of documentary sources. We must try and sketch the outline however.

Wealth was above all ownership of land, and economy was therefore a matter for each domain. Domanial economy dated back to the Late Roman Empire and persisted and developed under the Merovingians. The domains of the Carolingian period are known to us through texts dating from the beginning of the ninth century. Among the best known are administrative documents, such as the *Capitulary of villis* and the *Brevium exempla* – the former setting out the principles of management and enabling us to get an idea of the proportion of land devoted to crops and pasture and the relation of yield to stock, while the latter is a model description of a domain and the keeping of its accounts. Several abbey polyptyches are also famous, such as those of St Germain-des-Prés, dating from Irminon's abbacy, and of St Rémi at Rheims.

Most of the domains seem to have covered a vast area, though they varied considerably in size. The *Brevium exempla* was modelled on that of the fiscal domain at Annappes, near Lille. Calculations

Horse-drawn chariot. Manuscript of the *Psychomachia* of Prudentius, end of the ninth century. Paris, Bibliothèque Nationale, ms. lat. 8085, fol. 62. The Christian poet Prudentius (348–*c.*410) was one of the most read early medieval authors. His symbolic poem *Psychomachia*, or 'Battle of the Soul' describes a battle between the vices and the virtues. Here soldiers are about to surrender. Horses were still harnessed with a collar rather than a yoke, reducing their pulling power.

Cart drawn by oxen. Detail of a miniature
from Folchard's Psalter, ninth century.
St Gall, Stiftsbibliothek, Cod. 23, p. 12.
Cartage was a duty often imposed on
the peasants. Like the horses, the
oxen here are harnessed with a collar.

of the number of barrels of corn and other produce help to show
that this domain probably corresponded to the 2,500 acres of the
present *commune* of Annappes. A comparable domain at Palaiseau,
near Paris, belonged to St Germain-des-Prés, and was also an
ancient royal *villa*. The domain of Fontaine - Bonneleau in the
Beauvaisis, which was presented to the cathedral of Amiens in
about 850, included several villages, agricultural land and pasture;
the seigneurial reserve alone probably included 1,000 acres, and the
whole domain about 4,000.

These vast estates, many of them larger than modern French
rural *communes*, were exploited on a more or less uniform plan.
The land was divided between the seigneur's reserve and the
holdings worked by the peasants. It was cultivated by free peasants
or serfs (heavier work being demanded of the serfs) with the object
of getting the best out of the land, which was divided for the purpose into 'manses', or holdings varying in size according to value
and productivity, but each probably calculated to support a peasant

$\mathcal{S}$

family. In return for his tenancy, the head of each family owed his seigneur a certain rent in money and produce, as well as the amount of free labour fixed by custom and circumstances. Gradually, probably to avoid the confusion caused by a change of tenant, these services and rents began to be thought of as owed by the land rather than the man, as Irminon's *Polyptych* recorded. Thus manses could be held by freemen or serfs, so long as the services and rents were kept up. The increase in the population led to manses being shared. By the beginning of the ninth century two or three families might be found living on a single manse, each contributing a part of what was due, though this did not change, but remained what it had always been for this piece of land.

All the tenants living on a domain, whether freemen or serfs, cultivated their land, helped develop the reserve, and contributed to carting, fencing and the upkeep of outhouses, according to the conditions of their tenure. They had rights of grazing, and of access to the rivers watering the domain, and the neighbouring forests and copses where their pigs could be fattened. The serf families also provided servants, who lived on the reserve and were fed by the seigneur, women who worked in the female quarters at spinning and weaving or in the poultry-yard, and artisans who were supplied with wood and iron for mending agricultural implements.

Labourers often worked in co-operation, using the seigneur's plough and harness. But local customs regulated everything, particularly the rotation of crops, which was usually biennial. Medieval crops were always poor, and would probably amount to about fourteen bushels per acre in modern measures, or the equivalent of the yield of the poorest countries before 1914. As for stock farming, the half-wild pigs that strayed in search of acorns were probably of moderate quality, but the cows must have been poor specimens, because of the scarcity of grazing, nor was this adequately supplied by the commonland outside the domain.

Nevertheless the whole domain provided a livelihood for the seigneur, his stewards and the peasants, and formed a community represented by the parish, of which the seigneur was often patron.

Economically the domain played a far from negligible part, but it was a form of exploitation which produced a closed economy. Transport was very difficult: we have every reason to believe that the Roman roads had been neglected under the Merovingians. The best plan for a very rich man owning several domains was to move with all his numerous followers to each of them in rotation. This was what the Frankish kings did, and their successors continued to do so until the sixteenth century.

However, each domain produced a surplus of some sort which could be commercialised. We have some idea of what trade must have been like in the Carolingian period. There must have been internal transactions to do with the marginal activities of the domain. The products of the workshops, particularly stuffs, were almost entirely for home consumption, and may not even have been adequate for this. And any agricultural surplus must have been slight. Storage was a difficult problem, and from the *Brevium exempla* we learn that farm produce was very quickly distributed among the inhabitants of the domain. We find that a *casa indominicata*, consisting of 740 'journals' (as much land as could be ploughed in a day) of agricultural land, had no corn in its granaries: everything had been distributed for fodder until the next harvest. Stores of bacon and beer were kept, the livestock were counted, but there is no mention of produce being sold. From this document it seems that any surplus was disposed of immediately after the harvest, and that sales occurred only rarely, in times of shortage for instance. We can be sure that the sale of the produce of a domain was a regular seasonal affair. There are signs of an effort towards a closed economy: for instance the monks of the abbeys of Belgian Gaul acquired domains further south to provide wine for themselves, and the Irminon's Polyptych mentions cartage of wine from Berry to Paris. Every important landowner tried to be self-supporting. However there are indications that exchanges of goods did go on: for one thing, the importance and prosperity of abbey domains inevitably led to sales outside; for another, however good the economy of a domain might be, there were some provisions that could not be found everywhere and had to be bought – salt for instance. It is impossible to say how important these transactions were; they may have been very slight, but the existence of fairs and markets proves that there were some.

Trade

There were many fairs at the beginning of the Carolingian period: that of St Denis near Paris, on 9 October, dated back to the reign of Dagobert I early in the seventh century; that of St Matthias (24 February) lasted eight days and was first held in about 775. These fairs were frequented by foreign merchants, especially the English, and we know that wine, honey and dye-stuffs were on sale. In the north of Italy fairs were more common. The situation of Pavia, for instance, was especially suitable: it stood at the meeting-point of three routes used by traders on their way to the Adriatic, who had been driven from the shores of the Tyrrhenian Sea by Moorish pirates. New markets were constantly appearing in this region during the period between the eighth and tenth centuries. Professor Violante has shown that this development depended on the domanial system. Spontaneous social evolution had concentrated the land in the hands of the great seigneurs, and this could have resulted in a closed economy and the slowing up of real trade. But the founding of fairs and markets was a sure sign of a contrary trend. So also was the increase in tolls, payable in theory to the public authority, but gradually being usurped by the seigneurs: the great landowners sought and were granted the right to hold markets on their own land. And these markets were not only for transactions between the different domains of a single seigneur. Had that been the case it would have been pointless to collect market dues and tolls. The central government had forbidden such charges being made on people carrying merchandise for their own use and not with a view to trade, as we learn from Charlemagne's capitulary of Thionville. So that we are forced to conclude that these markets were intended for the disposal of any agricultural or industrial

St Germain-des-Prés, drawn
up by order of Abbot Irminon, is extremely
detailed. It indicates the different
tasks entrusted to them and the rent they
paid. The page shown here relates to
the domain of Palaiseau, near Paris.

De Palatiolo

Palatiolum

Habet in Palatiolo mansum dominicatum
cum casa et aliis stabilibus sufficienter.
Habet ibi de terra arabili culturas VI,
quae habent bunuaria CCLXXXVII, ubi possunt seminari de frumento mod. I·CCC.
de annona ari p. CXXVII. ubi poss. colligi de uino mod. DCCC.

Habet de prato ari p. e ubi possunt
colligi de feno. carra· CL·

Habet ibi de silua, sicut aestimatur, per
totum in giro leuua I. ubi poss. sagina-
ri porci·L·

Habet ibi farinarios III. exit inde
in censu de annona. mod. CL·IIII.

Habet ibi ecclesiam I. cum omni appa-
ratu diligenter constructam, aspiciunt ibi de terra arab. bun. XVII.
de uinea ari p. V et dimidium,
de prato ari p. III. excepto hab. ibi
mansu ing. I. habente de terra arab
bun. IIII. et ancp. II. de uinea ari p. I.
et dimid. de prato ari p. III. habet
ibi hospitia VI. quae habent de terra
arab. unusquisq; iornale I. et inde
faciunt in unaquaq; ebd. diem I.
pullum ouaV· Habet aliam ecclesiam in giro quem uuarod pbr tenet,
aspiciunt ibi hospitia VI. et hab. in ipsa
prebm. et hospites de terra arab.
bun. VI. et dimd. de uinea ari p. V.

de prato ari p. V. de silua no-
uella. bun. I. faciunt in u-
naquaq; ebd. diem I. si eos
pauperit· pullum ouaV· de-
nariosinj· exit inde in dona-
cabat· I·

Uualafred· cot. et maior.
auxorcii cot. n. eudi mia.
homines sci germani hab. secum
inf. II. hi sunt· uualabildis
leutgardis. tenet mansos ing.
IJ. hab. de terra arab. bun. VI.
de uinea. ari p. VI. de prato
ari p. IIJ. soluit denuu qdq;
mansu boue· I. ad aliud anni
soate I. in ligno et cia. denrum
de uino in pascione. mod IJ.
ueruicecu agno I. arat ad
hibernat pticas IIII. ad
tronis. pticas IJ. couuadas
carrop. manop. capita quan-
tu ei iube pult in ouaXV·
Ai r mundi. cot. et uxorcii cot.
n. hal drada ti. faciut· hab.
secum inf. V. hi sunt. n. elisom
hildegaud. eliseus. raidhil-
dis. hairuueo. tenet mansu
ingenuilem I. habentem
de terra arab. bun. X·
de uinea· ari p. IJ. de prato ari p
I et dimd· Soluit similiter·

surplus, and for acquiring necessaries unobtainable in the domain itself. Trade cannot therefore have been brought to a standstill or even localised; on the contrary, the concentration of landed property made external commerce possible. The increased charges for *portaticum*, *teloneum* and *ripaticum* show that the emperors were interested in the expansion of trade. Merchants had not disappeared as a class, and if the transit charges were being appropriated more and more by the landowners, this only reflected a displacement of political power, not a change in the economy.

The full significance of these commercial transactions escapes us, partly because documents are extremely rare, but also because what we have are inexplicit. They hardly provide us with a single fact that cannot be interpreted in several ways. For example, some capitularies give orders that serfs must not be allowed to hang about the markets: does this mean that the fairs attracted great crowds, or on the contrary that it was because so little was on sale that it was possible to loiter there? Is the increase in fairs and markets a sign that there were now more commodities to sell and that there was an ever-increasing surplus to dispose of, or can it on the contrary be explained by the growing difficulty in communications, paralysing trade and forcing it to become more local? It is all very obscure. One thing is certain, and that is that trade did exist, and that commercial life was going on in the towns.

But what were the towns of the Carolingian period like? We possess the rather summary information that they were fortified groups of buildings, still preserving their Roman ramparts. Some of them were quite important, as can be seen from the size of the area enclosed by the ramparts. We have practically no evidence about the size of their populations, but it is unlikely that they were smaller than under the Byzantine Empire. As in the eleventh and twelfth centuries, they were composed of houses, gardens and even some farmland. But they cannot have provided enough food to be self-supporting, and must therefore have depended on the surrounding country, a fact which presupposes a fairly active local trade. It is certain that towns such as Tours, Poitiers, Avignon, Arles,

Cologne, Metz, Paris and Milan each contained several thousand inhabitants. We know that a number of towns were sacked by the Normans, and that the loot collected by these barbarians came from private houses as well as churches. The citizens must therefore have accumulated some wealth, and this is not surprising in towns known as centres of commerce. Charlemagne's contemporary, Theodulf, described the goods stored in Arles; in the eighth century, Mainz traded with the Slavs, and a little later a colony of Frisian merchants settled there. Professor Vercauteren's description of Belgian towns creates the same impression; but this was undoubtedly a region more favourable to trade than the others; business was conducted on an ample scale, and in about 850 several toll bridges were established on the river Marne – a sure sign of prosperity. In 779, Amiens was one of the most important toll-booth towns in the Empire, and controlled communications between trading centres like the port of Quentovic at the mouth of the Canche Dunrstede on the Lek (not far from present-day Rotterdam), Maastricht and Rouen. At Quentovic there was a flourishing mint, and the task of collecting taxes – all indirect – was given in 787 to Gervold, Abbot of Fontenelle. In Italy the towns of the Po valley drained off most of the trade. In Germany Mainz and Aix-la-Chapelle, in Lorraine Verdun, in Provence Arles and Marseilles were all famous for their commerce. All this goes to show that even if urban economy had been reduced it had not been destroyed, and that trade was going on, to what extent we do not know, but even if it was not flourishing it cannot have been negligible.

But were there at this time any professional traders – in other words a merchant class? We know that such a class existed in the Merovingian epoch, but its survival into the next period has been questioned. The merchants from the Orient who had settled in the West during the sixth century do in fact seem to have disappeared, but there were certainly others of various different sorts. Scandinavians put in an appearance, and we find Jewish merchants, who kept up the link with the East by buying merchandise there and selling it in the West where it was unobtainable, and also engaging

Silver denier of Charlemagne's reign, minted at Quentovic. Cambridge, in the collection of Professor Philip Grierson. Mints had to be set up close to large centres of trade so that merchants could obtain currency. Coins struck at Quentovic, the great commercial centre on the river Canche, bear a ship as a symbol of the activity of the port.

in the slave trade when opportunity offered. We have evidence also that little colporteurs, like the *quidam pauperculus* of Orleans, used to go from town to town with a donkey loaded with goods, buying and selling; the business they did was on a very small scale, and they probably frequented the weekly markets. But there were also more prosperous merchants, who made trade their profession. For instance certain merchants from Mainz – a centre of the corn trade – used regularly to go up the river Main to collect supplies, and carried on a steady traffic between their town and Fulda and Thuringia. It is known that in the tenth century they pressed further east and did business with the Levant. In Sweden, in the middle of the ninth century, the town of Björkö on Lake Mälar was famous for the prosperity of its merchants and the abundance and variety of the produce sold there. A group of traders had existed since the ninth century at Verdun, and in the tenth it became the centre of the slave-trade; slaves were brought there from the eastern frontiers of the Christian kingdoms and sent on by way of Arles to Moorish Spain.

We have other evidence of the existence of merchants being engaged in business on a large scale: in 796, Charlemagne was negotiating with Offa, King of Mercia, with a view to securing mutual protection for their respective traders; he also granted the merchants of St Denis exemption from paying tolls. Some privileged merchants even seem to have obtained monopolies. At first these were the palace merchants, whose existence in the reign of Louis the Pious is proved by their mention in the *Formulae imperiales*. They enjoyed the king's special protection and various immunities, in return for which they had to perform certain services, such as keeping the palace supplied. But as they were chosen by court officials and their numbers were limited, there was no question of any extensive business organisation. They also acted as agents for the transport of the produce of the imperial villas (wine, building stone, lead, etc). Very similar were the abbey merchants, who also enjoyed exemption from tolls. Court and abbey merchants were in fact recipients of concessions; in return for supplying goods to the

establishments that employed them they used the circuits thus created to dispose of their own merchandise and conduct a profitable business.

There is evidence that a merchant class already existed in the north of Italy in the eighth century: a decree of Aistulf's concerning recruiting for the army fixes the military service required from merchants; they had either to serve as lightly armed foot-soldiers or as fully armed cavalrymen, according to their wealth. It is note-worthy that the property taken as a basis for service was exclusively movable; here we find the first instance of movable wealth being ranked with ownership of land. Later on, the Thionville capitulary equates recipients of a revenue of six pounds with owners of four manses; both were liable to pay *heriban* – the tax for immunity from military service. However, in the hierarchy of Carolingian society, owners of movable possessions were inferior to landowners, for even if they were rich they were not in a position of authority, and had no dependants to offer to the army.

The Thionville capitulary provides further evidence that a class of rich merchants did exist. In Lombardy, after the period when trade by river was controlled by the *milites* of Comacchio, professional merchants combined with landowners to form a commercial circuit, in return for which they were recompensed with privileges, protection and exemption from dues. They owned their own boats, had supplanted the inhabitants of Comacchio within fifty years, and were soon afterwards firmly established at Pavia and Cremona. The Milanese merchants mixed more and more with the great landowners, and bought land themselves – a sure sign of a rise in the social scale. The ninth century also witnessed the birth of the town of Venice and its important trade. Protected by the emperors, Venice captured the spice market and became the main centre for trade with the East.

A considerable amount of trade was obviously going on, although its importance has for long been questioned by some historians. A great many works have been published on the subject and we can now gather something of its nature, potentialities and limits. Of course commercial activity was partly conditioned by political circumstances, and taking the period as a whole there were fluctuations according to time and place. For instance, Mediterranean trade was in difficulties and therefore much reduced when the Moors settled in Spain, Septimania and Italy; trading in northern Europe decreased under the influence of the terror inspired by Viking raids; and central European trade had a setback as a result of the inroads of the Avars and the Hungarians. These were all cruel disasters whose results were felt for several years, after which there was a rapid revival.

Without embarking on the sweeping generalisations that have complicated the discussions of scholars, we must not lose sight of two features that have been brought to light by two contemporary historians. The first, emphasised by Monsieur L. Musset, is that though the ravages of the Scandinavian invaders made so great an impression on the minds of chroniclers, they were only temporary disasters, between which the North and West re-established commercial relations, even if only in order to redistribute the booty the former had taken from the latter; thus *emporia* were set up on the shores of the Baltic, for instance at Hedeby, where slaves, precious metals, horses and furs were traded for wine, arms, stuffs and glassware, to the great profit of the Saxons and Frisians, while the Christian depot at Duurstede was frequented by Scandinavians. The second point, clarified by Monsieur F. Himly, is that it is important not to think of the Moslem and Christian worlds as homogeneous blocs, and so fail to take account of regional differences, the independence of some individual governor from the purely theoretical central power, or the discords within these apparently united blocs. We must remember that Charlemagne had diplomatic and commercial contacts with Haroun ar-Raschid and the East, at the same time that he was waging war against the Moors in Spain. The importance of political struggles and their repercussions on the economy is sometimes greatly exaggerated.

It is certain however that piracy by sea, without completely putting a stop to trading – for it had been an endemic disease ever since ancient times, and had never brought circulation in the Mediterranean to a complete standstill – had nevertheless hampered and reduced it to a marked extent. Moorish pirates in the south, Scandinavians and Irish in the north, diminished the amount of trade carried on. Merchants were obliged to abandon their established routes, but they soon opened others.

Nonetheless, during the age of Charlemagne, trade routes which had been in operation since time immemorial still existed. To the east of the Empire, trade flowed along the great Russian river-ways connecting the northern regions with the Caspian Sea and Byzantium; to the west, communications with the British Isles, Gaul and the Lusitanian coast by sea had never been interrupted. Within the Empire, the most frequented land routes were those converging on the deltas of the Rhine, Meuse and Scheldt; this point was opposite London whose commercial importance was on the increase, thanks to its unique situation near the navigable mouth of the Thames and the great Roman roads that diverged from it – Watling Street leading to Chester, and Ermine Street to York. In the ancient kingdom of Austrasia, trade moved along the old Roman road from Rheims to Cologne, by way of Bavai, Tongres and Maastricht; further south routes through the Meuse joined the Rhône valley by way of Verdun, Langres and Dijon; and a cross-country route from Verdun to Strasbourg and the Swabian Jura joined the Danube at Ratisbon. Finally, Italy was accessible by three routes: the first from the Rhine to Bellinzona and Como, the second passing through the Jura and over the great St Bernard, and the third by the valley of the Saône, Maurienne and Mont Cenis. These three routes converged on Pavia, whose commercial importance can be further understood if it is realised that merchandise could be conveyed thence by land or river to Venice, the centre of trade with Byzantium, or to Bari or Rome.

These great routes determined the character of trade in the different regions of the Empire. Relations with the southern countries were different from those with the north. In the south, Mediterranean trade was directed towards Byzantium, Italy and Spain. Ever since the beginning of the eighth century Byzantine economy had suffered an undeniable decline, not so much as a result of an offensive blockade by the Moors as of a defensive one attempted by the Greeks. The latter no longer acted as middlemen in the traffic in spices, although these were still on sale in the markets of the West: in fact, protected by their kings, the merchants had divided this traffic, once a Byzantine monopoly, among themselves, and went in person to the East to get the supplies which no longer passed through Constantinople. In Italy, since the end of the seventh century, the Tyrrhenian Sea had been closed by the Spanish and African Moors, who were at the height of their period of conquests, and invaded Sicily and southern Italy, overcoming the defences organised by Charlemagne and later by Lothar. In spite of the Frankish reconquest of Septimania, and of some success in naval battles, the war went on, and piracy flourished unchecked. Trade now changed its course and went by land across Italy to the Adriatic; this was for a long time the only route to the East. Commercial transactions with Spain kept going in spite of the war. Under Pepin the Short and Charlemagne, the port of Marseilles was still used; and Arles remained a prosperous market, frequented by the Greeks. In 812, Theodulf saw Moorish coins there, as well as precious stones, Cordoba leather, silks and everything indicative of active trade with the Moslems. At the end of the ninth century, it was on the route of the slave-traffic between Verdun and Spain. We shall never know how much trade went on with Moorish Spain; it must have fluctuated with the political situation, but it did exist and there is no evidence of a break in relations between the Christian and Moslem worlds.

To the north, the most active trade was with the British Isles, Scandinavia and the Slavonic countries. Commercial relations with England had begun in the fifth century at the latest, and had never been broken off despite Irish piracy. At the end of the seventh century, English ships used often to put in at the mouth of the Loire, and the Saxon money found there shows that intensive trading went on along the whole coast from the Charente to Frisia. The conquest of Spain by the Moors led to renewed activity there, though the Aquitainians were temporarily cut off from this sector. Oriental produce like silk or papyrus, on its way anywhere north of the Pyrenees, was now sent to England with oil from Narbonne, salt from the Charente and lead from Melle. In the first half of the ninth century, progress in ship-building, with such new types of boat as the *scapha* (a coastal vessel) and the *barca* (for the high seas) replacing the old Mediterranean or Breton models, stimulated trade with the British Isles. This was also the moment when Charlemagne's defensive campaigns kept the Normans away from the shores of the Empire. A maritime march was created, with headquarters and a procurator of customs at Quentovic, lighthouses were built, and ports like Quentovic and Duurstede were improved. The Frisians were the most active professional intermediaries between England and the continent; they were busy from Denmark to the Seine, up which they travelled as far as St Denis, taking with them the famous garments known as *pallia frisonica*, though really made in England.

The chief cause of the economic decline of the Mediterranean countries during the ninth century was the arrival of the Scandinavians, who had profited from revolutionary nautical advances, begun to build large ocean-going ships a hundred years before, and overrun the coasts in search of plunder or trade. They now depended chiefly on plunder, though trading did not stop altogether. The trade route between the Frankish world and the Slavonic countries was probably established by them. The Normans were certainly known in Russia where, under the name of Varangians, they led expeditions to collect slaves and a great many different kinds of produce.

Thus we see that trade went on in the Frankish world, though on a reduced scale, after the middle of the ninth century, when a period of anarchy and perpetual warfare began among the Christian countries. There were phases of activity on one coast or another, its chief trend being towards the north. Trade in the Mediterranean became more difficult, because of the dangers to be met with on some of its coasts and the decline in the prosperity of Byzantium; the Moslem world was an open market for slaves or produce from the north, and the northern races were now mingling with the civilised world. These were the main influences turning Frankish trade away from the Mediterranean towards the Baltic, with certain consequences affecting the currency.

In the sixth century world markets had been dominated by the Byzantine *nomisma*, a gold coin of high quality, by means of which the Eastern Empire had tided over economic difficulties in the seventh century. But a new situation was created by the fact that the Moors had seized the sources of supply of gold. The Moslems did not only mint gold coins: in Asia the currency was all silver, while Africa and Spain held large stocks of gold. At the same time, gold coins were becoming scarce in the West. It was now that Charlemagne gave up striking gold coins, and they disappeared from Gaul, where nothing but silver deniers were minted. Only in Italy was gold currency still kept going, and in spite of large reserves, the gold-standard was abandoned as a whole in the West. There were several reasons for this: first, metal now played a less important part in trade, which was often carried on by barter (the increased number of mints only showed that more small coins were needed for the internal market); then again, transport of gold became more and more difficult as insecurity increased, and hoarding became more common; and finally, from the middle of the ninth century, money gradually ceased to be under the king's control. The last effort to preserve it was the Edict of Pîtres, issued in 864 by Charles the Bald, which laid down some regulations that were absolutely impossible to apply. It is certain that gold could no longer be considered the only means of settling a commercial account at this time; some historians have greatly exaggerated its importance.

But the commercial economy, however active it may have been at this period, only affected a very small part of the population. Throughout the Middle Ages, the great mass of peasantry had nothing to do with external trade which dealt mainly with luxury objects. Internal trade in corn and clothes concerned them more. Civilisation was above all agrarian, and wealth was concentrated in the hands of two classes, neither of them numerous – merchants and landowners.

Land and tenure

Wealth in this form was always greatly desired by those of high social rank: it was impossible to keep up a social position without being rich, and better still possessing land, and authority over the numerous inhabitants of a domain. But changes were taking place in the distribution of land. The Roman idea of full ownership had figured in the Frankish world as *allodium*, but it was beginning to be replaced by tenure, or possession that was in principle revocable, and in the ninth and tenth centuries this became the normal manner of owning property. Inherited wealth, *allodia*, absolute possession of land without obligation of any sort, was subject to limits. The custom of sharing an estate among an often numerous family made the individual portions smaller with each generation. Every member of the nobility was therefore anxious to increase his property, and he could only do this by marrying a rich heiress, or else by receiving a grant from his sovereign in exchange for faithful service. These grants of land, so sought after by the nobles, were known as benefices; and a layman of high rank might receive an even more generous mark of favour – the gift of an abbey.

The word *beneficium* had been current at least since the seventh century to describe any sort of tenure granted as a favour to the recipient. This form of tenure had the special advantage that it involved no obligation in terms of work, nor payment in kind such as the *agrarium* (a proportion of the harvest); it merely entailed the payment of a very low rent, having no relation to the value of the land – a token rent, whose sole object was to establish the fact that the land did not belong to the occupier but to his master, the beneficiary recognising by this means that he was only a tenant. But this rent was not always insisted upon. The earliest reference to benefices occurs in a charter of 735–7, conferring the abbey of Murbach on Eberhard, son of Adalbert, Duke of Alsace. The mayors of the palace did not own enough land to acquire followers by distributing it, but they gave away Church land. Charles Martel is known to have made this a general custom. When St Boniface remonstrated with the first Carolingian kings about this habit, they were unable to stop it; they merely regularised this form of pillage, and safeguarded the rights of the plundered churches, by insisting on rent being paid even if it was only a token sum. Charlemagne upheld the benefices granted by his predecessors, and gave away others, especially during the early part of his reign. One of the special features of his policy was to increase the number of double benefices, in other words those held jointly by the king and the Church: the capitulary of Heristal makes a clear distinction between the *precaria*, or precarious tenures, granted by request and conceded by order of the king (*verbo regis*), and those spontaneously granted by the churches, which were the only ones that could be revoked by them. But a benefice of Church land was only one form of those granted by the king, which might include his own property. For as a rule a benefice was a concession of land, whether it consisted of an entire domain (*villa*), or only a part. It seems probable that, chiefly in western Gaul, a benefice must include at least four manses. A benefice of twelve manses was granted to men who carried out their military service on horseback, fully armed. The legal status of a benefice was clearly indicated in the capitularies. It was not a property, but a tenancy, and the beneficiary had to submit to supervision, even as to the use he made of it: in particular, he was forbidden to employ people living on his benefice to cultivate his allodial property in times of labour shortage. Above all he must not let the land deteriorate, for the king or the seigneur who had made the grant was still the true owner. The question was, for how long did the concession last? In theory it would end with the death of the beneficiary. In practice, we know that in the ninth century certain benefices had been in the same family for two or three generations, for instance the domains of Baugy and Perrecy in the region of Autun; and one of Charlemagne's charters of 811 states that this was true also of the Italian church at Aquileia. These were matters of fact, but the legal principle did not change: a benefice was a temporary tenure, and the rights of the proprietor were pre-eminent. Benefices were one of the sources of wealth for the social class that was concerned in the administration of separate kingdoms or of the Empire.

Ecclesiastical wealth and lay abbacy

The most valuable form of benefice was the concession of abbeys. Abbeys had been founded as places of worship and work, where monks sought and found a life based on ideals of Christian perfection, but as a result of the generosity of believers they soon acquired large – sometimes vast – landed property; since they were administered more skilfully than the lands of the seigneurs they usually prospered, and brought in considerable revenues. Those established in pagan or thinly populated regions had been endowed with immense areas of uncultivated land, which they had reclaimed and turned into rich farmland. There is evidence that extremely valuable monastic properties already existed in the seventh century, and were multiplying during the eighth. The inventory of possessions of the abbey of Fontenelle (today St Wandrille) made by order of Charlemagne, shows that at the end of the seventh century, under a single abbot, the monastery received more than a thousand donations. At the beginning of the ninth century it was

recorded on Irminon's *Polyptych* that the landed property owned
by St Germain-des-Prés included more than 90,000 acres. The abbey
of Fulda needed fifteen thousand ploughs to cultivate its land.

There was an ancient tradition that these lands constituting the
abbatia should be administered by the abbot of each monastery,
but the bishops very often claimed rights of control over them, not
always with success. Some of the monasteries had been founded by
the kings, and although they were protected by immunity from
tax-collectors, the king was still their true owner. From this
circumstance, the notion soon developed that a monastery and its
land could be owned by a proprietor who left the profit and
administration to the abbot. Owing to the fact that, since Charles
Martel, the monastery had been in the hands of the nobility, the
juridical theory developed about the middle of the eighth century
that an abbot, whether bishop or layman, could hold the *abbatia*
or revenues of a monastery as a benefice. This term *abbatia* had at
first stood for the abbot's position and functions, both spiritual and
temporal, but henceforth it had a purely material reference, that is
to say to the ownership of the land belonging to the monastery and
the profit from it. An abbacy was now merely considered as a
pecuniary advantage. The abbot was thought of as the owner of the
property, and when the king nominated one of his chief vassals as
head of a monastery, it was implied that he was to enjoy the profits
from the land held as a benefice from the king. The two terms
monasterium and *abbatia* co-existed, but had different meanings:
an abbey was no longer a monastery, but enjoyment of the wealth of
a monastery. Although monastic organisation provided for all the
monks of an establishment including the abbot to hold the property
in common, a distinction came to be made between the abbot's and
the monks' income. This custom was legalised by Louis the Pious,
so as to guarantee the monks an adequate share. The king's power
over the churches was derived both from the ancient rights of the
Frankish aristocracy, and the more recent role of the sovereign as
protector of the Church. But protection tended to be confused with
ownership. The king could dispose of an abbey as a benefice, just

as he could any other land or source of profit; the lay beneficiary pocketed the revenues, and handed over the spiritual function to a priest. All this was fairly confused even in the minds of contemporaries, but it is explained in the capitulary of Heristal, where Charlemagne decreed that the beneficiary must maintain the abbey buildings, pay rent and a double tithe to the monastery, and sign an agreement of precarious tenure detailing these obligations. The beneficiary was considered to be the actual abbot. He lived in the monastery as much as he liked, and had authority over the clerics and monks; the monastery's wealth was at his disposal. Alcuin, a churchman of high spiritual integrity, owned several abbeys and invited his friends to enjoy their produce. These immensely wealthy domains were the finest rewards the king could give his faithful adherents: in the middle of the ninth century, Robert the Strong owned the abbeys of St Martin of Tours and St Aubin of Angers. When Theodulf of Orleans was disgraced in 818 he lost at one blow the abbeys of Fleury-sur-Loire and St Aignan of Orleans; in 831 Hilduin lost the abbey of St Denis as a result of his involvement with Lothar.

Most of the lay abbots were counts, to whom abbeys belonging to the treasury had been granted by way of remuneration. After Charlemagne's day, groups of abbeys formed the nucleus of the landed property of all the great noble families. Grants of abbeys were also the normal means for the king to endow his relations: Fulrad, Charles Martel's grandson, was Abbot of Lobbes and St Quentin; Adalard and Wala – also grandsons of Charles Martel – were both Abbots of Corbie; Hugh, half-brother of Louis the Pious, received St Quentin and St Bertin; Angilbert and his son Nithard were Abbots of St Riquier; Charlemagne's daughters and sisters were Abbesses of Argenteuil, Faremoutiers and Chelles. Lorraine contained a great many abbeys, and was coveted in 859 by both Charles the Bald and Louis the German, as an easy means of satisfying the greed of their important vassals now that their own lands were diminished in size.

Lay abbacies thus provided the most important examples of

those concessions of property on which Carolingian society was founded. Trade and movable wealth were means of acquiring rank, but they were on the fringes of the social structure. The Carolingian kings saw society as a hierarchy in which the power given by wealth played an important part, and they encouraged it to develop along these lines. An individual's rank was determined by ownership of land, and the conditions of ownership and the duties it implied established the social hierarchy. Economic power was of first importance and was used by the sovereigns to govern and enforce their authority.

5 The foundations of government

Personal ties and royal vassals

The chief problem for all sovereigns of the Middle Ages, particularly those of the early period, was to gain real and permanent authority over their kingdoms. The Carolingian kings, like many of their successors, had to contend with insuperable difficulties: the vastness of the territories to be governed, the lack of communications, rudimentary administrative organisation, too great autonomy and independence of local chiefs, the constant fear of faithlessness on the part of those to whom authority was delegated, and finally the general shortage of men able to carry out the tasks of government efficiently.

In Charlemagne's day the empire contained over 300 counties administered by counts. But how could these men, alone and almost unaided, put into effect the decisions of the central government, when they were at one and the same time judges, generals and administrators, and often had to leave home and come to court, or were chosen as *missi dominici* to go to other parts of the empire on diplomatic or military missions? The administrative structure was already inadequate, and was becoming more and more lax. Some means of controlling the population and assisting in the task of government had to be sought for in the structure of society itself.

A deeply rooted old Germanic tradition of personal fidelity still existed, a belief in bonds between man and man, and in the obligation of a rich and powerful man to give those who 'commended themselves to him' the means of living according to their station. Herein lay the importance of a personal pledge, but herein also lay its weakness, for fidelity was always an uncertain and variable quantity; hence came the custom of strengthening such bonds and giving them a religious character by an oath; hence also the need for benefices which, as revocable tenures, insured a vassal's fidelity and converted those personal pledges into genuine contracts.

The beneficiary who had been given the tenure of a rural domain was not merely an important figure in the locality, he also had jurisdiction over all the inhabitants of his domain. If he was faithful to his seigneur, he would direct the population in his interests. Thus the benefices made by the king to certain of his immediate dependants seem to us now, and must have seemed to contemporaries, a reasonably satisfactory means of bringing the population of the realm under the control of the central government. The natural result was a hierarchic society, in which the king's authority made itself felt both through officials such as counts and bishops, and through a social class linked to the king morally and financially, possessed of authority over one section of the lower classes, forming the solid nucleus of the army, and pledged to help the king's officers. These were the characteristics of the *vassi dominici*, or direct vassals of the king, at the end of the eighth century.

These men, without having either the rank or power of seigneurs of the upper nobility, formed a class apart, and received the consideration and respect their responsible position deserved. One proof of their importance was that when the oath of personal allegiance to Charlemagne was made by all freemen, as happened several times during his reign, the *vassi dominici* made it to the *missi*, as the counts did, whereas all other subjects made it to the counts. Like all other vassals, the *vassi dominici* had the right to adequate maintenance by their master – in their case the king. There were some who received no land, and who lived in the palace at the king's expense, but most of them were given a benefice and lived on the profits from it. We have no evidence as to the number of *vassi dominici*, but they are so often mentioned in the capitularies that we may assume them to have been very numerous, and increasingly so in Charlemagne's day. It was the need to administer the realm that caused them to multiply, for we find them particularly in regions conquered by Charlemagne or his father: Aquitaine, Italy and Bavaria. If all the king's subjects were 'faithful' to him, as was officially implied in the oath of allegiance, the *vassi dominici* were especially so: the bond attaching them to the king was an extremely close one. Those who lived at court were however considered less favoured than the holders of benefices.

Towards the end of Charlemagne's reign, a vassal who had carried out his duties at court satisfactorily could always hope to be rewarded with a benefice. Once they were settled in the region where they held a benefice, the *vassi dominici* would be employed in the administration, or to assist the counts. Some were given the task of supervising the king's own domains; all normally attended the count's tribunal; they served in the army as a matter of course, and made up its essential strength. In the course of time the *vassi dominici* were absorbed into the local nobility, and intermarried with exalted families. By now they ranked as seigneurs, and thanks on the one hand to marriages with princely or even royal houses, and on the other to the fact that they settled in their domains and their descendants became the local seigneurs of the eleventh century, it is probable that the entire landed gentry of the Middle Ages was in part descended from the Frankish aristocracy, and often from the Carolingian kings.

The power of the seigneurs, and immunity

The part played by rank and wealth in the social structure and the government of the realm had been clearly apparent in the institution of the *vassi dominici*, but it was not confined to them. The privileged position of these faithful servants of the king was soon eclipsed by the creation of regular retinues, or groups of vassals. Here again, social evolution was relentlessly at work, annulling the effects of vassalage to the king though based on the same principles. Although the king could establish his vassals on his own territories, these were not limitless, and next to them lay the often vast domains of the aristocracy. The same ancestral pledge, the same need to own land was seen in those who were not direct vassals of the king, but of princes. Already in Charlemagne's day, we find these retinues made up of the vassals of great men, who had granted them benefices and received their allegiance. The Carolingian Empire seems to have been a mosaic of properties in the hands of lesser landowners whose livelihood depended on one or two

Nobleman of the ninth century. Malles,
fresco in the oratory of San Benedetto.
Charlemagne encouraged the increased power of the
nobility, and his government depended on it.
The man shown here is probably
a benefactor of the church of Malles.

domains; some holding their land directly from the king and forming the aristocracy among vassals, the others holding it from some very rich and powerful prince, himself a vassal of the king. Thus the *vassi dominici* were only a special instance of the huge social phenomenon of vassalage, and of the combination of dependence on the seigneur, ownership of land, and power, which were the essential features of the ruling classes all over the Empire.

The seigneur's power was in theory directed in the interests of the monarchy, but it was not long before it became independent and a hindrance to the central government. This tendency was already apparent in Charlemagne's reign; it was to become more marked. The great landowners often had a potent means of evading royal authority, and one granted by the king himself: immunity. This was a privilege that had already existed in Merovingian times, but the Carolingian kings distributed it liberally. As a result of the immunity which only the king could grant, it was forbidden for any official or agent of the king to enter the privileged domain, even to collect taxes, even to pursue malefactors. The policing of these often vast territories was left entirely to the privileged owner, who was called the 'immunist'. The purpose of immunity was to liberate him from the powerful counts, who were often tyrannical, especially in the Merovingian epoch. The immunist thus became responsible for most of the count's functions. He collected taxes (tolls and other dues) on behalf of the king, handed over the men from his domain to the army, and pursued brigands, who were greatly tempted to take refuge in a region where the count had no right of entry; he presided over a tribunal where disputes were settled and the small offences committed by the inhabitants of the domain were judged; and if any of them was accused of a serious crime, it was the immunist's task to seize him and carry him before the count's tribunal. Immunity did not remove a domain from the power of the king: the king could always enter it in person and do as he liked there; but it did remove it from the activities of officers of the crown and their personnel; the immunist carried out their functions in his domain and was himself the king's agent. In practice this immunity, conceded mainly to churches but also to laymen, accustomed the immunists to exercising regalian rights. The royal power was far away, the king rarely put in a personal appearance, his representatives were kept away by privilege: the immunist seigneur became a person of considerable importance, and the power he wielded in the locality was almost unlimited.

Later, when the power of the central government declined and the habit of handing on benefices from father to son became common, the existence of regions where the seigneur behaved like the king was bound to strengthen the tendency towards a seigneurial regime disastrously. But under Charlemagne, and during the first half of the reign of Louis the Pious – when Carolingian civilisation was at its height – the immunists remained faithful to the king and fulfilled their obligations towards him. At this period immunity had its place in a coherent society whose organised hierarchy helped the king to govern.

Maintenance of control

If society as a whole is conceived of as a hierarchic organisation founded on the social status of its members, government presupposes the existence of definite principles and the means of carrying out the sovereign's wishes.

In both these respects the essential features of the Carolingian monarchy can be seen: a compromise between Germanic and Roman traditions, and the undeniable influence of the Church. The king was not an omnipotent tyrant: he was surrounded by counsellors, he had to conform to the wisdom of his ancestors as represented by the law, and carry out the mission entrusted to him by God; but it was he who wielded the power, and decisions made in agreement with his followers and under divine inspiration had the force of law. Also, although the king's decisions were according to Germanic tradition the verbal expression of his will, they began to be put in writing more often: there were signs of a renaissance of the art of writing, so important in the Roman State.

The Franks understood the law in terms of ancestral custom. It was the expression of wisdom; it could not be argued about, abolished or modified. Originally transmitted orally among illiterate races, the law was a practical code designed to keep order, without regard to principles. This code was still very much alive under Charlemagne, and most of it was drawn up in the eighth century. After conquering the Saxons, Charlemagne himself gave orders for their laws to be drafted. But such documents were essentially practical, and almost exclusively concerned with individual rights. As the need for order and uniformity grew, the laws had to be more exactly defined. But they still had no bearing on administration.

From the beginning of Charlemagne's reign, we find him issuing legislative decrees having the force of law, either so as to settle questions not covered by national laws, or else to clarify certain points in them. These new decrees were often applicable to the whole Empire, and tended to unify the law. They were called capitularies. They were generally divided into clauses (*capitula*); hence their name (*capitulare*) which first appears in the capitulary of Heristal in 779, and later became part of the official vocabulary of Frankish legislation. Capitularies derived their authority from two sources: the king's *bannus* and the *consensus* of the people. These two aspects of power belonged to the Germanic attitude of mind: power entailed an obligation for subjects to obey, and the people participated in the king's decisions – a relic of the old tradition of a people's assembly. But while the *bannus* (or king's right to command, forbid and punish) was immutable and beyond discussion, the value of the *consensus* varied in different epochs and according to the authority of the reigning sovereign: under Charlemagne it became a pure formality. In any case, the *consensus* was limited to nobles; there was no question of what we now call 'the people' having any part in it. In the Carolingian epoch, as in other periods of the Middle Ages, only men of rank and social importance were considered, and these were the only ones referred to by the word *populus* in documents. The *consensus* was the recognition that a given general rule or individual measure conformed with the law, and implied that it must be complied with in the future; this use of the verb *consentire* signified that the king's subjects recognised their obligation to obey an order given them, but not in any sense that they had the right to accept or reject it. It was simply a solemn undertaking to respect it. A letter from Charlemagne to Pepin, King of Italy, dating between 806 and 810, clarifies this point; in it the Emperor speaks of men who will not *consentire* to the dispositions of a capitulary of 803, and orders Pepin to force them to do so. The same applies to the capitulary of the *missi*, issued in 806, which orders the *missi* to force the people to *consentire* – that is to say to accept the partition of the Empire as established in the document known as *Divisio regni*. The King consulted no one except technical experts before these documents were drafted.

The capitularies were therefore definite manifestations of the king's absolute authority, and one can see them as a return to the imperial edicts of Roman times. The ordinances contained in them often appear to be arranged without system, but it is usually possible to distinguish the general legislative measures from administrative ones inspired by circumstances. We have an example of the way they were drawn up in a text dating from the end of the ninth century, Hincmar's *De ordine palatii*. It calls for two preliminary operations: investigation by a commission and deliberation with the nobles. The investigation could take place either before or during a meeting of the assembly. After conversations between the king and his closest advisers, lists of points to be dealt with were drawn up, then a plan was outlined by a group of men in the king's confidence; the *Annals of Lorsch* tell us that in 802–3 when the *capitula legibus addenda* (to formulate national laws) was in preparation, experts in the different legal systems currently in force throughout the Empire were brought together; this happened also for the capitulary of Aix-la-Chapelle of the same period; the drafting of a clause designed to enforce the dispositions of Frankish law throughout the Empire (that is to say one of the groups of laws effective at the time), was entrusted to experts in Frankish, Burgundian and Roman law. These commissions sometimes consisted entirely of laymen, but more often of bishops and abbots, as was the case for the *Admonitio generalis* of 789.

Such flexibility shows the principle dominating the king's council: there was no fixed formula or definite framework, but anyone whose advice the king valued could be summoned to appear. The king took part in the discussion and explained the object he had in mind, and his councillors adapted the text to express the royal will. This happened in 817, before the meeting of the assembly of Aix-la-Chapelle which proclaimed the unity of the Empire, and also in 823, when Adalard, Abbot of Corbie, and the Arch-chancellor Helisachar prepared the *capitula* which were to regularise the status of Church property owned by laymen, and submitted them to the Emperor, who deliberated with his councillors and then made drastic alterations in the original drafts. In this work of preparation, both king and councillors expressed their opinions freely. Afterwards came the meeting of the assembly and the deliberation of the nobles, who were gathered together in two colleges, the clergy in one and laymen in the other – the laymen did not have to consider matters that only concerned the Church. This discussion was very important: the meeting of the nobles already foreshadowed the 'service on the council' which in feudal times became one of the chief obligations of a vassal. Nor was it limited to the meetings of the general assembly; the king could always consult anyone he liked, for instance smaller gatherings of *missi*, bishops or abbots. In 828 Louis the Pious and Lothar announced that they had held an assembly 'with a few of their faithful adherents'. After the nobles' deliberation, the result was proclaimed to the entire assembly, the essence being the king's verbal statement of the decision arrived at, and his *bannus* (or order that must be obeyed) which constituted the legal act. This order (*verbum regis* or *verbum imperatoris*) sometimes took the form of a short address. In any case, it was followed by the reading of the capitulary. Next came the *consensus*, which the assembly could not refuse to give. The circulation of capitularies was the task of the counts and *missi dominici*. A great many copies were often made and sent to different parts of the Empire. The *missi* had to see that their provisions were carried out, and sometimes explain them in public and insist on the counts conforming to them. This was the means by which the king administered and legislated for the whole of his realm. After 803, we find capitularies with clauses revising the old laws; this certainly has a connection with the revival of the Roman attitude to public institutions, and the restoration of the Empire. Deeply conscious of his new dignity as Roman Emperor, Charlemagne took it upon himself to be a legislator like his predecessors. As instruments of government, the capitularies were in any case well adapted to the times and circumstances in which they were issued. They gave the government effective control over the population, and they contributed to that restoration of the State of which we have other evidence.

The whole work of administrating the Empire was carried out by means of an active correspondence between the king and his agents, including local administrators; notes were sent out from the central government and reports were received from officials. According to Frankish usage, a legislative act was essentially verbal, the king's word; this was a formality dating from the time when writing was not in use. The formality remained but the Franks were attracted to Roman habits, and also borrowed ideas from Burgundian law, which had been much influenced by Roman law. We therefore find writing beginning to figure in Frankish law at a very early stage: the Formulary of Marculf mentions written administrative decrees. Writing made a modest reappearance in Pepin the Short's reign; in 768, when Pepin sent commissioners to the recently subjugated Aquitaine, he gave them a written note of the chief points in their instructions. This is the earliest reference we have to writing being used in this way, and there is no evidence that departments devoted to administrative correspondence existed at this time. They developed under Charlemagne, who set great store by writing, and did his best to spread it throughout his domains. His admiration for Roman customs was boundless, and from his reign onwards we begin to see an increase in written statements furnishing proofs of the king's rights. In the interests of both State and Church, legislative decrees were collected and published, and new ones drafted and announced. Obviously there could be no uniformity in the laws of such a vast Empire unless they were preserved in writing. We know that the day after the imperial coronation of 800, there was an unsuccessful attempt to redraft the national laws. But already, in 794, a capitulary had been issued showing the increasing importance attached to writing, at least in the matter of procedure, for it ordained that when a case was heard by the king's tribunal the parties to it should provide themselves with memoranda. This was an entirely new idea. The same trend was shown in administration, with the result that more writings appeared expressing or explaining the king's wishes.

We know of the existence of a whole series of documents of this sort, issued by the palace or addressed to it. Among the earliest are some important acts, such as Bavaria's solemn renunciation of independence, signed by Duke Tassilo in 794, and preserved in the archives; or the Division of the Empire, drawn up in 806, a copy of which was sent for the Pope's signature; or the resumé of the

Seal used by Charlemagne to ratify documents. Paris, Douët D'Arcq, no. 15. It is an antique intaglio, probably of the head of Antoninus Pius or Commodus, set in a ring with an engraved inscription on the bezel: XPE PROTEGE CAROLUM REG[M] FRANC[O]R[UM].

assembly's decisions; or instructions to the *missi* and *tractoriae*; or charters authorising them to requisition transport; or circulars addressed either to the king's lay agents (as in Italy in 779–81) or to the clergy to fix the form of the liturgy; or mobilisation orders to abbots, immunists and counts, often in extreme detail; or various instructions addressed to the king's sons, to private individuals, or councils indicating the points they must discuss – all these make up a mass of written documents bearing witness to the activities of the palace and the effective control of all administrative departments by the central power.

The second category included writings addressed to the government by the king's local representatives: some of these were requests for details and explanations from the *missi* or the counts; or reports from the *missi* announcing that the king's orders had been executed (for instance one from the *missus* Garnier, who in 780 gave a detailed account of the state of the Church in Marseilles and his domains). These reports presuppose the existence of a number of other written documents, sent by the counts to the palace through the different grades of the hierarchy. After the imperial coronation, these reports and their written justifications increased in number, and the government became more and more anxious for exact information, especially about benefices granted by the king, their upkeep and usurpation. The *missi* were not the only ones to supply these reports: the *judices*, or head stewards of the royal domains, had to render an account of financial revenue once a year and yield three times a year; after 802 the wool and linen woven in the workshops and the number of garments made from it had also to be recorded. In 787 Charlemagne instituted inventories of the property of royal abbeys. All these documents were preserved in the palace, in the *archivum palatii* kept by the chancellor.

Professor F.L.Ganshof has stressed the importance of writing; it contrasts with the modest part it played in Pepin the Short's administration, and shows Charlemagne's genius as an administrator, his concern for order, and his desire to return to the methods of the Roman Empire, all of which were emphasised after his coronation as Emperor. This was the principal innovation made by the Carolingian period in the sphere of government.

Like all the public institutions of the Empire, the administration of this period was based on two principles: first, responsibility entrusted at every stage to the men acting as agents of the government; secondly, constant supervision of these men by officers of superior rank, who insisted on their keeping permanent contact with the central power, furnishing reports of their management and submitting to inspections. As an administrative machine it should have given the Carolingians effective control over the whole country, provided that the sovereign's power was firmly based.

In the reign of Charlemagne the monarchy was founded on a compromise between Germanic, Roman and ecclesiastic notions of power, and was threatened by no real difficulties. After his day, there was a rapid decline in the power of the monarchy, while the aristocracy quickly became a force to reckon with in the State, and the Church – once guided by Charlemagne as leader of the Christian world – now aspired to take precedence over the sovereign.

6 The Church

The bishops

The part played by the Church at this period cannot be too greatly stressed: it was essential to society. At the beginning of our period at least, the clergy were the only educated men. It was among them that the thinkers were to be found who influenced the development of politics, civilisation and culture. It was from among them also that the king chose his most efficient assistants in the task of government. In the *regnum Francorum* the bishops' functions were administrative as well as religious. Charlemagne wanted to have an organised Church in his Empire, and gave much thought to it. Though genuinely devout and determined to rule as a Christian prince, he kept control over the Church during the whole of his reign, but under his successors the bishops began to claim a dominant part in government, until they finally succeeded in setting themselves up in a position of superiority to the king himself.

Before the reign of Pepin the Short, the Frankish Church and the episcopacy were in a state of abject decadence. Ever since the time of Clovis, the kings had claimed and obtained the principal say in the choice of bishops – a matter of great importance, for the pontiffs were essentially the spiritual heads of their dioceses, and at a period when men of outstanding merit were rare they were in fact virtually the leaders of the people. At first the bishops refused to accept the king's intervention in their election, as being contrary to the most ancient traditions of the Church. Gradually they began tacitly accepting it, and official candidature became the rule in the Frankish Church – in other words bishops were to all intents and purposes chosen by the king. Another ancient tradition was the solidarity of the episcopate. Each bishop was master in his own diocese, but he had to keep in contact with his colleagues, and the decisions taken in the assemblies known as synods or councils had to be generally applied. To make these contacts easier, ecclesiastical provinces were created, following the old administrative divisions of the Roman Empire: where the provinces of the Empire had consisted of several *civitates*, the ecclesiastical provinces were made

Liturgical comb in ivory. School of Metz, second
half of the ninth century. Cologne, Schnutgenmuseum.
This admirably carved ivory is known erroneously as
'Heribert's comb'. The central scene is the Crucifixion;
on either side are pierced motifs symbolising the Tree of Life,
a frequent iconographic theme of Byzantine ivory reliquaries.

St Gregory giving a blessing. Miniature from St Gregory's *Homilies on the Gospels*, about 800, Vercelli. Biblioteca capitolare, ms. 148, fol. 9v. This is a typical miniature of the first Carolingian Renaissance, probably executed in Italy, but influenced by early Frankish, Irish and Anglo-Saxon techniques. Gregory the Great, pope and doctor of the Church, author of theological and liturgical works, restored the prestige of the papacy and inspired the missions which completed the conversion

of England. He is here
represented blessing the world,
against a background
framed in a strapwork arcade,
a design very commonly
used by the Celts and Germans.

up of several dioceses, under the supervision of the bishop of the chief city, who held superior rank to the others of the province. But since about the middle of the seventh century these assemblies and this hierarchy had practically disappeared; no councils were held, and the metropolitan bishops were idle. The bishops were very often favourites of the king, and when a see fell vacant he either nominated one of the clerics from the Royal Chapel, or even a layman, who at once took orders, but went on leading the same life as all the other great seigneurs. Under Charles Martel these practices continued: Charles left certain sees vacant, such as Lyons and Vienne, for several years, while he bestowed the sees of Paris, Bayeux and Rouen on his nephew Hugh – a plurality expressly forbidden by ecclesiastical canons.

Some reform was necessary. It was advocated by St Boniface, an Anglo-Saxon monk and missionary to Germany, and was carried out by Carloman and his brother Pepin the Short, and afterwards by Charlemagne. A papal delegate gave advice, the king took action and regular councils were resumed; the strong hierarchic Church of the Carolingian Empire resulted after about twenty years. But the kings refused to give up their strict control over the episcopal elections, and their wishes still dominated the choice of bishops. The idea that the temporal leader had a spiritual mission was natural at this period. Even Carloman, a pious man who renounced his position as mayor of the palace to become a monk, would not have admitted that the reform he had worked for could be carried out in his realms without his consent. Inspired by St Boniface, who was deeply influenced by the hierarchic organisation of the English Church under an archbishop, Carloman created an archbishopric for his kingdom of Austrasia, and Pepin followed suit by creating three in Neustria. When Carloman abdicated and his kingdom was annexed by the energetic and authoritarian Pepin the Short, St Boniface's reform, which had been designed to remove the Frankish Church from royal control, had in fact the effect of uniting and organising it, but under the direction and domination of the king.

Charlemagne went on with his father's work, but his object was to organise the Church not merely as the framework for the religious life of the kingdom and afterwards the Empire, but as an organ of government. He made no distinction between civil and religious power; in his eyes the *regnum Francorum* was identified with Christianity, and he sincerely believed it to be his duty to lead his subjects to safety and watch over their religious life: he was both a political and a religious leader, and the Church had to be the agent both of temporal and spiritual welfare, which were indivisible.

At the outset of his reign he seems to have given some sort of primacy in the Frankish Church to Wilchar, Archbishop of Sens, described in the *Liber pontificalis* (a chronicle written in the Pope's circle) as the 'Archbishop of the Gauls'. Wilchar appears to have acted as minister for ecclesiastical affairs at court, and even after the archbishoprics of Rheims and Mainz had been restored, he always headed the list of Frankish bishops. His contacts both with the Pope and the King greatly helped the reorganisation of the episcopate, which took the form of a return to the ancient Roman canons. Charlemagne held these canons in high esteem, and in the capitulary of Heristal in 779, he declared that the suffragan bishops must obey their metropolitans. By 794 the work of reform had progressed a long way: the synod of Frankfurt laid down that the metropolitans should act as judges in ecclesiastic courts, helped by their suffragans. In 798 Bavaria was created an ecclesiastic province with Salzburg as its cathedral city. By the end of the reign reorganisation was complete; the old cathedrals, except Aix, Eauze and Narbonne, had been given archbishops, and new archbishoprics like Mainz and Salzburg had been created. Henceforth it was established that only the pope could create an archbishop; sometimes this was done on purely personal grounds, without giving him jurisdiction over the other bishops, but all metropolitans must be archbishops. This hierarchic system helped Charlemagne control the episcopate, through which he wielded an almost absolute power over the whole Church. The archbishops, who now had authority over the bishops in their province, had to give an account of themselves to the Emperor, and if the need arose were themselves under the control of the *missi*. A letter has been preserved from Archbishop Laidrad to the Emperor, written a short while after he had been nominated to the see of Lyons; it gives Charlemagne details of what his church needed.

Charlemagne was not the man to allow the rights of choosing bishops assumed by the Merovingian kings to go by default. In practice it was he who nominated them, for no election could take place without his assent: it was he who created Willehad Bishop of the Saxons in 787, and who founded the bishopric of Munster in about 805, and gave it to Liudger. He was not thought to have usurped this prerogative inherited from the Merovingians, Pepin and Carloman, though it was contrary to ecclesiastical canons, but to be doing the Church a service and carrying out one of the duties of his position. Never admitted in the canons, it had become a custom through long use, and no one was shocked by it at the time. There was no longer any question of free election by clergy and people, although this was the absolute rule laid down by canon law. The King thus controlled the Church in its own interests, and at the same time satisfied the ambitions of some of his followers – for the great aristocratic families coveted ecclesiastical dignities and the wealth that went with them.

It seems in fact that a great many bishops came from the nobility in Charlemagne's day, while others had once been clergy of the Royal Chapel, or else famous scholars and writers. Thus we find Gervold, chaplain to Queen Bertrada, made Bishop of Evreux; Angilram at Metz, and Hildebald, the King's chaplain, at Cologne; at Orleans the poet and theologian Theodulf, who probably came from the Visigothic nobility; Maginhard at Rouen, Madalbert at Soissons, Ebroin at Bourges – all certainly belonging to aristo-cratic families. And many more. Some clans succeeded in acquiring sees for several of their members – such was the noble Frisian family from which came Hildegrin, Bishop of Châlons in 804, his brother St Liudger, Bishop of Munster, and their uncle or cousin Gerfrid, also Bishop of Munster. The civil and religious duties entrusted to bishops by Charlemagne made them essential to the mechanism of ruling the Empire, as well as persons of importance in society, and left them little time to evangelise the inhabitants of their diocese, some of whom were still uncivilised although Christian in principle, while others belonged to newly conquered pagan countries. The spiritual activity of the Church was left entirely in the hands of the monks.

Monasticism

The social phenomenon of monasticism had a profound influence on the whole of the Middle Ages. In Charlemagne's day it developed some features that were to persist for centuries.

The expansion of monasticism in the reign of Charlemagne had profound repercussions on the artistic and literary life of the time, and was of capital importance from every point of view. This was the moment when, after rapidly gaining ground, the Irish form of monasticism introduced by St Columba began to lose influence. His somewhat unpractical rule soon relaxed its hold, and at the end of the seventh century that of St Benedict began to spread; those monasteries that did not accept it in its pure form adopted a mixed rule, inspired by both these great ascetic currents and sometimes also by the spirituality of St Caesarius. The Anglo-Saxon monks who had gone with St Boniface to convert the Germans favoured the growing influence of the rule of St Benedict of Nursia at the end of the eighth century. This was an event of supreme religious and social importance. Thenceforth each monastery devoted itself to evangelising the surrounding country, stimulating worship in the parish churches, and infusing new life into ritual, study and manual labour. This was the period when the great abbeys developed and became centres of culture, in spite of the practice of creating lay abbacies. But although Charlemagne took a personal interest in reforming these monasteries, it was not easy, and he was by no means always successful.

The very ancient abbey of St Martin of Tours, founded in the fifth century, observed a rather indefinite rule, and its monks had discouraged two attempts at reform. In 796 Charlemagne entrusted it to Alcuin, one of the great minds of the time. He was struck by the laxity of the monks and tried to re-establish observance of the rule, but he had to proceed prudently and with caution. Soon after his death, it became clear that his efforts had failed, and the monks were sent away and replaced by canons. The case of St Martin of Tours illustrates Charlemagne's monastic policy: in order to re-establish order, he chose a man of outstanding gifts, took a personal interest in reform, and even at times intervened energetically himself. The monastery of Echternach, near Luxemburg, provides another example. It had been a royal abbey since the reign of Pepin the Short, and the abbots were treated with the utmost consideration and respect. Until 775 it was governed by the Anglo-Saxon Aldebert, friend of St Willibrord, and afterwards by another abbot of the same nationality, Beornrad, whom Charlemagne nominated Bishop of Sens in 785. As at Tours, the monastery had a flourishing school, but observance of the rule was very lax; in any case the monks refused to accept the rule of St Benedict. Here also they were replaced by canons. The abbey of Corbie was active in missionary work: the monks swarmed into Saxony after its conquest, and founded a branch known as 'New Corbie' or the abbey of Corvey, near Paderborn, under Abbot Adalard. Charlemagne also took a great interest in the abbey of St Amand, west of the Ardennes, and entrusted it to such very important men as Gilbert, Bishop of Noyon and Tournai (who died in 782), Arn, who became Archbishop of Salzburg in 785, and finally Adalric; here also the abbots nominated by the King had a struggle to impose the Benedictine rule. At St Bénigne of Dijon the Benedictine rule was not introduced until 865. At St Victor of Marseilles there was no longer an abbot; the bishop administered the monastery as well as his bishopric, a situation that lasted at least until 822.

Some abbeys were cultural centres and contained flourishing schools in Charlemagne's reign, but the true Benedictine observances which were later to inspire their highest achievements, were

accepted with reluctance. Charlemagne had two very definite aims
in view. Struck by the lack of unity in the monastic life, the vague-
ness of the rules, and the fact that it was sometimes doubtful
whether a community was made up of monks or canons, he
attempted to remedy the situation by insisting on each monastery
living according to an exact code. All monks were directed to adopt
and practice the rule of St Benedict. Secondly, whatever rule a
monastery might follow, it had to conform to certain principles
designed to keep order: he insisted that vows must be observed
and seclusion and stability preserved; he set himself against the too
common vagrancy among monks, and the anarchy caused by their
not knowing to what authority they were answerable; he defined
the relationship between monasteries and bishops; he forbade the
monks to be involved in commerce or apply to the lay courts of
justice; and he laid down rules for the internal organisation of
monasteries and for the regular holding of services. In everything
he did, the same concern for order and uniformity is to be seen – a
concern which led him to establish a definitive version of the rule
of St Benedict and have it circulated; we still possess the transcript
of a re-copy from St Benedict's own hand, made at Monte Cassino
in 813 by order of the Emperor and Abbot Theodemar. This
is manuscript number 914 in the library of St Gall; it was copied
by the monasteries and became the basic text setting out the
behaviour to which monks must conform.

However, in spite of his desire to spread spiritual reform
throughout his Empire, Charlemagne was himself influenced by
the customs of his time in treating the monasteries first and foremost as centres of intellectual life and agriculture. His efforts to
further spiritual reform were hampered by these entirely temporal
aspects of monastic life, and he was the first to deviate from some
of the principles published in his own capitularies. We find him,
carried away by the customs of a society wherein Church and State
were inextricably linked, demanding that abbots should serve in
the army, or uniting several abbeys under the rule of a single
abbot who obviously could not administer them all himself – such

IN NOMINE DNI NOSTRI IHESU
XPI INCIPIT REGULE
PATRIS NOSTRI BENEDICTI

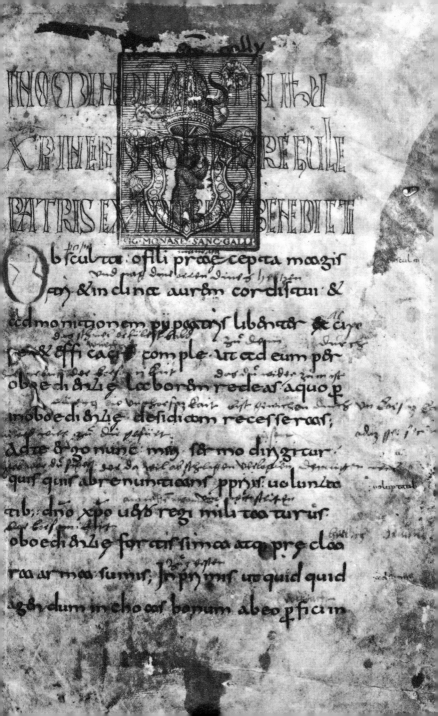

SIG · MONAST · SANC · GALLI

Obsculta o fili praecepta magistri &
inclina aurem cordis tui &

admonitionem pii patris libenter excipe
& efficaciter comple ut ad eum per
oboedientiae laborem redeas a quo per
inoboedientiae desidiam recesseras;
Ad te ergo nunc mihi sermo dirigitur;
quisquis abrenuntians propriis uolunta-
tibus dno xpo uero regi militaturus
oboedientiae fortissima atque praeclara
arma arripis; In primis ut quidquid
agendum inchoas bonum ab eo perfici

as Alcuin, who possessed at least six, or Theodulf, who was head of all the large monasteries in his diocese; finally, like his ancestors and his successors, he often nominated lay abbots. As for the special imprint he left on monastic life, it was what one would expect from his practical mind: he made use of the monks as missionaries, which if not exactly their vocation was at least in the tradition of Anglo-Saxon monasticism. He sent them to Frisia, Saxony and the Slav countries. Some of the larger abbeys were given the task of spreading Christianity in newly conquered or unchristian regions: thus Fulda, Hersfeld, Amorbach and Corvey became outposts of Christianity and the spearheads of religious penetration in Saxony; while Schledorf, Innichen, Kremsmünster and Chiemsee played the same part among the Slavs of Carinthia. Charlemagne defined his monastic reforms in a great many capitularies; they were the active expression of a theory. Owing to him, and even after his day, the rule of St Benedict took first place and became the only monastic rule in the West. As early as 811, Charlemagne was asking an assembly to consider whether it would not be advisable to forbid all other rules, 'since this one', as he said, 'seems to be so excellent'. His efforts bore fruit and his hopes were realised shortly afterwards. Charlemagne was an organiser and pioneer in a period of transition; monastic reform was to be completed under Louis the Pious and St Benedict of Aniane.

Louis the Pious had received an excellent education from priests and monks. As King of Aquitaine he had met a monk called Witiza in the south of France; a descendant of a noble Visigothic family, he had renounced the world to devote himself to the monastic life, and changed his name to Benedict out of veneration for the founder of the Benedictine order. Dedicated to Christian ideals of perfection, he had been struck by the decadence of the monasteries, and had founded on his inherited lands the abbey of Aniane, over which he presided, and where the rule of St Benedict of Nursia was followed in all strictness and purity. Benedict of Aniane had a profound influence on Louis the Pious, who made him his chief adviser in religious matters and helped him spread the

Benedictine rule throughout the monasteries of Aquitaine. When he became Emperor, Louis summoned Benedict of Aniane to his side and founded for him the abbey of Inden, not far from Aix-la-Chapelle, giving him the task of reforming the monastic life of the whole Empire. Benedict of Aniane aspired to give new life to monasticism everywhere, by insisting that the Benedictine rule should be faithfully observed and its spirit once again honoured, and by reviving a perfect community life, of union with God in prayer and contemplation. This Benedictine ideal, as a rule for living rather than a call to direct action, now took the place of the missionary ideal inspired by St Columba and the Anglo-Saxon Benedictines, and also of the intellectual ideal, which saw the abbeys of the eighth century as centres of culture rather than of communal Christian life.

St Benedict of Aniane initiated these reforms in 816 or 817, but they were far from complete when he died in 821. However the general trend had been fixed: from now on monks were considered as men dedicated to worship and prayer, rather than as preachers or missionaries.

At the same time, reforms were by no means limited to the monastic life, but affected the entire clergy, as well as nunneries and chapters of canons – already ancient institutions: in some churches, particularly cathedrals, certain of the clergy were employed to hold services and assist the bishop; they formed a sort of college, but were not obliged to live as a community in the monastic manner. In the eighth century, St Chrodegang, Bishop of Metz, tried to put down abuses and induce the canons to lead more regular lives by drawing up a rule for them: they were to live inside the cloisters, meet for the holding of services and confess their sins frequently. This rule was first applied at Metz but later in other places, and under Louis the Pious it was enforced in a great many cathedral chapters.

To sum up, there was an effort to induce the clergy to lead a more regular life: there were now fewer priests living a worldly life almost like laymen. The bishops felt this trend as well and devoted

Statue of Charlemagne, ninth century. Church of St Jean, Müstair. One of the very few surviving examples of Carolingian sculpture in the round. The aim of the artist, no doubt inspired by a late antique model, was to represent Charlemagne, founder of the church at Müstair, as successor of the Roman emperors. The ceremonial dress and serene expression conforms to the idea of a revival and continuation of the Roman Empire, in which Charlemagne firmly believed.

themselves more to their spiritual mission. At the same time an effort was made to obtain greater freedom in the episcopal elections.

The episcopacy as an influence in politics

As a result of these reforms, the secular clergy once again began to direct the Christian crusade which had for the last century been in the hands of the monks. After Charlemagne's death a real episcopacy was established in the *regnum Francorum*, founded on notions of collective responsibility that had been dormant for two centuries. Aware that their mission was to control the Frankish Church, the bishops eagerly desired and planned religious reforms, but were inclined, like all their contemporaries, to confound spiritual and political government, and so claim a role in the State. These were the same politico-religious views that had existed under Charlemagne, but the prelates' political role had now become superior to that of the sovereign.

In these changed circumstances, conscious of the supernatural character of their mission, and with intellects sharpened by the renaissance in scholarship and culture, the bishops elaborated a political and basically theological theory which was finally put in practice and accepted by the sovereigns themselves.

The Carolingian Renaissance had created a generation of educated clerics, among whom certain distinguished intellects were outstanding: Agobard, Archbishop of Lyons and a famous writer; the Arch-chancellor Elisachar; Hilduin, Abbot of St Denis and Arch-chaplain; Wala, Abbot of Corbie and Charlemagne's cousin; Raban Maur; Jonas, Bishop of Orleans, and many others. The intellectual, spiritual and political direction of the country had previously been in the hands of men imbued with the principles of Roman law and favourable to imperial absolutism. The new thinkers, on the contrary, had formed their minds by studying theology and canonical law. There had been a marked revival of the latter ever since Pope Hadrian sent the Emperor the documents forming the basis of Church law – the collection of canons known as *Dionysio-Hadriana*, which Charlemagne adopted and circulated through the Empire as its ecclesiastical code. Now canonical law, although partly inspired by Roman law, made a sharp distinction between spiritual and temporal power, and proclaimed the superiority of the spiritual. This distinction was set forth in a passage of a letter from Pope Gelasius to the Emperor Anastasius, which had profound repercussions on political theory: the pontiff declared that a bishop's function was superior to the king's, since on the day of judgment he would have to account to God for the king's actions. This was an affirmation of pontifical authority as against secular power; it now became part of canonical law, and was studied and adopted by the more educated clerics. But the clergy and the bishops went even further. At the beginning of the ninth century, they constructed a theory of the Christian State founded on the ideas expressed by St Augustine in the fifth century, in his treatise on the City of God.

This theory, latent in Charlemagne's day, began to be openly voiced by the clergy at the beginning of the reign of Louis the Pious. It was known as political Augustinianism, although it gave a distorted picture of the thoughts of a mind too subtle to have reached the conclusions drawn from them in the ninth century. St Augustine in fact begins with the fundamental notion that peace and justice produce perfect order, or in other words obedience to God's designs: this order must be realised in the family and in the State. The State must be founded on that perfect justice which gives every man his due: from which it can be logically deduced that a true State must be founded on Christian principles, otherwise it will not give God His due, and *justitia* cannot be perfect. It was a theoretical view of the world, but ninth-century commentators drew practical conclusions from it. The Fathers of the Church had already affirmed the primacy of the spiritual element in the lives of the faithful, a doctrine implying also the primacy of the bishops as Christian leaders, and the need for all State institutions to be impregnated with Christian ideas. Pope Gelasius's doctrine follows logically from these ideas. So also does the statement of St Gregory the Great: 'Power is granted from on High . . . so that the earthly kingdom shall be at the service of the Kingdom of Heaven'; or the doctrine of Isidore of Seville, a learned Spanish bishop of the sixth century, who believed that the civil power should protect and help the religious power.

In 829, when Louis the Pious consulted a synod of bishops at Paris about the nature of his duties as king, they replied with a detailed exposition of political Augustinianism. The gist of this advice was repeated in 831 by Jonas of Orleans, a well-known writer, who set down in his *De institutione regia* a complete account of the ideas held by educated clerics at the beginning of the ninth century. Jonas sent his book to Pepin, King of Aquitaine, with an exhortation to carry out his duties as a Christian prince. This treatise reflects the thought of the majority of the bishops in about 830, and the theories that were gradually evolving in their minds.

The ideal and purpose of life being peace in this world and eternal salvation in the next, it was the king's duty to ensure that his subjects received these blessings; he was responsible for the people's safety and this mission was the basis of his authority. His power was given him by God, and the election of high officers of Church and State was only the manner in which God's will was shown – it was not a right exercised by the people. Jonas did not mention the king's consecration, which he obviously held to be a consequence of the divine choice, though it created no rights in itself. The essential feature of his doctrine was that it made the king's power conditional. It was not the sovereign's property; it was a trust, an office, a ministry. If he carried out his trust badly he was no longer a king but a tyrant. The king had duties: he was leader of his people, he governed God's people – that is to say the Empire or Christianity, since these two notions merged; he must rule with fairness, exercising his power righteously, with piety, mercy and justice. The word 'justice' was used here as a theological term opposed to 'sin'; to St Augustine, 'justice' summed up perfect government. Jonas followed the philosophy of the Bishop of Hippo, and drew practical conclusions from it, although only moral ones. He emphasised the role of the bishops, and departed from the formulas used by Gelasius and Isidore of Seville. He concluded that temporal power was only the secular arm of the spiritual power. This belonged to the bishops, who wielded the *power of keys* – the keys to the Kingdom of Heaven – and who must show the king where his duty lay. Bishops were superior to kings; they too had a strict duty to perform: to prevent the kings from sinning or leading their people into harm, to admonish and instruct them. The Church must be free, the episcopate was the head of the Church to which the king belonged like every other Christian, and the episcopate was thus responsible to God. It was the bishops' pastoral duty to sanctify the consciences of the king and his subjects, and to advise the king and be responsible for his decisions, even if they did not actually intervene in matters of State.

It is noticeable that in the whole of this treatise, which reproduces the canons of the council of Paris, the superiority of the spiritual power is constantly affirmed, but there is no allusion to any right of this power to depose the head of the State should his conduct fail to conform to spiritual teaching. However it seems as if the underlying idea were that submission of his subjects should depend upon the king's 'justice', that is to say his fidelity to his essential duty as judge, administrator and protector of the righteous. Nowhere is the notion expressed that subjects have a right to rebel against an unjust sovereign. The first explicit statement of political Augustinianism obviously never goes beyond theory; all the same it was the first affirmation of the supremacy of the spiritual power in the Frankish realm. Even if the intervention of the bishops is not envisaged as a concrete reality, but remains in the sphere of moral abstraction, it is an extremely important manifesto. It marks a turning-point in the development of ecclesiastical thought – a development that was soon to find expression in the government of the Empire.

As early as 822, under the influence of these as yet unexpressed doctrines, the Emperor made up his mind to advocate a general reform of the State through the personal conversion of its leaders, and he set an example by publicly confessing his own faults. This was the Penance of Attigny, which took place in a Christian State where Christian morality prevailed, under the control of the bishops: it raised the question of reforming individuals as well as institutions. The bishops who urged the King to perform this ceremony certainly had no idea of weakening the monarchy; their plan was to bring it, and the whole State, more in line with the ideals of Christian society as defined by the theorists. But things turned out very differently. The Christianity of society was mainly an official façade, and the nobles therefore naturally concluded from the Penance that the Emperor's power was limited and reduced. So that it was the nobles' aspirations towards independence and even anarchy, rather than the idea of Christian government, that were strengthened. The struggles and rebellions that characterised the reign of Louis the Pious clearly show the difficulty of establishing authority – whether that of emperor, bishops or pope; in 850 a form of government was arrived at whereby the real power was in the hands of factions, some made up of ecclesiastics but others of laymen, and the latter began to play a more and more prominent part.

In the reign of Louis the Pious, the Pope did in fact make several attempts to free himself from imperial ascendancy. In Charlemagne's day his power had been subject to the Emperor's. It was true that Pepin the Short had founded the States of the Church in Italy, but the administration of the domains thus conceded to the Pope still remained under civil control. Charlemagne governed them, sent his *missi* there, and remained the supreme authority even for the administration of Rome. Although he consulted the Pope about religious matters, and saw that his decisions were carried out by the Frankish Church, he was still head of the Church and his consent was required for the election of popes, just as it was for bishops. Leo III had been dominated by the Emperor. At the beginning of his reign, Louis the Pious, while showing the Pope the same deference as his predecessor, had ordered his own officers

to inquire into a rebellion which had ended in a papal triumph, thus
demonstrating once again that the Pope's temporal power was
inferior to that of the Emperor. After 816, the relations between
the two powers underwent a change. Stephen IV was elected
successor to Leo III, and began to govern the Church without
waiting for imperial ratification. Soon afterwards he went to
Germany and renewed the coronation ceremony of Louis the Pious,
in which his predecessor had taken no part. This was the first step
towards a theory that would last all through the Middle Ages – that
imperial power could be conferred by the pope alone. When
Stephen IV died in 817, Pascal I was freely elected and no confirma-
tion was required; he merely announced his election to the Emperor.
In 824 Louis the Pious allowed Lothar to issue the *Constitutio
romana*, re-establishing the Emperor's control over the States of
the Church, but he repeatedly refused to intervene in the internal
affairs of the Church, as his father had done before him. Whereas
Charlemagne had settled the problem of iconoclasm by submitting
it to a council of the Frankish Church, his son still summoned
councils, but sent the question under discussion to the Pope for his
final decision. This increase in the pontiff's power seems to have
reached its zenith in 833, when the sons of Louis the Pious rebelled
against their father and pretended to ask Gregory IV to arbitrate,
feeling confident of his support: but when, having secured the
person of the Emperor, they believed success was within their grasp,
the Pope realised that he had been tricked, and had to retire into
Italy, leaving the nobles and bishops to do as they pleased.

For it was the bishops rather than the Pope who were trying to
impose political Augustinianism. It was the bishops who now set
themselves up as judges of the Emperor's political conduct, and
this was only a beginning. It was in their presence that Louis the
Pious declared himself unworthy of his Empire, and resigned his
office at St Médard at Soissons. A year later, when the nobles
became divided among themselves and grew tired of being ruled
by Lothar, they tried to restore Louis the Pious, but he showed his
recognition of the bishops' power by saying that since they had

disarmed him, only they could give him back his arms. They
became from that time arbiters of the quarrels among the princes,
and their doctrine agreed with the theoretical principles laid down
by Jonas of Orleans. However the assembly of bishops gathered at
Soissons did not dare judge the Emperor, much less to depose him:
they contented themselves with airing the grievances of the spiritual
power and extorting a voluntary abdication from Louis the Pious,
while contriving to give his action the appearance of a public
penance. An erudite cleric well versed in canon law, Raban Maur,
Archbishop of Mainz, was not taken in: a short while after the
ceremony at Soissons he declared that this action had confused two
very distinct issues – penitence, which was a personal affair, and
judgment, which presupposed jurisdiction – and that this confusion
had flawed and vitiated the whole proceedings at Soissons, render-
ing them invalid.

After the restoration of Louis the Pious to the throne in 834
there were apparently no further developments, and we do not
find the bishops openly intervening in political quarrels until the
end of his reign in 840. During the struggle between Louis the
Pious and his sons, and at the time of the dissolution of the Empire
– a period of total anarchy – the bishops were induced by the
princes themselves to lay claim to being the only stable and
transcendant power, and to intervene frequently in politics in the
name of morality. In 842, when Lothar was abandoned by everyone
and fled from Aix-la-Chapelle, his brothers entered the town and
discussed what should be done with the subjects he had abandoned.
'Their first thought,' says the historian Nithard, 'was that they
must put the problem to the bishops and priests, most of whom
were present, so that a solution might be found and a decision
taken on their advice – that is to say by divine inspiration.' In view
of the fact that Lothar had broken his promises, been guilty of
homicide and incitement to perjury, and shown himself incapable
of governing, the bishops unanimously pronounced him deposed
and handed over his realm to Louis and Charles. This was the first
instance of bishops passing sentence on a sovereign. It was of

Charles the Bald, King of western France. Miniature from Charles the Bald's Psalter. Paris, Bibliothèque Nationale, ms. lat. 1152, fol. 3v. This book is dated between 843, when Charles became King, and the death of Queen Ermentrude, whose name figures in the litanies, in 869. It is written in letters of gold and was the signed work of the scribe Liuthard. The style suggests the school of Corbie. Note the hand of God blessing the King (cf. page 22).

course done in compliance with the wishes of the conquerors; but the fact remained that the bishops had judged the political conduct of an emperor, in the name of Christian principles and at the request of two kings, and had pronounced him deposed. As for the kings to whom they entrusted the *regnum Francorum*, there was as yet no question of exacting any pledge from them.

A further step was taken in the following year by Charles the Bald, King of western France, at the assembly of Coulaines. Returning from an expedition to Brittany, he gathered together his followers to consider the organisation of his realm and the relations between nobles, bishops and king. Article 3 of the document drawn up at this assembly deals with the king's duties, and includes a promise on his part to protect the rights and dignities of them all. Article 5 shows the changes that had taken place in the last thirty years, for the king told the assembly: 'If our good faith is found wanting, as a result of human weakness, it must be the concern of your tried devotion to . . . advise us to make reparation suitable to the cause.' This important document strikingly demonstrates the point that had been reached: hitherto the Frankish king ruled as an absolute sovereign; now he admitted that his authority was limited, and that if he committed an injustice or broke his pledges, his followers had the right to remonstrate with him. The bishops, who had only gained independence under Louis the Pious, were now the chief moral authority in the realm. Yet their power was already declining, for the royal decree was addressed to important laymen as well as to the bishops. The nobles were now entering the scene and would soon share the controlling power which the bishops had just successfully claimed.

The assembly of Yütz, in 844, merely gave the three sons of Louis the Pious advice inspired by a similar view of a king's earthly mission without entering into details as to the limits of his power, and tried by exhortation alone to instal a peaceful government of the West, founded on the mutual love of the three brothers; but everything had changed fifteen years later, when Hincmar of Rheims was leader, spokesman and chief theoretician of the

Frankish episcopacy. In 859 Hincmar had saved Charles the Bald from extreme danger, when the King complained to the bishops at the council of Savonnières, that Archbishop Wenilo had taken sides with his enemies, and asked them to condemn him. The document drawn up by Charles and his followers recognised the supremacy of the bishops more explicitly than any other hitherto produced by the clerics. The King complained that Wenilo had attempted to have him dethroned, and declared that no one had the right to deprive him of his dignities 'unless he had been heard and judged by the bishops, whose advice and criticism he had been and still was ready to accept'. This was the first time the question of penalising a prince who had misconducted himself had been raised, and the principle formally accepted by the king. It was a triumph for the doctrines of Augustine and Gelasius, as modified by Hincmar.

The final stage was accomplished ten years later, in 869, when Hincmar consecrated Charles the Bald King of Lorraine. The promises made by the King and the ritual of consecration implied that royalty was a religious ministry, instituted and controlled by the Church, and Hincmar gave a supernatural flavour to the ceremony. Although on other occasions Hincmar rejected the principle that the pope could intervene in political affairs, and declared that temporal and spiritual powers were distinct – even though he stood for control of the State by the bishops – he was obliged to include the lay nobility; and the King's promise at the time of his consecration was addressed to everyone, and introduced for the first time the conditional and reciprocal nature of the duties of king and subjects. This was a very serious event, illustrating the developments in thought that had taken place during the last fifty years.

The Church had now become a secular power, reformed by the emperors so as to enable it to carry out its spiritual function as well as that of assisting the established order assigned to it by Charlemagne; its institutions and its clergy had been purged and reorganised. Monks, clergy and bishops alike had faith in their mission, and sincerely wished to carry it out either through the monastic life or the ministry. At the same time the bishops were now involved in the life of the State, and under the influence of theologians and specialists in canon law (because thinkers of the period could not refrain from projecting religious ideas into politics), they desired a form of government in which the temporal power would be subsidiary to and under the control of the spiritual power represented by the episcopate. This idea had been barely formulated before it was modified by the seeds of anarchy spread by attempts to realise it: the Church would not long continue to exercise sole control and supreme authority – the responsibility was to be shared by important ecclesiastics and laymen. This development degraded, weakened and soon afterwards destroyed the monarchy. In the tenth century it was to be no more than the memory of a splendid dream, and a necessary fiction to unite the realm. But the Church was to play a part in restoring its brilliance and so preserving the values it stood for. The role of the Church in the Empire, and the Augustinian theory evolved by the clergy, made up by no means the least important aspect of Carolingian civilisation. And the mutual support given each other by Church and Emperor produced the Carolingian Renaissance.

7 The renaissance of literature

A guided movement

The end of the eighth century and the whole of the ninth saw a remarkable advance in all branches of culture, which has been described as the Carolingian Renaissance. The sovereigns took an active part in this movement, which was inspired and directed by the Church.

It was indeed a kind of renaissance, for the whole of the seventh century and the first half of the eighth had been a period of almost complete barbarism in the *regnum Francorum*. Of course a few scattered centres of culture still existed and remained active. Without them, and the tradition they preserved, and without certain intellectual currents whose manifestations can now and again be traced, this renaissance would have been impossible. The secrets of ancient culture were not discovered afresh, nor were literature and the arts reinvented all at once. A long period of preparation, in one or two monasteries where a few books had been treasured and an extremely small number of men still devoted themselves to study, led up to the dazzling achievements of the reigns of Charlemagne and Louis the Pious.

When the barbarians conquered the West during the fifth century, culture was already in a deep decline, especially in certain regions such as the northern provinces, the north of Gaul, Germany and Armorica. Here there was a smaller Roman population; intellectual life, less firmly rooted, had offered no resistance to barbarism. The Romans had been submerged by the invasion and the population returned to paganism and a tribal existence. In the neighbourhood of the Mediterranean, on the other hand, Roman culture and thought had in part survived. In Italy and southern Gaul, regions conquered· by the Visigoths who had been Christians since the fourth century and whose kings were to some extent Romanised, Latin culture appears to have persisted. The Visigoths were dazzled by the culture they found, and helped preserve it.

But what sort of culture was it that existed at the time of the invasions? Centres of learning and schools were to be found throughout the Roman Empire. At Pavia, Milan, Ravenna and Rome they had been kept going in Theodoric's time, although the authorities had made little attempt to preserve scholastic life. At Arles, Avignon, Vienne and Clermont, flourishing schools still existed in the sixth century; at Narbonne and Barcelona small groups of scholars kept an essentially literary and oratorical culture alive: the principles of eloquence, rhetoric, grammar and poetry were studied, and there was some interest in extending learning, to include subjects such as history, geography and natural history. The civilisation of the ancients seems to have been handed down in this way; but in fact ignorance of Greek, and the consequent impossibility of drawing on the springs of Greek culture and philosophy, led to an impoverishment of knowledge and thought, in spite of the efforts of rare spirits like Boëthius and Cassiodorous. The sciences classified by Boëthius – such as arithmetic, music, geometry and astronomy – had fallen into complete neglect and were only to return to favour after the Carolingian Renaissance, when they would form a basis for education during the Middle Ages. The culture the barbarians had found in the West was thus a mere relic of the true civilisation of the classical period.

In spite of this, the barbarians were greatly impressed by it; but they found it difficult to understand. Their leaders adopted different attitudes towards it. It was encouraged by those who were already Romanised, and had held power under the Emperor, like the first Visigothic and Burgundian kings. Others, such as the Frankish conquerors, or even Euric, a Visigothic king of the end of the fifth century, were uninterested. Later, in the sixth century, the glamour of culture won over the sons and grandsons of Clovis, who were not unresponsive to Latin civilisation. An important event was the adoption of Latin as the cultural language of the aristocracy, and it seems certain that even Roman juridical customs, such as the drafting of acts, began to figure in barbarian law, as also did all practical and scientific skills hitherto unknown to the invaders (surveying, medicine or architecture for instance). Techniques were taking the place of true culture, but Roman educational methods were rejected as of little use to the victorious warrior races. Moreover, if they wanted to earn their living in the barbarian States, Romans of the original stock had to adopt barbarian values and customs. It was therefore left to the Church to preserve the ancient heritage, and an ecclesiastical culture, blending together Christian and classical themes, began to appear.

The growth of monasticism also contributed. The monastic ideal was the pursuit of personal perfection through a life of prayer and study. Consequently, by their assiduous reading of sacred and profane books, the monks helped preserve Latin culture without actually spreading it, and imprinted upon it the blend of classicism and Christianity to be found in the works of the Fathers of the Church, whose writings were often read. Although Latin was the normal language of culture, the form it took in the few works written at the time was incredibly barbarous: phonetics, morphology and syntax were all modified in popular Latin, a simplification and distortion of classical Latin. However, scholars of the middle of the seventh century still conformed to the essential rules of grammar, prosody and rhetoric, and writers such as Virgil were read, as well as the Fathers of the Church.

During the second half of the seventh century the level of culture sank even lower. Neither in Aquitaine, Provence nor Burgundy was it possible to find scholars of the old style. The senatorial families mixed more and more with the Franks, and adopted their way of life; education underwent a complete change. Some degree of culture could still be found at court, where what might be described as a worldly and refined life still existed. But the only real centres were the episcopal and monastic schools. The abbeys following the rule of St Columba were in touch with the Celtic world, which had preserved a very ancient tradition of Latin learning, but this influence affected only a chosen few.

The wars waged by Charles Martel during the first half of the eighth century to crush the movement for independence in Aquitaine, the Lyonnais and Provence, completed the destruction of centres of culture and learning. Ignorance became general.

Whereas under the Merovingians influential laymen still knew how to write, it was rare to find one who could even sign his name in the eighth century. A few of the clergy could write, and this had the important result that offices formerly held by educated laymen now passed into their hands, and they became the sole custodians of culture. Anyone who wanted to devote himself to study now retired into a monastery, and these were the only places where manuscripts were copied and texts studied. The *scriptoria* of Corbie, Laon, St Denis, Fleury-sur-Loire and St Martin of Tours, like those of Fulda, St Gall and Bobbio, worked hard at copying ancient texts, and these monasteries also produced some hagiographic works; but they no longer studied the profane authors of antiquity, except in the form of extracts illustrating some moral or grammatical commentary. Culture had sunk to a very elementary level, and its decline had brought with it a dearth of ideas.

This was the state of things at the beginning of Charlemagne's reign. A few men of exceptional intelligence, such as St Chrodegang of Metz, deplored the decadence of learning and enlightenment. Scholarly members of the clergy, like St Boniface, educated in Anglo-Saxon schools where the intellectual level was higher, were disquieted by the effect of the general ignorance of the ministry and clerical life. Realising that a fresh impetus must be given to education, Charlemagne set in motion the great enterprise which was to reach its apogee under Louis the Pious.

This renaissance seems to have been a widespread movement with several definite characteristics. Its inspiration was Christian, and its aim the expansion of the Church; yet although it was addressed principally to the clergy, laymen and even women were urged to profit from it, and schooling was in theory to be provided for everyone. It was exclusively Latin in character, for the Greek world was at this time entirely cut off from the West, and in spite of the influence of certain men who had been affected by Hellenism, such as Paul the Deacon, the sources referred to were purely Latin. Nor was it confined to literature, but embraced all branches of human knowledge, considerable work being done in the fields of

Abbeys, archbishoprics, bishoprics and scriptoria. Under Pepin the Short and his brother Carloman, a religious renaissance began in the *regnum Francorum*. Bishoprics and abbeys were restored; new monasteries were founded which contributed to the wealth of the sovereign. Besides exploiting the land and so helping the economic development of the country, the monasteries were centres of culture containing studios and schools. The region richest in abbeys seems to have been the ancient domain of the Arnulfians, Austrasia.

---·--·--	The Western Empire of the mid-ninth century
□	Archbishoprics
■	Archbishoprics with scriptoria
○	Bishoprics
●	Bishoprics with scriptoria
△	Abbeys, priories, convents
▲	Abbeys, priories, convents with scriptoria

Utrech

AIX-LA-CHAPELLE

St Bertin   Nivelles   Liège
Arras   St Amand
St Vaast   Lobbes   Stavel
Amiens   Prüm
Corbie   Laon   Echternach
m
St Riquier   St Maxin
Jumièges   Mettlach
Rouen   Rheims   Me
St Wandrille   Chelles   St Denis   Hautvilliers
Paris   Meaux
St Germain-des-Prés   Faremoutiers
Ferrières   Troyes
Le Mans   Sens   Langres
Orleans   Germigny-   Luxeuil
St.Calais   des-Prés   St Germain
Tours   Auxerre   Flavigny   Dijon
Marmoutier   Fleury-   Besançon
Angers   St Martin   sur-Loire
Noirmoutier   Poitiers   Bourges   Nevers
St Philibert-de-Grandlieu   St Croix   Autun
St Hilaire   St Sulpice
St Maixent   Couches
Limoges   Lyons
Saintes   St Martial   Menat
Solignac   Clermont
Périgueux   St Yrieux
Vienne
Conques
Bordeaux   Embrun
St Didier
Avignon
Eauze-Auch   Arles   Aix-en-
Toulouse   Provence
Aniane
Gellone
Narbonne

canon law, Roman law, theology and science. Finally, it was not a spontaneous movement but a guided one, and Charlemagne's wishes played an extremely important part in it: he gave effect to them by legislation, by collecting scholars around him at court, and by personally stimulating study. The renaissance developed steadily. At the beginning of the reign culture was almost exclusively monastic, but as a result of legislation, other centres opened later on, and schools were to be found close to the royal palace and the cathedrals, and even in country parishes.

The first efforts were directed at producing more books. From about 780 the *scriptoria* were kept hard at work; specialists in calligraphy were employed on the long, arduous and delicate task of reproducing the works of great writers or liturgical books, while as time went on the more valuable of them began to be more and more elaborately and even sumptuously decorated. Papyrus had vanished, parchment was scarce and had to be used sparingly, but the need for books was so great that this activity steadily increased. A real revolution in the art of writing was in progress: instead of the unequal, irregular Merovingian script, cluttered up with confusing flourishes, or the angular writing imported from the British Isles by Irish and Anglo-Saxon scribes, a new style was gradually appearing, with small, separate, rounded and perfectly legible letters; it was called *Caroline minuscule*, and its advantages were so great that it was adopted by virtually all sixteenth-century printers after Gothic type was broken up. It has obvious links with the printed letters of the present day.

Libraries were growing richer. At the beginning of the eighth century there was general neglect in the monasteries, and only the remains of their old collections were left. After about 750, however, conscientious abbots began to add to their possessions and collect new treasures. At St Wandrille, for example, the three abbots who succeeded one another between 747 and 807 – Wando, Witluic and Gervold – acquired a hundred volumes for their monastery. At the end of the century, Alcuin realised that his abbey of St Martin of Tours was short of books, and sent emissaries to Britain to get some.

Page of Caroline minuscule. Loisel Evangeliary.
Paris, Bibliothèque Nationale, ms. lat. 17968, fol. 1.
A typical example of this type of writing, regular
and easy to read in contrast to the confused
forms of Merovingian script. (cf. Gregory's
Historia Francorum on page 19.)

BEATISSIMO PAPAE DAMASO
HIERONIMUS

Nouum opus me facere cogis ex ueteri · ut post exemplaria scrip-
turarum toto orbe dispersa · quasi quidam arbiter sedeam ·
& quia inter se uariant quae sint illa quae cum greca consentiant
aut ueritate decernam · Pius labor · sed periculosa praesump-
tio · ludicare de ceteris ipsum ab omnibus iudicandum · senis mutare
linguam · & canescentem mundum ad initia retrahere paruu-
lorum · Quis enim doctus pariter uel indoctus cum in manus uo-
lumen adsumpserit · & a saliua quam semel inbibit uiderit discre-
pare quod lectitat · Non statim erumpat in uocem me falsarium
me clamans esse sacrilegum · qui audeam aliquid in ueteribus
libris addere mutare corrigere · Aduersus quam inuidiam du-
plex causa me consolatur · Quod & tu quis summus sacerdos es
fieri iubes · & uerum non esse quod uariat etiam maledicorum
testimonio conprobatur · Si enim latinis exemplaribus fides est
adhibenda respondeant · quibus tot sunt exemplaria pene quod
codices · sin autem ueritas est quaerenda de pluribus · Cur non
ad grecam originem reuertentes · ea quae uel a uitiosis inter-
pretibus male edita uel a presumptoribus imperitis emendata
peruersius uel a librariis dormitantibus aut addita sunt aut
mutata corrigimus · Neque uero ego de ueteri disputo testamento
quod a LXX senioribus in grecam linguam uersum tertio gradu
ad nos usque peruenit · Non quaero quid aquila quid symmachus
sapiant · Quare theodotion inter nouos & ueteres medius incedat ·
sit illa uera interpretatio quam apostoli probauerunt · De nouo

Their chief need was for books to copy, and they sent for them to Ireland, Italy and Spain. This practice lasted for a long time, and even at the height of the Carolingian Renaissance, during the first half of the ninth century, books were being searched for everywhere: whether gifts, purchases or loans, they could be copied and so multiplied. We still possess the catalogues of some of these libraries: for the most part they contained sacred books, the works of the Fathers of the Church and the Greek fathers (evidently translated into Latin), but also everything that might help teach young clergy the Latin tongue, now no longer spoken in its pure form, and revive its grammar and literature. In the middle of the eighth century, Corbie certainly possessed a sixth-century copy of Livy; Fleury-sur-Loire some extracts from Sallust; St Amand a manuscript of Pliny the Elder; St Martin of Tours a copy on papyrus of a commentary on Cicero's *Topica*; often there would also be some volumes of ecclesiastical history in these libraries.

In the monasteries or bishoprics where these libraries were to be found, there were also schools for the education of the clergy. The syllabuses were vague and depended entirely on the teachers, but they left great freedom to those who wanted to read, study and educate themselves: thus the Venerable Bede and Alcuin had been taught the elements of science by their masters, and afterwards acquired much wider knowledge in Anglo-Saxon schools. The organisation of schools all over the *regnum Francorum* was in a rudimentary state, and was left in the hands of the clergy and monasteries; the chief object was to train clerics and monks. Charlemagne's contribution consisted in seeking out and bringing to his realm foreign scholars, particularly from countries where schools still flourished like Italy and England, in legislating to provide modest educational foundations as the spearhead of culture, and establishing a centre of science, art and literature at his court. This work was begun in 780.

It was in no way revolutionary; there was no change in the orientation of studies, and the principal aim remained the education of the clergy. But the measures taken by Charlemagne opened vaster horizons, and had results that were felt far outside the educational sphere.

In a capitulary published between 786 and 800, Charlemagne declared: 'Because it is our duty at all times to improve the state of our churches, we are concerned to restore with vigilant zeal the teaching of letters, which has fallen into abeyance through the negligence of our ancestors.' And he gave orders that books whose texts had been corrupted by careless scribes should be corrected, that schools should be opened (the very word had almost been forgotten, he said) all over his realm – restored in Gaul and founded in Germany, where they had never existed. His objects were that divine service should be conducted correctly and with dignity, that monks and clerics should be educated, and Gregorian chant should be properly sung according to the principles laid down by his father. And besides these ecclesiastical aims, he wanted all his subjects to receive the benefits of instruction.

He achieved his end by general measures included in his capitularies, and also by giving personal instructions to bishops and abbots. A mandate addressed to all the archbishops, and to be passed on to their suffragans, ordered that all bishoprics and royal monasteries must be able to provide an education conducive to a regular life and literacy, for all those capable of receiving it. Schools must be available to all for the encouragement of a Christian way of life, although their chief aim must still be to recruit and train the clergy, and the episcopal churches should concentrate on educating those they needed in their own diocese. This was also the drift of a reprimand contained in a letter to an archbishop, probably the Archbishop of Mainz, who was training clerics for other dioceses. A capitulary issued in 789 contained an article on schools. This time it did not deal only with episcopal schools, but was addressed to ordinary priests, advising them to win over as many children as possible to the service of God, and ordering them to open country schools where they could be taught to read, as the first rung in the ladder of education. Charlemagne also gave instructions to the bishops to draw up a course of study for episcopal and monastic schools: the psalms must be read, music, singing, calculation of dates and grammar must be taught.

These measures combined to form a complete educational programme: children were to learn to read, sing, take part in divine service and recite the psalms, as well as to acquire the rudiments of calculation and even of medicine. Some schools gained a special reputation for the high quality of their teaching in one or other of these branches, for example Metz for singing and music. The schools at Lyons, Orleans, Mainz, Trèves, Ferrières, Aniane, St Wandrille, St Riquier, Murbach and St Martin of Tours were becoming famous. At Tours, Alcuin varied the education according to the talents of his pupils; some studied singing, others reading, writing, the liberal arts or Holy Writ. Charlemagne's directions were often observed and had an undoubted effect. He stimulated the renaissance of study and the opening of schools. Teachers of the next generation, such as Eric of Auxerre or Lupus of Ferrières, praised his efforts, and have handed down to us the respect scholars felt for him. As Lupus wrote: 'Scholars are so greatly in debt to Charles that they will remember him always.'

Charlemagne in fact created an educational structure which lasted for several centuries. Elementary teaching and education in the liberal arts were kept separate. The former could be given in private houses, parish schools and abbey priories, as well as in schools attached to cathedrals, collegiate churches and monasteries (where a more advanced education could also be obtained). It was an elementary course designed for beginners. But we must remember that learning to read involved not only the deciphering of texts, but also the art of reading aloud distinctly; and that singing was a direct preparation for celebrating divine service – one of the main purposes of this basic education; nor were learned men, like Eric of Auxerre, at Laon Cathedral, too proud to teach it to children. The psalms, canticles and hymns that must be learned by heart were normally sung. The technique of writing and the elements of grammar formed the highest grade of this elementary teaching.

A course in the liberal arts was the highest form of education. The programme was fixed in the eighth century and remained the same until the twelfth; it was based on the views of Martianus Capella, Cassiodorus and Isidore of Seville, and included the Seven Arts classified by the ancients. This course was entirely dependent upon the classics, and consisted solely in making commentaries on ancient books; ninth-century teachers seem to have felt unable to add anything to the results produced by scholars of long ago. They held that these arts fell naturally into two separate series: those aiming at developing the intellect alone, and those that could be applied to the physical world and its features, such as number, space, the heavenly bodies and harmony. Alcuin distinguished three aspect of 'logic': grammar, rhetoric and dialectic; next came 'physics', divided into four groups: arithmetic, geometry, music and astronomy. These two great series were given the titles of *trivium* and *quadrivium* two centuries later, and remained the basis of education during the classical Middle Ages. For Alcuin they were the seven pillars of wisdom, or steps by which to ascend to perfect knowledge. He himself wrote treatises on grammar, rhetoric and dialectics, and we know that he taught all branches of 'physics'.

However this complete course was not taken in all schools. In the middle of the tenth century, Gerbert did not start his pupils with grammar, but plunged them straight into dialectics, or the science of reasoning, then into rhetoric, and finally embarked them on studying the style of the classical poets. Each of these sciences needed a special method of teaching: thus grammar included the study of rules and examples taken from writers of antiquity – Virgil, Statius, Terence, Persius, Juvenal, Horace and Lucan; rhetoric studied the art of oratory among the ancients. Dialectics, or the rational method of distinguishing true from false, through definition and discussion, was Alcuin's favourite branch of learning. He knew that Aristotle had thrown light upon it, but was only acquainted with his works indirectly, since no Latin translation existed in the West. The different branches of 'physics' were less commonly taught than 'logic'. Of course it was thought necessary for clerics studying singing to know the rules of musical theory, but in 831 the library at St Riquier contained twenty-six volumes of *libri grammaticorum*, one on medicine and not a single one on physics itself. This course could be followed up by philosophy, that is to say the entire field of learning outside logic and physics, including ethics or the study of the four cardinal virtues. Raban Maur did not hold that the seven liberal arts embraced the whole of learning. It was beginning to be realised that the field of investigation by human intelligence was unlimited.

As for methods of instruction, they all started from one principle: a text must first be read by the teacher or a pupil, this to be accompanied by a grammatical, rhetorical or dialectical explanation, and the study of examples from other branches of learning; next came a dialogue or discussion, carried out according to the methods of dialectical reasoning, the highest form of scholastic exercise. This method was adhered to in all schools throughout the Middle Ages. The influence of the ninth-century teachers who had devised it was therefore a determining factor in the development of the human mind: in spite of the exaggerations and aberrations of scholasticism, this method taught generations of students how to discipline their thoughts; on it was founded the scientific exactitude which made it possible for a chosen few to apply certain accepted facts to science; it formed the minds of several men of outstanding intelligence who flourished in Charlemagne's day, and (in greater number) under Louis the Pious and his sons.

The intellectual environment

It is not surprising that after a period of such complete barbarism, Charlemagne's work in organising education yielded no brilliant results until the next generation: men who had been students during his reign reached maturity at the time of his death. Nevertheless, several intelligent, and some genuinely learned or talented men, made their mark during his lifetime. The elite among these thinkers were self-educated, having developed a taste for learning after receiving elementary teaching in one of the few surviving intellectual centres. Most of these were to be found outside the Empire, but they contributed greatly to the revival of learning.

As always when a few intelligent men dominate a backward society, they kept in touch with one another, mainly through letter-writing, and so developed ways of thought, a community of interests, and a particular style of literary or scientific production, which had an influence on their contemporaries and successors. This is what is meant by the literary movement of Charlemagne's reign. They took classical writers as their models, and after a return to pure and correct Latin, developed their style in the direction of literary originality. In all their works we can trace the old Germanic background, the influence of Holy Writ and the Fathers of the Church, and lastly the rediscovery of the values of Roman civilisation after centuries of neglect. These different contributions created a way of thinking and a form of original expression peculiar to Carolingian civilisation; like the educational structure it persisted throughout the medieval period, and helped to shape the history of human thought.

By about the year 760, several main currents in literary aesthetics could be distinguished. First, the influence of antiquity, not directly but through more recent authors like Isidore of Seville (560–636). This Spanish bishop and aesthetician left his mark on the Carolingian period by making classical authors available to eighth-century scholars. He introduced them to Latin theories of versification, based on the arrangement of long and short syllables and stress, and also to the rules of rhetoric, grammar and literary creation. He stood for the traditions of classical culture in the latter half of the eighth century, and served as a model for many writers, Theodulf in particular. The influence of the Orient, with its love of brilliance, effect and colour, came from study of the Bible by scholars; it was brought to the West by the works of an Anglo-Saxon, the Venerable Bede (673–735), whose aesthetic theory was based on classical correctness of style enriched by the inspiration of the Bible, to which he was highly responsive. He introduced a new form of rhythmic versification, easier to appreciate than the Latin forms; it gave the unaccented syllables the same value as the short syllables of classical writers. He enriched poetry by Christianising the chief literary forms and taking examples of style from both Virgil and the Bible. Above all, he imitated biblical figures of speech, arrangement of words, and metaphor. He appreciated the beauty of the Bible as literature, and took delight in translating it into the purest Latin possible. He was largely responsible also for the allegoric interpretation of the Bible, and so indirectly for the deplorable popularity of allegory during the Middle Ages, which finally affected aesthetic and even scientific theory. Bede was as important an influence as Isidore of Seville on the writers of the Carolingian period.

Both these men emphasised the importance of writing correct Latin, as close as possible to the classical language. Charlemagne had himself been struck by the decadence of Latin; in a letter to Baugulf, Abbot of Fulda, he insisted that grammatical correctness was necessary so that errors of thought should be avoided: to arrive at the true meaning of Holy Writ one must have a perfect knowledge of the language and of the literary habits of sacred writers. This conviction of Charlemagne's was the basis of his educational reforms. He took lessons himself from Alcuin and Peter of Pisa, the grammarian, and he had a school directed by eminent teachers close to him in his palace. From a passage in Einhard, and an even more important extract written by an anonymous monk of St Gall, a picture of the Emperor has been reconstructed, as the creator of a palace academy, bringing together fine intellects to discuss rhetoric or philosophy, and taking part himself. This legend is probably based on the fact that Charlemagne certainly did not scorn to take part in such discussions; but there is no evidence that he kept a group of scholars permanently at court, and even if many of them taught at the palace school they took turns to do so. But whatever doubts may be thrown on the existence of this supposed academy, we know for certain that the best scholars were consulted, and that the palace school played an important part in the literary renaissance.

Soon after it was founded, Charlemagne sent for two Italian grammarians, Peter of Pisa and Paul the Deacon. Peter of Pisa, educated in his native town where traditions of Roman culture still survived, had met Alcuin in 767. Charlemagne put him in charge of the grammar department of the palace school. He was imbued with the purest classical doctrines, as we see from the treatise he wrote and dedicated to Charlemagne, in which he goes into the peculiar characteristics of gender and declension. His teaching may be considered as the first step in the reform of Latin scholarship and the return to the pure form of the language. But he was also a poet, and we still have a letter from him to Paul the Deacon, containing a eulogy of Charlemagne. Paul came from a Lombard family of Friuli, and had been educated at Pavia; his high degree of literary culture made him welcome at the Frankish court. After spending four years in the Moselle district, he had to return to Italy. He left behind a large quantity of writings: grammatical treatises, poetry, Roman history, histories of the Lombards and the bishops of Metz, a life of St Gregory the Great and a commentary on the rule of St Benedict. He was of great assistance to Charlemagne. He was a genuine writer, nourished on the classics, and his teaching did much to encourage Latin studies. Grammar went on being treated as a subject of great importance until the end of the reign, when Clement Scotus, author of a treatise on barbarisms, was also teaching at the palace.

But Charlemagne sent for other important scholars as well as grammarians – philosophers and theologians, all of them churchmen whose chief interest was in apologetics. At a period when learning was universally regarded as a means of arriving at revealed truth, it is not surprising to find these intellectuals using profane knowledge for the defence of their faith. Paulinus of Aquileia occupied several important positions, such as that of *missus*, and lived at court teaching grammar for several years. He was nominated patriarch of Aquileia in 787, and ruled over his diocese

Alcuin's handwriting, late eighth century. Paris, Bibliothèque Nationale, ms. lat. 1572, fol. 79. Alcuin was one of the greatest scholars of the eighth century. He was a great teacher and an energetic searcher after manuscripts, which could be copied for the use of students. This page contains annotations made by him for the guidance of his assistant.

wisely, while still continuing to take part in the affairs of the realm and in theological controversy. He was an adversary of the adoptionist heresy, and attended several councils. He left behind some theological treatises and a *Liber exhortationis*, a moral work addressed to his friend Eric, Duke of Friuli; all were written in fairly correct language inspired by the classics and the Bible.

His friend Alcuin was even more closely connected with educational reform. He was an Anglo-Saxon, educated at the episcopal school of York; Charlemagne met him at Pavia in 781, got him to join him and gave him several abbeys. In 796 he was Abbot of St Martin of Tours, and acted as it were as Charlemagne's minister of cultural affairs. His reputation was due more to charm of character and encyclopedic knowledge than to his creative genius, which was in fact not remarkable. It was he who listed the branches of learning and dictated how they should be taught. We have treatises written by him on all sorts of subjects: grammar, rhetoric, liturgy, philosophy, hagiography, theology and history, as well as poems and literary works. His style is affected, founded on knowledge and imitation of ancient writers; he used classical metres and turns of phrase. Alcuin was the most remarkable of the learned men who came from the British Isles to the West, and represented the combined influence of classical antiquity and biblical tradition originated by Bede.

Theodulf of Orleans exemplified a different branch of culture. Also a theologian, apologist and poet, in love with classical traditions, he had come under the direct influence of the teaching of Isidore of Seville. Finally, a Frankish nobleman called Angilbert, who had a son – the historian Nithard – by Charlemagne's daughter Bertha, had such a great reputation as a poet that the intellectuals of the day gave him the surname of Homer. He too imitated the ancients.

These writers, all of whom were in contact with Charlemagne and often called upon by him to help in his work of reviving culture, were all notable for their eagerness to restore the Latin language and go back to classical texts. From a literary point of view they

secundum impiissimum manich&m sed non esse q...
ph&nt&sia est s&c. ur nostr& · N& quod corporis solu
red totius hominis anime · & corporis ... c...
scela s&c& ee est thū cenum · nec turelit . quod &
m&ri se f&tundum diuinces s corpor& res & uerum
... scelu& torus · ꝑ

I Pr&dicticc au . eu tem &c& plenitudinem fi & a ide
& indel nec &ur de an gine m&ri& di filius & indu bi
t& s& In hominibus · Non In homine ꝑ&c& ur hoc
enim In prophe&is est & postolis ꝑ f&c& us In spu
non cludas filii · u . us quidem pr&prie filius cessumens
hominem · Alter& &u& non mortalis arrumpt& is sec̄do
sed unius unigenitur In c&elo · unig&tur inter r& ed&r · ꝑ ·

De incarn&tione & cu&m uerbi & fide credim .
In& dm nostrum In̄m xp̄m · de an gine m&ri&
nic& um qui ap̄e est s&mpiter mas di filius & uerbum
& non homo cel̄o cessump& ut uel ter& esse ꝑ& ce&ir
illum · N& que enim hominem cessumprit di filius ut sit uel
ter& ꝑ& ce&ir ipsum sed d̄r ge r& d&r · ꝑ f&c& us f&c& us
est & simul & homo · ꝑ f&c& us In car nec& ur de an gine · ꝑd ·

ꝗ de Incarn& & homi p s&c& ur

were purely imitative: their works were modelled on Latin writers and the Bible, and it must be admitted that they often lack inspiration. However, together they produced an original body of work: never had such reminiscences of pagan classicism and of Christianity been so intimately mixed, and the authors of this alliance were many of them of Germanic origin: the Lombard Paul the Deacon, the Anglo-Saxon Alcuin, Theodulf the Visigoth, and Angilbert the Frank. Thus Charlemagne's reign saw the development of new literary forms born of contacts between different civilisations. This fusion is even more plainly seen in the spheres of philosophy, theology and law.

Naturally enough the revival of culture led the clergy to examine problems concerning the Church, particularly the liturgy, theology and canon law. Liturgy laid down rules for the official forms of prayer and religious observance. Its development had been slow, and partly along local lines – there were Roman, Gallic, Celtic, Moorish and Greek rituals – so that, although the essential elements had been made uniform, and Mass always included readings from Holy Writ, singing and sacrificial prayers, marked variations could be observed in the respective importance given to these elements. And, because of the general ignorance of the seventh century, liturgical books were often disgracefully badly copied. With his love of order and unity, Charlemagne took an interest in this question, and instituted reforms bearing on the copying of books, the introduction of Roman customs, and return to the Gregorian chant. He asked the Pope for his advice on this subject.

The revision of liturgical books was very largely the work of Alcuin. First he rewrote the *Comes*, or lector's book of extracts from the Old and New Testaments, to be read aloud to the congregation during services; he made it easier to read, and adapted the text for various different occasions. Thus he composed a lectionary conforming to the liturgical cycle fixed by St Gregory the Great, and so to Roman usage. When it came to reforming the sacramentary – or book of formulas pronounced by the priest when

Table of Canons. Theodulf's Bible, early ninth century. Paris,
Bibliothèque Nationale, ms. lat. 9380, fol. 248. These tables of
concordance between the verses of the four Gospels were common from
the eighth century onwards. The characteristics here are the sobriety
and proportion of the design. The rose-work decoration of the
principal arch recalls the architectural style of Aix-la-Chapelle.

administering the sacrament – he asked Rome what was the official procedure. This too went back to St Gregory the Great, and the Gallic form, founded on an ancient sacramentary dating from Gelasius and not used in Rome since the end of the sixth century, was abandoned. In reply to Charlemagne's request, Pope Hadrian sent him books and a monk to bring the Franks up to date in the matter of Roman usages. Alcuin's Sacramentary was made obligatory by a royal decree in 785. It was the same with the Gregorian, or Roman chant as with the Roman liturgy. Pepin the Short and Chrodegang of Metz had already introduced it in *Francia*. Metz became a centre of Roman music, and clergy were obliged to learn the Gregorian chant by the Royal decrees of 789, 802 and 805: Charlemagne was therefore personally involved in this unification and Romanisation of the liturgy.

He was no less interested in theology, and its attempts to discover, by reasoning based on Holy Writ, definite ideas on which to found the Christian faith. At the beginning of the eighth century, the lack of Church councils in Gaul and Germany had led to the decay of theological activity; the religious revival caused by St Columba and his disciples had more effect on piety than on research into dogma. The Carolingian Renaissance brought with it a renewal of theological study, because it was a form of intellectual activity available to scholars who were all churchmen, because the councils were beginning again, and because it led to the study of doctrines coming from countries where culture had persisted, such as the Byzantine East or Moorish Spain. Charlemagne's advisers were asked to make a decision on three questions: adoptionism, iconoclasm and the Procession of the Holy Ghost; and contemporary scholars wrote countless treatises on these subjects. Adoptionism, widely held especially in Spain at the end of the eighth century, was the belief that Jesus Christ was not truly the Son of God and the Word incarnate, but God's adopted son; it had been spread by Elipand, Archbishop of Toledo, and Felix, Bishop of Urgel. The latter was suffragan to the metropolitan of Narbonne, and had propagated this doctrine (condemned by

Hadrian I in 785) throughout Septimania. In 792 Felix renounced his errors before the council of Ratisbon, but he returned to them later, and Charlemagne encouraged Alcuin to confute the heresy in writing. Alcuin thereupon wrote his *Adversus Felicis haeresim libellus*, in which he treated adoptionism as a form of mono-physitism; Felix's reply, in a letter to Charlemagne, was passed on to the Pope and afterwards examined by Paulinus of Aquileia, Theodulf of Orleans and Richbod, Bishop of Trèves. After Paulinus had written his *Libellus sacrosyllabus* and *Contra Felicem Urgellitannum*, Alcuin published another treatise with the same title and followed it up with a letter to Elipand, but the quarrel did not end with the death of the Spanish protagonists, and Agobard, Archbishop of Lyons, evidently thought it necessary to write yet another tract on the same subject after 818. The battle against adoptionism seems therefore to have been inspired by Charlemagne, the Pope and the councils, but the whole doctrinal controversy was set out in writings attacking the heresy by a few well-known scholars. Their intellectual methods of approach to the subject were typical of the Carolingian Renaissance: their arguments were always supported by textual quotations from the Bible or the Fathers. The discussion was philological as well as theological and patristic, often depending on the interpretation of terms used by writers on sacred subjects. This use of philological and gram-matical data as a basis for theological argument was the result of the efforts of Charlemagne and his circle to organise studies so that perfect knowledge of the language should lead to mastery of sacred texts. The tone of Alcuin's arguments is no less remarkable: he was neither bitter nor abusive about his adversaries, but full of moderation and charity; he showed an extensive knowledge of the Latin Fathers, some contact with translations of the Greek Fathers, and a talent for subtle reasoning which served as a model for the dialecticians.

The iconoclastic quarrel had begun in the East a long time before Charlemagne's reign, and made a breach between the Churches of Rome and Constantinople. In 754 veneration of images

HIERONIMVS ROMA EGRESSVS BA[...] HIERVSALEM INGREDITVR LEGIS MONO[...]

[...]TERIO SIC[...]MOS PAVLE DIVINA[...] [...] HIERONI[...]VLTVS VBIQVE DO

[...]RONIMVS TRANS[...]XIT OM[...]DO [...]E TRANSTVLIT AL[...] OLLIS HIC TRIBVIT QVIS EA CON POSVIT

Life of St Jerome. Miniature from Charles the Bald's Bible, about 141
846. Paris, Bibliothèque Nationale, ms. lat. 1, fol. 3v. This Bible
was produced at St Martin of Tours, by order of Count Vivian, lay
abbot of the monastery, and presented by him to Charles the Bald.
It marks the apogee of the school of Tours, which came to an end in
853 after the Normans burned the abbey. The three sections of the
miniature represent scenes from the life of St Jerome, translator of
the Bible: above, he leaves for Jerusalem; in the centre, he explains
Holy Writ to a few disciples, who include the noble ladies, Paula and
Eustochium; below, he distributes copies of his translation. This
miniature belongs to the Carolingian Renaissance, a time when the
Bible's text was being widely disseminated abroad. The book itself
and the circumstances of its production are evidence not only of the
remarkable skill of the school of Tours but also the pomp of the lay
abbot who, with the vast resources of the abbey at his disposal,
took an active interest in its artistic life.

had been forbidden in the Byzantine empire, but the council of
Gentilly, convoked in 767 by Pepin the Short, would not accept
this decision. Twenty years later the empress Irene convoked an
oecumenical council at Nicaea; it was attended by Pope Hadrian's
legates, but the Frankish bishops refused to come: the council
returned to the question and declared it lawful to venerate images.
When the conclusions of this council were conveyed to Charlemagne, he had them studied by theologians, probably headed by
Alcuin. They declared that respect should be paid to images of
saints, but were careful to distinguish this from the adoration due
to God alone; their attitude contained more nuances and reserva-
tions than that of the council. Thanks to the action of Charlemagne
and his advisers, a more exact definition of the dogmas concerned
in this subject was arrived at, and the king of the Franks was
recognised as virtually the head of Western Christianity.

Even more important controversies took place over the dogma of
the Holy Trinity. The ancient belief of the Church was that the
Holy Ghost proceeded from the Father and the Son at the same
time. When the council of Nicaea declared in 787 that the Holy
Ghost proceeded *through* the Son, this doctrine seemed suspect to
Charlemagne, who had a sharp criticism of the council drafted in
the *Libri Carolini*, which upheld the view that the Holy Ghost
proceeded from the Father *and* the Son: 'ex Patre *Filioque* procedit'.
This was the famous controversy of *Filioque*, in which Paulinus of
Aquileia, Alcuin and Theodulf all took part. Following the same

methods in their writings as they had with adoptionism, and all of them (especially Alcuin) treating their adversaries with consideration, they evolved a doctrine which was approved by the council of Aix-la-Chapelle in 808, and was to become a permanency in the Churches of the West. Here again we see the work of Charlemagne and the chief scholars of the Carolingian Renaissance.

Their influence was just as great in the field of canon law, or in legislation concerning the Church as a social unit. In the barbarism prevailing during the seventh century and at the beginning of the eighth, the canons issued by councils and the papal decretals had been forgotten; these, together with the Bible and the opinions of the Fathers, constituted the sources for Church legislation and the texts used as references. Occasionally some texts would still be collected and summarised, but without checking their authenticity or making them into a proper code. First Carloman and then Charlemagne set out to frame a legislative code founded on ancient usages, and this was revived when the councils began meeting again. In 789, in his *Admonitio generalis*, Charlemagne invited the clergy to observe a tradition that was universal and very old. An official code was sought for among authentic legislative texts. This did in fact exist in the shape of a canonical collection compiled by a sixth-century monk called Denys the Small. Charlemagne received it from Pope Hadrian in 774 and quickly circulated it. It was the collection known as *Dionysio-Hadriana*, and it became the basic text referred to by councils, and to which were added any new texts bearing on the subject and derived from different national sources, such as the Spanish councils. A new collection thus formed, and known today as *Dacheriana* (because it was rediscovered in the eighteenth century by Dom Luc d'Achery) became the source of canon law from about 800 onwards. But in this field, as in other forms of intellectual activity, only a start was made in Charlemagne's lifetime.

Later, under Louis the Pious, experts in canon law exerted themselves to spread authentic texts, and to organise the Church and the customs they wished laymen to adopt, in particular those concerned with penitence and marriage. Although Charlemagne had tried to impose Roman customs in all these matters, his success was very limited. About thirty manuscripts from the *Dionysio-Hadriana* collection, written in the ninth century, have come down to us, and from 845 the interest in canonical collections was so great that forgeries began to be made: the best known are the *False Decretals*. Their very existence proves the importance attached to such texts, but they do not seem to have spread rapidly. We must not forget that in Pepin the Short's reign ecclesiastical reform had been undertaken by Anglo-Saxon monks, and that the form of monasticism widespread at the time had been inspired by Celtic customs and the religious outlook of St Columba. His influence had established among the clergy certain usages to which he was attached, particularly to do with penances. Books known as penitentials listed possible infringements of the law of the Church, in other words sins, and indicated the required penance for each – prayers, fasting or pilgrimages. Such schedules might be useful to ignorant clergy finding themselves in charge of even more simple-minded worshippers; a good many were to be found in Britain, whence they came to Gaul, but they revealed a tiresome tendency to misunderstand the spirit of canon law and neglect the notions of the sacrament, the grace obtained by the Redeemer, and individual conscience, to which the Roman clergy had always been deeply attached. Specialists in Church law began a campaign against these manuals in the reign of Louis the Pious. In 829 the council of Paris ordered that they should be searched out and burned. Two archbishops, Ebbo of Rheims and Raoul of Bourges, drew up a detailed criticism of these books, and called for a return to Roman unity and regularity. They had to be replaced, because of the widespread ignorance of the clergy. But the new penitentials, particularly the penitential of Halitgar, and the *Quadripartitus*, substituted a system borrowed from the best sources of canon law for Celtic usages, and were preceded by a doctrinal exposition. Raban Maur, who was certainly one of the most intelligent men of his day, composed two penitentials in 841 and 853, based entirely on the *Dionysio-Hadriana* and the *Dacheriana*. It was also necessary to redraft the little manuals used to instruct the clergy in rural districts in their duties and the rules established by the bishops: these were the *capitula episcoporum*, of which the best known were by Theodulf, Haiton, Bishop of Bâle, Gherbald, Bishop of Liège, a bishop of Freising, and later on by Hincmar of Rheims and Raoul of Bourges. All these books were intended to strengthen the hierarchy and the authority of the bishops, to stop laymen interfering in sacred matters, and see that canonical rules concerning penance and marriage were strictly observed. Public penance, an old Church custom for the expiation of serious and notorious offences, had returned to favour in 813, as a reaction against the penitentials. But secret auricular confession was still kept up. An effort was made to condemn and put an end to abuses, such as consanguineous marriages or abductions, by defining the impediments to marriage; in 847 consanguineity in the fourth degree was definitely made an impediment. Thus canon law was made uniform and usages were regularised, all the more effectively because, by the very constitution of the State, legislation was carried out by civil and ecclesiastical authorities in co-operation, with the help of the councils and learned members of the clergy. Roman law was beginning to be studied again, and its influence is often visible in the tendencies that triumphed at this period.

Civil law also benefited from the Carolingian Renaissance. The whole Roman Empire had shared a single legal system, and many thinkers were attracted by this universality, which was based on logical norms very different from those governing Germanic law. In spite of invasions, and the adoption of national laws, Roman law had always been studied in certain centres like Bologna and Pavia, but it only began to have a general influence during the eleventh century. The differences among national laws were attacked in capitularies, and in books by certain broadminded clerics. As with canon law, collections of capitularies were made, for instance that of Ansegis, Abbot of Fontenelle, which dated from 827 and became quasi-official under Louis the Pious and Charles the Bald, and an attempt was made to classify the texts methodically so as to make it easier to consult them. As with canon law, too, texts were faked in order to support some individual pretension. The general purpose behind these compilations, whether authentic or fabricated, was to create a single legal system for the West, and to fight against the particularism of national laws.

Among contemporaries of Louis the Pious, Agobard of Lyons was most forcibly impressed by the absurdity of multiple legislation and the barbarism of some of the national laws. In a treatise addressed to the Emperor, entitled *Adversus Legem Gondobaldi*, he proved himself a high-minded and well educated man, capable of dealing with far-reaching problems. Criticising the Burgundian law which was in force in his diocese, he attacked the principle of separate laws for different nations, showed the abuses it led to, and called for the abolition of national laws and a unified legal code. His object was first and foremost to destroy this system, which was bound to lead to such relics of superstition as trial by ordeal or judicial duel. But Agobard was too much in advance of his time to have a chance of success. Even so distinguished a man as Hincmar, who belonged to a younger generation than Agobard, defended the system of trial by ordeal, and called on his knowledge of the scriptures to prove its excellence. The national laws were eventually replaced by a code with a narrower scope, but the principle survived in some regions until the middle of the tenth century. The reforms started by the contemporaries of Louis the Pious and Charles the Bald in the field of canon and civil law nevertheless continued the work initiated under Charlemagne.

It was the same with theology. The first Carolingian Renaissance produced distinguished intellectuals, who were masters of logical method, able to apply it with all subtlety to the study of difficult problems. But all intellectual advance depends on its framework and surroundings. In the Carolingian period, theology was only studied in abbeys and episcopal schools, where it was taught by the men actively responsible for their administration. It was therefore more inclined to tradition than innovation, and – like philosophy –

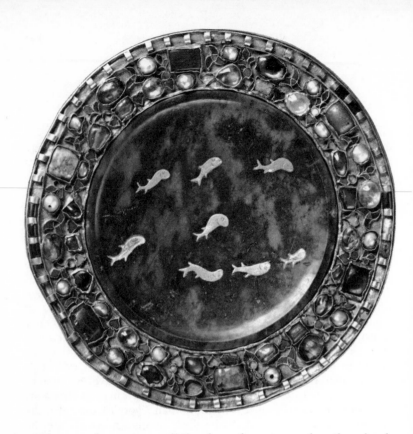

made no real progress until the eleventh century, when the schools became more independent.

In the reigns of Louis the Pious and his sons, theologians considered problems concerning predestination and the eucharist. The problem of predestination raised an important issue for Christians; it arose in the sixth century, and again at every period when man's future and his relationship with God were subjects for reflection, particularly in the sixteenth century during the Reformation, and in the seventeenth with Jansenism: did God mean to save all men or, on the contrary, to lead a chosen few to eternal life? From the first, three texts from St Paul, relating to divine prescience, man's freedom of will, and grace respectively, were brought to bear on the subject. In the fourth century a Celtic monk called Pelagius rejected the necessity for grace. When attacking his

Paten, known as Charles the Bald's, ninth century. Paris, Musée 147
du Louvre. It is made of hard, clear green stone, clouded
with darker patches to look like plants growing in deep water.
It is encrusted with eight minute goldfish, and set in
a gold mount. Though some have dated it to the tenth century,
it has recently been ascribed to the time of Charles the Bald.

doctrine St Augustine insisted that grace was a free gift from God,
and his belief was later distorted to support the conclusion that
God did not bestow grace on all men alike, but predestined some
to be saved. By a slight further twist, the conclusion was reached
that God predestined one part of humanity to eternal life and the
rest to damnation. Of course St Augustine did not approach these
problems from man's point of view: he was theocentric, and for
that very reason left certain aspects of the problem in obscurity.
But he had many disciples in Gaul: at the end of the sixth century
it was accepted that God predestined man's salvation, but the
council of Orange refused to accept that man could be predestined
to damnation. At the beginning of the Carolingian period, the
problem was again presented. It seemed as if the whole question
must be considered afresh. A theological controversy on the subject was initiated by Gottschalk, and led to many theological works,
and intervention by several councils. Gottschalk was a learned
monk from the monastery of Fulda, who had studied with
enthusiasm the works of St Augustine and his disciple St Fulgen-
tius, and collected a whole series of extracts from the Fathers,
which often – taken out of context – seemed to support the doctrine
of predestination. He was in contact with the most famous writers
of the day: Ratramn, Jonas of Orleans, Lupus of Ferrières and
Raban Maur, archbishop of the ecclesiastical province in which
he lived. Hearing that he had been preaching this doctrine in Friuli,
Raban Maur wrote a treatise to refute it, in the form of another
collection of extracts, with a moderately Augustinian conclusion.
In 848 the council of Mainz condemned Gottschalk, and in 849
this condemnation was renewed by the council of Quierzy, owing
to the intervention of Hincmar. Gottschalk was put in prison, but
many theologians took up his case. Ratramn of Corbie supported
him; Lupus of Ferrières, consulted by Charles the Bald, wrote a
treatise on predestination in 850; Prudentius, Bishop of Troyes,
was on his side. Hincmar, who supported his condemnation,
obtained the advice of one of the most learned contemporary
scholars, John Scotus Erigena, a very original thinker, the best and

perhaps the only true dialectician of his day. But his reply to Gottschalk's supporters was clumsy, and contained more than one heresy according to several theologians. Prudentius of Troyes replied in a work prefaced by Wenilo of Sens, Hincmar's rival. The quarrel was embittered by personal factors, but it proved that a party wholly dedicated to Augustinianism existed in *Francia Occidentalis*. Prudentius, Lupus, Ratramn and Wenilo believed that the doctrine was threatened not by Gottschalk but by his adversaries. In Lothar's kingdom the reaction was similar: the entire school of the Church of Lyons, including Amolon, Remi, and above all the scholaster Florus, whose opinion carried great weight, declared that his interpretation of several passages of the Scriptures was correct, attacked John Scotus Erigena, stated that Raban Maur (now dead) had been wrong, and made a bid for appeasement. Between 855 and 860, four councils summoned to consider the doctrine of the council of Orange of 529 – it had declared in favour of moderate Augustinianism – attempted to pour oil on the troubled waters; so also did the papal legates at the council of Metz in 863. This quarrel in which the opinion of Raban Maur and Hincmar, two men of action who saw the danger of extreme doctrines, was confronted by that of studious men only interested in logic and pushing their theories to the furthest possible limits, clearly shows the keenness of purely intellectual speculation among these brilliant, learned, subtle minds trained in the art of argument.

Passions just as great were aroused by the eucharistic controversy. One of the essential beliefs of the Church since earliest times had been that the body and blood of Christ was actually present in the bread and wine consecrated during Mass: the members of the congregation who received them in the sacrament of the eucharist were receiving the body of Christ. In every period there had been some who were shocked by this belief, and had questioned the reality of transubstantiation, seeing it purely as a symbolic rite; but the Roman Church always condemned them and held firm on this point. Under Louis the Pious, the desire to understand and explain, born of the revival of learning, led to a controversy con-

EXRECVMDOMINVSMVNDVMDICIONEGVBERNANS
MPERITACSCEPTRVMREGNANSQIIVREPERENNI
NMORTALETENES CVMCRIMINAMVLTAPARENTVM
AXAST CEIVSTITIAECVMFRENALOCARAS
MNIBVS ERGOTVISSERVI SVPERASTRABEATAM
PERAREHINC VISTE CHRISTEDEDISTI
ONIQVE TMODOCREDENDO PATRISQVETVIQE
VNCNOME DRI TI GLORIAMCVNCTASTVPEBANT
AECVLADVDVMNERT CEQDCESTATVRAMICA
VMMIXPICOLAED NAT RITEGERINDVMHOC
RIVSTA THAO NVMAVID OD TOLLERELEGEM
EDCE T TOTVMAVGVS NVTVEXCOLATORBEM
NAMHOC ONVS ANTO RANDOCARDINEPRODIT
RBSSCI VTCALEDV SVLT CAESARISORET
VGVSTOPVRE TA MAM HINCLAVDECORONAM
AMOPTIM DEXRAMVIRTV DIVINAPARETARTE
TIPSIES VTODETVTRIN POSCIMVSOMNE
AMALMVM VTO IVSTITIAEQVODREGNITETVBIQE
AECSILI ARATAQVELLIGATVCIRETAMICO
VMAFFER TLORICAPLACITVSICIPSAPARATVM
PTEMVSNO SSE ERAMICVMSVEMPIECHRISTVS
RETVTATO RMANNILLVSIACVLOPREMITASTFVR
ASVELIN ILLOPOTERATHOSTISCRIMINEDIRO
DEFENSOR ARTIS BIR MMONSTRATAMANDVM
VSOANAT VIANE TCESARISOBTINETHAVSTVM
MENFITQ OAMNEA TVMIMPERIVMMANETORBE
NRECNAC AIVMONN PERAEVVMMVNERADONANT
TPERSAD ALSICQVEIVSGOBOLISLATVSAMBIT
ENSPLEB LETAPRO VCRINAIMPLEDONANT
MVSAMVIV TEDEN CITVRAMARE
PEMECSV SCETRATANENO DV SATVBIQ
REMHAVST DONE LLITABARTE
RAEFORMO SEIVRATENEBRI ELAVEPASSINT
TSEDARE RVIAM
QVAMESTS SOLIDVSPERMANE TRACTVOVILE
TRANSFOR ATOR CRISTI LARATRIBVTA
VRECOLE INTNO NVGIOMEANSDOTVMABORE
RVAEHOCS INTNO MEANSICOTVMABORE
NEMPETON STVRGETVIPROBE TVDDINAMARI
SITTREMO NESTQVEBONADIV FAMAE
PROFICIT INDEORBEMDVM IGITAQ
SICABICI RPORTCRVCEDAT SEQITVRQ
VNCTIBI NIMINODATVMOCAS TOPIISQ
CAESARLA GEMODOVISTVCAS VICIAST
KERRESS OMQETIMORA INIM NSDAT
VPIVSET GRATNIMIVMP NVMRO HAECGENS
DVENIAM IREAMVSNOBISADIVSSAPARENTIS
CONSCRIP SIDVDVMNACRISTILAVDELIBELLVM
VERSIBVS ETPROSATIBIQMENVNCINDVPERATOR
OFFEROSANCTELIBENSCVIVSPRAECEDITIMAQO
STANSARMATAFIDEVICTOREMMONSTRATVBIQVE

cerning the eucharist. In 831, one of Raban Maur's pupils called Paschasius Radbertus, a scholaster of Corbie, humanist, man of letters, hagiographer and theologian, wrote his chief work, *De Corpore et Sanguine Domini*, which he revised in 844 and sent to Charles the Bald. In it he affirmed that the eucharist was both real and symbolic at the same time. As it was thought that the somewhat vague treatment of the subject might give rise to controversy, the King consulted John Scotus Erigena and Ratramn of Corbie. The latter wrote a treatise with the same title as that of Radbertus, in which – without going so far as to make the eucharist purely symbolic – he questioned the identity of the body of Christ (the historical personage), with the body present in the sacrament (which could be taken as the *essential virtue* of Christ). In a letter to the Abbot of Prüm, Raban Maur returned to this question, subtly distinguishing between the essence and the mode of presence, while John Scotus Erigena seems to have tended to a spiritualist and mystical view by speaking of a 'memory' of the body of Christ. These controversies show the revival of speculative reasoning, which had been dormant for two centuries. The method used was literal explanation followed by theological analysis of the Scriptures and the Fathers. Thus Remi of Lyons reproached Pardulus of Laon for having made use of apocryphal texts. But none of this amounted to dialectics, except in the case of John Scotus Erigena, who was justly accused by his contemporaries of using nothing else; he was gravitating towards the dialectics of the eleventh and twelfth centuries, and was already using subtle and exact methods of reasoning. But besides this scientific criticism, a new allegorical form of explanation was beginning to appear, used particularly by Raban Maur; Amalar of Autun pushed it to the extent of symbolism without relation to logic, which was described by Paschasius Radbertus as nonsense. However, the allegories and symbolism originating in the Carolingian period were to remain in favour for a long time, and invade and sterilise medieval science and literature. The religious beliefs of all these men were unshakeable, and they only thought of learning as the foundation of apologetics.

The most remarkable feature of the reigns of Louis the Pious and his sons was the great number of writers who were at work. There were at least forty whose books had some merit. Many of them tried their hands at different forms, and beside the works of scholars and theologians we find history, hagiography, poetry, and encyclopedic works embracing the whole of culture.

History at first took the form of dry and apparently accurate annals, which were simply lists of events in chronological order. Often begun before the new dynasty, they were usually kept going in monasteries, such as Lobbes, St Gall, Fulda, St Vaast of Arras, and Lorsch. But official records were also beginning to be kept at court: the Royal Annals, begun in 741, were still continuing in various centres after 829. There were also works by individual authors who had tried to imitate the great historians of antiquity. Einhard, a friend of Charlemagne's, a learned humanist famous for his knowledge of Latin, and head of the artistic activities at court, set himself to write the Emperor's life modelled on the lives of the Caesars by Suetonius. The *Vita Karoli*, though a sort of pastiche, has undoubted literary value, for its author was faithful to his subject, and envisaged history as a branch of eloquence; its historical value is more dubious, since instead of collecting information from eye-witnesses he was content to follow the text of annals that are still available in a more complete form. Biographies of Louis the Pious were written by Thegan and an anonymous author nicknamed 'the Astronomer' because of his interest in meteorological phenomena. The same subject was treated by a versifier, Ermold the Black, who celebrated his hero's reign in a long poem. Very different qualities are to be found in Nithard's *History of the Sons of Louis the Pious*. This cultivated nobleman, grandson of Charlemagne and lay Abbot of St Riquier, who fought for Charles the Bald and was killed in his service in 844, found time to write a book describing the political and warlike opposition to the sons of Louis the Pious before the Treaty of Verdun. It is a work of the first importance, very carefully thought out and composed. Nithard was not only a man of action, he had a clear and acute mind, and was able to make balanced judgments about men and events. His work bears witness to the solid education received by important laymen during the flowering of the Carolingian Renaissance. Chronicles of world history had been in existence for a long time, for there had always been a few inquisitive minds eager to go back as far as possible into the past; the subject was revived by men like Freculphus, Bishop of Lisieux, who rewrote and completed the ancient chronicles of Eusebius, St Jerome, Prosper of Aquitaine and Orosius; another attempt of a similar sort was made in Charles the Bald's reign, by Adon of Vienne.

A literary form close to history, but more concerned with the edification of readers than with faithfulness to facts, was hagiography. Cultivated even in the Merovingian epoch, it had been revived in Britain by the Venerable Bede. In Charlemagne's day, Paul the Deacon wrote the lives of the bishops of Metz. Under Louis the Pious, Agnellus compiled those of the archbishops of Ravenna – a work remarkable for its careful research into historical sources. The lives of the abbots of Fontenelle by an unknown author, of Sturm, Abbot of Fulda by Eigil, of Wala by Paschasius Radbertus, and many others (quite apart from earlier works rewritten in more polished language) are all examples of hagiography in the reign of Louis the Pious. This interest even led to the creation of legends, such as those invented by Hilduin, Abbot of St Denis, and his followers.

Poetry was also in favour. The collected Latin poems of the Carolingian era take up four fat volumes of the *Monumenta Germaniae historica*. But they are on the whole mediocre. Poets inclined more and more to write in rhythmic verse, better adapted than classical prosody to ears that were unresponsive to the sound of the Latin language. A number of the poets of the period had some talent: Milo of St Amand, Raban Maur, Eric of Auxerre, Ermold the Black, Sedulius Scotus, Walafrid Strabo, Moduin and Prudentius are among the best.

There was also an interest in the didactic exposition of scientific learning. Theologians like Gottschalk, Raban Maur, Paschasius

Radbertus, Prudentius, Ratramn and Lupus of Ferrières wrote treatises on philology and scientific subjects as well as theology. John Scotus Erigena was not only a theologian and dialectician; he was also a metaphysician, trying to construct a philosophic system that was neither rationalistic nor pantheistic, but which attempted to analyse such notions as God and Man, using a vocabulary largely borrowed from the neo-Platonists by way of St Augustine. A dozen years after he had written about predestination, he produced his *De divisione naturae*, in which he divided the whole of Nature into four classes (founded upon the creative power of beings and their condition as creatures, and leading to the notion of non-created and almighty God); he was aware of the problem of universals; he distinguished the different departments of theology. It is to his credit that he was not satisfied with merely collecting sources, but combined and transformed them, and evolved his own arguments from them. His works had a great influence throughout the Middle Ages.

In the intellectual intoxication that fermented after the barrenness of the previous period, some writers made inventories and summaries of knowledge. Encyclopedias were compiled, such as Raban Maur's *De rerum naturis*, which is merely an incomplete version of Isidore of Seville's. Lupus of Ferrières, another encyclopedist, was of noble Frankish stock, and showed an eager appetite for every branch of learning, sacred or profane. Theologian, hagiographer, Latinist and humanist, he devoted himself entirely to culture, and his correspondence with princes, prelates and scholars is a monument to the intense intellectual activity of the contemporaries of Louis the Pious and Charles the Bald. But the high quality of the works produced in this period is a function of the habits of thought and the mentality of the elite.

The different currents of ideas during the Carolingian epoch are not easy to study, and the work has hardly begun. One can however glimpse the sources of literary inspiration, and the working techniques used by intellectuals.

Not all the influences orientating the vast movement that began about 780 and went on until the end of the ninth century are yet known, but it is certain that the Irish and the Anglo-Saxons played an important part. Alcuin, John Scotus Erigena, Sedulius Scotus, Dunchad, Dungal and many other writers came from the British Isles and brought the Franks treasures of Latin literature that had been preserved in their country. The exact circumstances of their preservation we know little about, but it is certain that in the seventh and eighth centuries experts in literature like Aldhelm of Malmesbury and Bede were living in Britain, and that books which have since vanished, like Lucan's *Orpheus*, were preserved there. British libraries greatly influenced the Carolingian Renaissance, as did the patronage of important lovers of literature. Charlemagne was the most illustrious of its patrons, but all the sovereigns descended from him followed his example, and Louis the Pious, Charles the Bald and Louis the German counted their books among their most treasured possessions, and were surrounded by brilliant and cultivated courts where intellectuals were in high favour.

The Church was a prime influence because it was open to the world of ideas, because of its power and wealth, and its frequent and easy contact with schools and artists' studios; and of course some intellectual activities were the special domain of ecclesiastics. It was the Church that directed and encouraged the mingling of ideas on a vast scale that went on at this period. And it was the Church's efforts towards educational reform, and a more complete understanding of sacred writings, that led to the writing of so many books on language and grammar. As for the models studied, some of them – especially the poets – were thought to be a danger to faith. However Virgil, and to a lesser extent Horace and Ovid, were avidly read and annotated, in spite of the mythological allusions their works contained. Imitation of them even led to a change in the orientation of the literary renaissance: an artificial style developed, a sort of playful literary paganism, very far from the original aims of the movement. Thus imaginative literature was born of imitation of the ancients.

Hellenism too had a part to play in all this. Some ancient Greek works were preserved and studied in the Byzantine Empire. But Byzantium was still closely connected with Italy, and some works or literary themes were handed on to the Empire of the West through the intermediacy of Greeks from Italy, such as the Neapolitan deacon, Paul. These two sources, Latin poetry and mythology and some relics of Greek culture, influenced the intellectual climate: and side by side with the literature of ideas derived from school teaching, a number of literary forms began to be cultivated for the sake of pure entertainment. But emotional, passionate, or psychological sensibility was virtually non-existent at the time; it was imagination as an intellectual pastime that dominated medieval literature. Legends were accepted, Virgil and Lucan were constantly read and commented on, and an *Ilias latina* – or 'Latin Iliad', a collection of Homeric legends – was compiled. There was a public eager to read of the exploits of heroes and fabulous beings – purely imaginary creations. As for thought with a purely religious content, it was expressed not only in learned works, but also in sermons for Christian audiences. Here we have valuable evidence of the development of a mentality which began in the Carolingian period, for anyone who reads these works can easily see that their main theme is not the New Testament's religion of love, but the vengeful God of the Old; here we see spirituality dominated by an oriental current, hardly tempered by intermediate figures closer to man – the Virgin and the saints.

The most interesting mental development of the time was certainly the birth of philosophical argument, though only a few profound intellects grasped the fact that speculation could lead to two different spheres of thought: philosophy, ruled by pure reason, and theology, which presupposed an initial assumption.

Such were the general intellectual characteristics of our period. The student is struck by its genuine humanism, its eager desire to rediscover and absorb all human knowledge and find a rational method of acquiring it. 'Science', wrote Lupus of Ferrières, 'must be pursued with science'. In these words he expresses the disinterested cult of learning which was the fruit of Charlemagne's educational reforms, though not part of the Emperor's original purpose. The great and admirable impulse he gave to learning, creative activity and method, resulted in a complete revolution in the minds of educated men. The flowering of culture, inspired by Charlemagne's efforts in the middle of the ninth century, changed the direction of men's minds and led to a renaissance of literary invention and methods of thinking, in fact to the formation of a new cultural climate. It was the result of long and patient endeavour and the contributions of outstanding minds, and would probably have led to even more striking progress but for the misfortunes suffered by the West in the ninth and tenth centuries. Nevertheless the two great trends of the movement – the importance of method, and interest in imaginative literature – continued after this troubled period, and directed the course of medieval learning and literature. The Carolingian Renaissance of learning and literature cannot therefore be considered merely as a brilliant moment in the history of the human mind; it was the fount and origin of an indefinite evolutionary process. This is also true of the revival of the visual arts.

8 The renaissance of the visual arts

Architecture

A combination of influences led to a renaissance of the visual arts comparable to that of literature. Germanic habits and techniques, the rediscovery of Roman traditions, Byzantine and oriental innovations were fused together to create an original art. Carolingian art, with its response to oriental, northern and Mediterranean influences, was very complex. And in spite of wholesale destruction, the little that still remains to us compels admiration as an undying manifestation of civilisation. The few surviving examples of architecture, mosaic, the goldsmith's craft, work in ivory, painting, illuminated manuscripts, and to a lesser extent sculpture, are among the most interesting achievements of human genius.

When they have not been disfigured by later artists or nineteenth century restoration (sometimes as bad as complete destruction), the remains of Carolingian architecture show a striking formula inspired both by Charlemagne himself and by the good taste of the men to whom he had entrusted the embellishment of his palaces – Alcuin and Einhard. Apart from a few great monuments destined to house a large number of people, like some of the abbeys, buildings were generally small and intended for a few occupants. This was of course due to the small population of the Empire and its towns, the largest of which contained a few thousand inhabitants at most. But several great collections of buildings were devised, like the monasteries of Aniane (of which nothing now remains) and St Gall, whose plan has been preserved. These monuments kept more or less to earlier local architectural styles, and were at first chiefly made of wood – a familiar material to the half-nomadic German tribes. The heads of important noble families must have lived in wooden palaces of the same type as one of a later date, whose remains have been discovered at Lojsta in the island of Gotland. The large monasteries were probably built on the same quadrangular plan. But this indigenous architecture was so simple that it hardly lent itself to artistic development, and architects soon began seeking inspiration from Roman monuments. A desire for greater

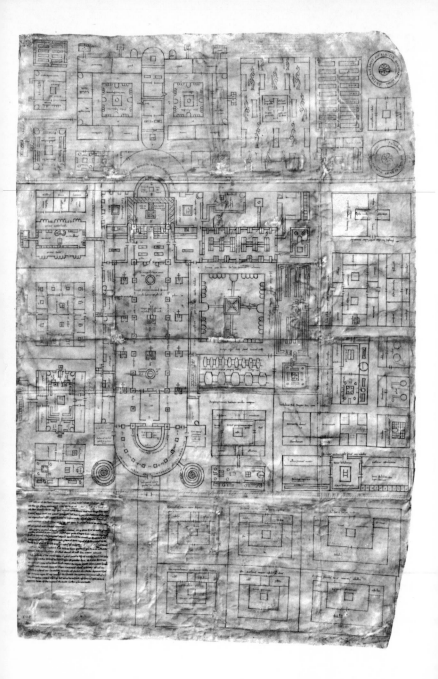

Left Plan of the abbey of St Gall, beginning of the ninth century.
St Gall, Stiftsbibliothek, ms. 1092. This is either the original plan
made during the abbacy of Gozbert (816–36) for the reconstruction
of the monastery, begun in 830, or else a copy of it. It was probably
carried out under the direction of Haiton, Bishop of Basle (803–23)
and Abbot of Reichenau. All the buildings are indicated by
inscriptions on the plan.

Below Model of the abbey of St Gall, carried out after an exhaustive
study of the ninth-century plan, by W. Horn, C. Born, C. B. Lund
and S. Karschunke, with the co-operation of the University of
California. The elevation of the church has been based on the
dimensions indicated on the plan (central nave 20 feet wide, and
10 feet for each aisle). The living quarters and agricultural buildings
were reconstructed from the remains of wooden buildings discovered
in northern France and in England, where this type of architecture
remained traditional for a long time. We see the south side of the
church, the cloister and adjoining buildings. The unfinished roof on
the right belongs to the dormitory over the heated common-room.
In the foreground are the farm buildings.

security produced a return to building in stone, and thenceforth the Roman style of building was taken as a model. Hardly anything of this art remained except temples, commemorative monuments, and public edifices such as gardens, amphitheatres and arches. The Carolingian period produced more or less imperfect imitations, according to the materials used and the skill of the builders. Nowhere was the tradition more firmly established than in the construction of churches, which were modifications of Roman basilicas, with very slight regional variations. The Carolingian epoch represents a transition between Roman and early medieval architecture. Techniques appropriate to stone and wood were combined. The tradition of building arches in stone had not been entirely lost under the Merovingians, though it was certainly on the decline: but the Byzantine cupola was still taken as an almost unrealisable ideal in the seventh century. In general, Carolingian architects had to be content with less extravagant forms, and great basilicas were generally covered in timber. Oriental influences were hampered by defective technique, resulting in works blending Byzantine and indigenous influences in an original way, rather than slavish copies. And the tradition of building places of worship in the Roman manner helped preserve their uniformity of style.

During the latter half of the eighth century, churches were designed on a rectangular plan with a narrower sacrarium at one end and a narthex at the other. Recent excavations have brought to light the plan of the churches of St Saviour of Paderborn, built in 777, of Niederdornberg dating from 790, and Minden from the beginning of the ninth century; at the same time churches were also being built on the basilica plan, with the three traditional naves of Roman buildings. Soon modifications were introduced: often a transept was added to provide more space for the congregation, and a lantern was placed at the junction of the transept and nave to give more light and solve the problem of connecting two perpendicular naves. The use of bells led to the construction of towers, and in this way large buildings came to have various additions modifying the general plan. They were considered aesthetically successful, and were much imitated afterwards: the basilica of St Martin of Tours must certainly have influenced the design of the abbatial church of St Riquier. Building techniques were still rather crude however. Even during the Merovingian period the art of building walls of ashlar had not been entirely lost, but there was an increasing tendency to use quarried stone embedded in strong mortar, often containing rows of bricks to give a decorative and regular appearance. The whole effect was thick and massive. The chief buildings constructed for Charlemagne show a skilful marriage between Byzantine influence and Roman techniques. On the whole, plans for building were carefully thought out and well ordered. At St Denis, the old fifth-century church where the royal tombs stood was replaced by a building begun in 754 and consecrated in 775. Recent excavations have shown that it must have been a timber-covered basilica, decorated with columns, and with a spacious but only slightly projecting transept and a lantern. At the west end was a narthex containing Pepin the Short's tomb. At St Riquier an immense abbatial church was in process of construction when Angilbert became abbot. Charlemagne had entrusted the building of it to experts from Rome and Italy. There was a church built on the basilica plan with nine towers, two centrally placed as at St Martin of Tours, and two enclosing the narthex designed for Angilbert's tomb. The superstructure was of wood, another instance of a compromise between nordic and Mediterranean traditions. The architectural masterpiece of this period was without doubt the Royal Chapel at Aix, begun in 792 on the designs of Odo of Metz, and consecrated by Pope Leo III in 805. In spite of the restorations of 937, and alterations carried out in the Gothic period, important traces of the original building still exist. It was undoubtedly inspired by the Lateran Palace, and by the Ravenna monuments, for its great doorway was reminiscent of the basilica of San Vitali, as were also the galleries on two levels and the tribune with its niche where the Emperor appeared in public. The whole was disposed round a central octagonal space. The beauty of this building depended entirely on the proportions of the arches and the

...QUI CONSTRUIT AULAM EFFECTUSQUE PIIS DAT STUDIIS HOMINUM QUORUM PERPETUI DECORIS STRUCTUR...

Left The Royal Chapel, Aix-la-Chapelle. The tribune of the Octagon with the Imperial Throne, 792–805. The Royal Chapel stood opposite the rest of the palace buildings, on the far side of a courtyard big enough to hold 7,000 people. It is octagonal in shape, covered with a dome, and surrounded by a vaulted aisle supporting the tribunes and leading into two side chapels. It is an admirable monument, worthy of its founder. The inspiration is mainly Roman, though it bears a resemblance to San Vitali in Ravenna. Marble columns support richly decorated capitals in the classical style, and the vaulting is divided into triangles as in Roman architecture. A stone throne in the tribune marks the emperor's place; it contained relics. The building was partly rebuilt in the Ottonian period and also in the twelfth century, but there are important remains dating from the foundation.

Below Bronze balustrade from the Royal Chapel. These railings, masterpieces of their kind, are in two different styles. The panels represented here are the oldest, probably in the Frankish or Lombard tradition, and have a certain rigidity of line. The more recent panels show a return to classical antiquity. The whole of this balustrade has fortunately survived alterations to the Chapel, as well as destruction and looting.

rich mosaic decorations. Yet, in spite of these Byzantine features, it
was probably inspired even more by Rome than Ravenna. In about
806, Theodulf of Orleans had the little church of Germigny-des-
Près built as an oratory for one of the palaces. It was still practically
intact though dilapidated in the middle of the nineteenth century,
when a savagely executed 'restoration' destroyed almost all that
remained of this little building with its five apses and three naves
covered in mosaics. Belonging to the same period were the abbey
of Aniane (vanished today), the churches of San Benedetto of
Mals near Trent, of Near-bei-Münster in Switzerland, and of St
Peter of Fulda. All these buildings had sprung from the same
inspiration. The revival of architecture in Charlemagne's day may
seem to have been archaistic, but it was in reality more than that. It
was the expression of a synthesis of elements tending to revive
Roman classicism: Aix-la-Chapelle was the Frankish interpretation
of a Romano-Byzantine theme: Germigny showed a peculiarly
Gallic sensibility to Byzantine and oriental influences. Architecture
was already an original art.

This originality became more marked during the ninth century.
Then under Louis the Pious and his sons, it began to be
recognised that architectural beauty depended on the proportions
between the different parts of the building, the design of arches, and
harmony between decoration and plan. All the surviving monuments of this period are religious buildings, whether great abbatial
churches or little country chapels. Although Ansegis's masterpiece,
the abbey of Fontenelle, has completely disappeared, a few other
buildings have come down to us. At Rheims, the cathedral rebuilt
by Archbishop Ebbo with the help of Louis the Pious, and finished
by Hincmar, had a lead roof and a marble floor, and was almost as
large as the existing thirteenth-century cathedral; at St Riquier,
there was a vaulted construction at the west end, occupying almost
a quarter of the total floor-space, and a tribune including an altar
and baptismal fonts. The abbatial church of St Philibert-de-Grandlieu has been preserved almost intact. In 853, Abbot Heribold had
a vault erected over the saint's tomb and added three apses; the

nave was built a little later. The whole edifice, with its massive columns and roughly chamfered capitals, its apse vaulted with a semi-dome and narrow windows, is a good example of ninth-century architecture. It is one of the very few complete monuments of the period still to be found in France.

A good many crypts have survived: that of St Quentin reproduces the most typical features of St Médard at Soissons, which was destroyed in the first world war. There are others at Flavigny, St Germain at Auxerre, St Rémi at Rheims and St Bénigne at Dijon. In Germany there still exists a jewel of Carolingian art, incrusted with baroque ornamentation: the abbatial church of Corvey on the river Weser, dating from the second half of the ninth century. The antechapel, built between 873 and 885, is in a splendid state of preservation, and the oldest building of its type now in existence. The lower part of the façade is extremely simple; its three doors have semi-circular arches corresponding to the gable and the two towers framing it. The most striking architectural feature is the height and narrowness of the shallow porch, crowned with a triangular gable and a statue of Christ in a niche. Inside, the impressive three-storied elevation is somewhat reminiscent of

The Ark of the Covenant between two angels. Early ninth-century mosaic.
Germigny-des-Prés. This mosaic, dating from 806, decorates the half-dome
covering the eastern apse of the little church of Germigny. The angels are
pointing to the Ark, which is also indicated by the hand of God emerging from
a rainbow of gold, green and blue. The Ark is at the centre of the composition
and thus links the church of Germigny to the Temple in Jerusalem. It can also
be seen as the symbol of biblical kingship revived by Charlemagne. The design
is clearly imitated from contemporary miniatures.

Aix-la-Chapelle, and the vaulted entrance leads into the high
square body of the church, surrounded by the aisles and tribune.
All the large churches of this period have raised choirs reached
by steps, very much in keeping with the ritual pomp that was being
reintroduced in church ceremonies. The vaulting, where it existed,
was of the barrel type, or occasionally groined, supported on square
columns that were already tending to be shaped according to the
stress they had to take and the arches converging upon them,
while pilasters gave them the appearance of cruciform supports.
The apertures were narrow, the arches supported either by voussoirs,
or springers without groins, or simply by a mass of mortar; the
bell-towers were built on a massive foundation, often arising from
the antechapel. The tribunes on the aisles were reminiscent of the
traditional plan of early Christian basilicas. Architecture, then made
a considerable advance: although still archaic, and imitative of
Roman styles, it was sufficiently original to endure, and in the
following period it became a basis for the magnificent achievements
of the Ottonian and Romanesque styles.

Decoration

All these buildings must have been brilliantly decorated. The roofs
were often made of gilded metal, the vaulted ceilings covered in
mosaics; the capitals and sculptures were of marble. Many of the
ciboria, crosses, reliquaries, candelabra and candlesticks were
marvellous examples of the goldsmith's art, set with precious

stones. Very little has survived, for these objects were often melted down for the sake of the precious metal they contained, but there is enough to give us an idea of their rich and delicate workmanship.

The art of mosaic reached Gaul in the fourth century and remained in favour throughout the Merovingian period. In Charlemagne's day it was revived, and used a great deal. It was at this period that a great mosaic was made for the Royal Chapel, representing Christ in glory, and (at the base of the dome) the figures of the Apostles and twenty-four old men of the Apocalypse on a blue background with gold stars; and the techniques of Constantine's day were revived in the mosaic of the Scala Santa in the Lateran. At Germigny, as at Aix, the background of the principal mosaic was deep blue with gold stars; it represented the Ark of the Covenant and two archangels, with the hand of God above. Before this building was 'restored', the western apse (now

Theodora, mother of Pope Pascal I. Detail of a mosaic,
817–24. Rome, church of Santa Prassede, chapel of
San Zeno. Pascal I intended this chapel, dedicated to the
martyr honoured on the Via Flaminia, to be his mother's
mausoleum. The square halo about her head (cf. page 111)
suggests that the portrait was executed in her lifetime.

destroyed) consisted of blind arches decorated with large palm-
leaf mouldings; the same pattern ornamented the entrance arch
into the eastern apse, with palms against a pale ochre background.
An incredible number of mosaics were executed all over the
Empire during the Carolingian epoch, and they usually imitated the
Byzantine style.

Buildings were also decorated with designs in terracotta or
plaster. At Germigny, terracotta modillions were found supporting
the roof, as well as clay tiles made in a mould and ornamented with
figures in relief, and fragments of stucco: fluting on the intrados of
arches, foliage decorating the archivolts, and so on. At St Riquier
plaster panels ornamented the secondary altars.

There was some revival of the art of sculpture in the Carolingian
epoch, but it was still rather primitive. Whereas in the seventh
century only marble had been used (in the capitals of the crypt at
Jouarre for instance), in the eighth century sculptors began using
stone; but their work was still very rough, and no startling progress
was achieved in the reign of Louis the Pious. The main trouble was
lack of technique. Sculpture in the round was rarely attempted, and
artists preferred to carry out a design in relief, by the primitive
method of hollowing out the stone between the lines: it was the
same technique as that used in *champlevé* enamel and had the same
cold charmless effect. Sculptors also found it difficult to represent
human beings, or indeed anything except simple ornamental
motifs, strapwork or palm-leaves. Fine examples of these had come
from Britain, and monumental sculpture was strongly influenced
by Irish and Anglo-Saxon art, as is shown by the few ninth-century
works that have come down to us: the strapwork crosses from
Bregenz and Romainmôtier, gables at Cortona and Spalato. The
output was very small compared with the perfection and profusion
of ancient sculpture.

The art of working in relief was seen at its most original and best
in objects made of gold and silver. The technique of working in
metal had been highly esteemed in the Orient since very early
times, and handed on to the Germanic tribes. There is evidence

Top left Early ninth-century ornamental sculpture added to part of an antique architrave. Rome, church of Santa Prassede, chapel of San Zeno. The architrave dates from the second or third century and was decorated with roses and strapwork in the Carolingian style when Santa Prassede was built.

Bottom left Early ninth-century capital, church of Germigny-des-Près. Sculpture imitating the antique style. This is among the very few pieces of sculpture that were preserved when the church was disfigured by restoration between 1841 and 1870.

Top right Fragment of a marble arch, probably from a choir-screen, early ninth century. Cortona. Accademia Etrusca. The nave and choir of the church were often separated by a screen where ambos, or lecterns, framed a sometimes decorated passage. Screen, passage and ambos all figure in the plan of the abbatial church of St Gall, at the east end of the central bay (cf. page 158).

Bottom right Fragment of a sculptured altar frontal from Lauterbach (Austria) eighth to ninth century. Bregenz, Vorarlberger Landesmuseum. The cross on the right was originally in the centre, but the remainder of the plaque has not survived. Archaic decoration of this type occurs in very early Anglo-Saxon sculpture. The whole is in flat relief.

172

that even before the great invasions there were skilled goldsmiths in towns like Rheims, Trèves and Arles. By the seventh century, works on a large scale like altarpieces were being made, and in the ninth, images of embossed metal in high relief, whose convexities were filled with plastic material such as wax, resin or cement: the reliquary offered by Pepin of Aquitaine to the church of Sainte Foy at Conques is an example of this technique. From time immemorial craftsmen had worked in *cloisonné*; the designs were made by soldering a filigree pattern on to a metal plaque, and filling in the spaces with different coloured enamels set with precious stones. This very old technique spread through all the Germanic races, as can be seen from Frankish belt-buckles and Visigothic or Anglo-Saxon jewels. The finest works of this description came from Childeric's burial-place, discovered at Tournai in the seventeenth century, and from that of an Anglo-Saxon noble, probably a king, found at Sutton Hoo in 1936. The technique was still being improved in Charlemagne's time. Some pieces of bronze furniture, such as 'Dagobert's armchair', dating from about 775, in the Cabinet des

Médailles, were also made at this time. But in the ninth century the greatest advance was in liturgical furniture: chalices, patens, reliquaries and bindings were produced in profusion – examples are the Nuremberg cross, the Victoria cross at Oviedo, and Charles the Bald's paten in the Louvre. Some typical bronze reliquaries of the period were shaped like a leather purse; they were always decorated on one or other of their faces with a somewhat stylised cross. The best known are at St Bonnet d'Avalouze in France, Enger in Germany, and Andenne in Belgium; they are so loaded with ornaments that they look like collections of precious stones, pearls and gold. The famous Stefansburse from the imperial treasure at Vienna, dating from about 830, is the most perfect example of such works of art, in spite of being restored in the nineteenth century. The goldsmiths did not confine their efforts to small objects such as these: they created great works like the altar at St Denis, now lost, but known to us through a fifteenth-century miniature representing it, now in the National Gallery in London. The Munich ciborium, a sort of baldachin supported by arches

The Ardennes Cross, about 825–50. Height 29 inches. Nuremberg, Germanisches Nationalmuseum. This cross is of embossed copper and gold leaf, decorated with precious stones and rock crystal and mounted on a wooden framework. A few pieces of metal have been lost. The treasures of important churches often contained valuable crosses of this kind, but very few have survived.

Binding from Lindau, ninth century. New York, Pierpont Morgan Library, ms. 1. Liturgical books were no less sumptuously produced and decorated than other pieces of religious furniture. The binding was often of precious metal. In this case the upper side, shown here, is a plaque from the school of goldsmiths at the court of Charles the Bald. The under side, no less magnificent, dates from the eighth century with decorative animals and curved lines of Anglo-Saxon style.

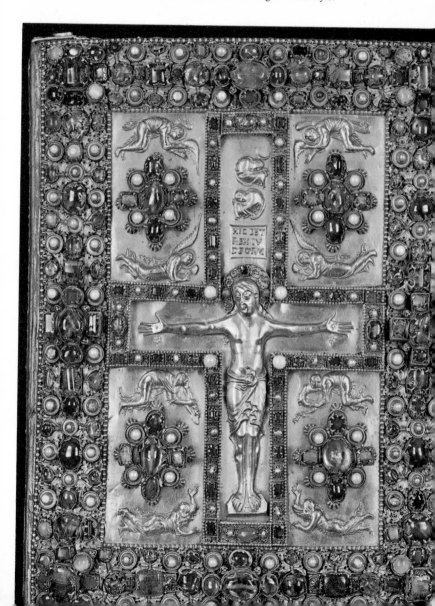

and columns at the corners, the Aldershamen and Essen-Werden altars, are relics of this amazing goldsmith's art of the ninth century. Even larger objects in bronze came from their workshops: at Aix-la-Chapelle the great doors and balconies of the tribune, admirably designed and beautifully executed pieces, are still preserved; and we know that in the abbatial church at St Riquier six bronze statues of animals, birds and men used to stand on top of the columns of the blind arcade enclosing the high altar. We do not know whether they were sculptured in the round. It is clear that by the ninth century goldsmiths and metalworkers had developed a technique enabling them to produce work of the highest quality.

Besides the art of the goldsmith, ivory-carving reached a point of perfection at this time that has never been surpassed. Here again the impulse was not original, but had been inspired by the double influence of Byzantium and the Anglo-Saxons. The themes treated by ivory-workers bear witness to a new breadth of outlook: the iconography of the ancient paleo-Christian sarcophagi was revived, with a leaning towards subjects from the New Testament. The influence of miniatures is undeniable: the sides of the binding of the Lorsch Evangeliary and Charles the Bald's Psalter show that ivory-carvers and miniaturists were inspired by the same models. Ivory-carving was chiefly the work of the monks in the studios of the great German abbeys, and gradually developed in the direction of the masterpieces of Ottonian art. The only individual artist known to us is Tuotilo, a monk of St Gall, whose signature is on the plaque of a binding still preserved in the abbey; some facts about him are given us by the works of the writer known as 'the monk of St Gall': he lived at the end of the ninth century. The style of ivory-carving was influenced equally by classical and Byzantine art: the Christ is usually beardless, and the folds of his clothes and the other draperies are reminiscent of antique and Byzantine miniatures alike. The decoration is incredibly skilful, and only matched by that of Byzantine marbles; many ivories of the period show traces of the gilding with which they were once decorated and the glass beads which gave life to the eyes of the figures.

Left One side of the binding of the Lorsch Evangeliary. Carved
ivory from Charlemagne's palace school, about 810. London,
Victoria and Albert Museum. (The other side is in Rome, in the Vatican
Museum.) The Virgin is enthroned, holding the infant Jesus
on her knee, with St John the Baptist on the left and the high priest
Zacharias on the right; below, scenes of the Nativity and the angels
bringing tidings to the shepherds. This beautiful work was probably
inspired by paleo-Christian and Byzantine models.
Below Adoration of the Magi. Detail of the other side of the
same binding. The figures are treated in relief.

In the same way figurative painting had developed out of what
had been a purely decorative art. We know that a good many mural
painters existed in the eighth and ninth centuries. The art of fresco,
so highly esteemed in Rome, had never been forgotten, and the
painters of the Carolingian period were eager to revive this
technique, like all the others practised by the Romans. It is difficult
today to get an impression of these works from the few surviving
fragments, or even to date them exactly, as they have often been
repainted in the course of time. Glass windows were also certainly

used, but nothing remains of them but a memory: the chronicle of St Bénigne of Dijon, written in 1031, describes a window found in the church illustrating the martyrdom of St Paschasius, which had been executed 'in very early times', but had 'resisted the passage of the years'. We do not know if this was a work of the ninth or the tenth century. Nothing at all is left of these works, and in order to appreciate the quality of Carolingian painting we must make do with a few fragmentary murals and a great many manuscripts, both of which, however, enable us to realise that this was one of the very great periods in the history of painting.

Even during times of artistic stagnation, there were regions where local activity persisted and brilliant works were produced, obviously by great artists: such are the ninth-century frescoes in Asturias and Catalonia, and some illuminated manuscripts. But in the earliest Frankish period, the technical and artistic traditions, methods and inspiration of the Romans were only to be found in Rome itself; even at Milan, Ravenna or Trèves, the tradition had been interrupted by the invasions. The art of painting was of course still practised in some of the monasteries, but very few examples exist today, and those are only sporadic efforts, each with its own style and quality. Occasionally an artist of genius evolved his own technique and inspiration, but there was no real school or established tradition of painting. Works of art were rare individual phenomena. Only after Charlemagne's day does one find the artists of the West expressing their individuality, and perfecting, adapting and transposing traditional methods with a certain uniformity of style. The sole tradition that survived was the use of iconographic themes in painting: for example in the seventh, eighth and ninth centuries a place of worship was often decorated with the tall figures of saints. But these influences must sometimes have been interrupted: during the iconoclastic period, the popes encouraged the iconophilist Greeks to represent God and the saints; after the oecumenical council of 787, numerous representations of the human figure were made in Italy; while in Gaul and Germany, where Church doctrine was less favourable to images, decorative rather than figurative art prevailed.

Other influences made themselves felt: the revival of classical antiquity and the taste for mythology apparent in literature also affected painting, and the iconographic themes and styles of the fourth and fifth centuries reappeared. Imitations of the antique were to be seen in the mural paintings of north Italy, but this art flourished also in other parts of the Empire. We know that the great rooms of the palaces at Ingelheim and Aix-la-Chapelle were also decorated with paintings. The characteristic feature of these murals was that purely decorative motifs were rare, and figurative themes, such as representations of the Trinity often seen in apses, were the rule. The paintings at Auxerre and Müstair were narrative frescoes. We still possess some fine ensembles. At the abbey of San Vincenzo, at the source of the river Volturno, there is an oratory built on a cruciform plan having the walls and vault decorated with frescoes; they can be exactly dated between 826 and 843, by the portrait of an abbot among them. The general effect is Roman: there is a procession of saints holding a crown; in the apse is a Virgin surrounded by angels; these themes are the same as those of the mosaics at Ravenna. The church at Müstair, in a valley in the canton of Grisons near the Italian frontier, is entirely decorated with frescoes dating from the end of the ninth century, retouched in the twelfth and restored in 1947; they depict eighty-two scenes from the Old and New Testaments arranged in five rows. In the Italian Tyrol, at Malhes near Bolzano, a collection of descriptive frescoes painted before 881 treats numerous figures in a very original manner reminiscent of Müstair, and at Naturno there are others that cannot be exactly dated. While none of the frescoes at Oviedo, Tuñon and Valdedios in Asturias contain figures, the crypt of St Germain d'Auxerre has paintings that can be dated between 841 and 859; the scenes are treated in an original manner, and the human figures have extraordinary movement and life. This church is above all remarkable for the very close connection between these figurative scenes and the decoration of other parts of the building. In St Maximin at Trèves, the crypt of a very ancient sanctuary has

Martyrdom of St Stephen. Fresco dating from 841–59. Church of St Germain d'Auxerre, France. A fine series of frescoes has recently been discovered in the crypt of this church. They can be exactly dated, as the crypt was built in 841 and St Germain's relics were installed there in 859. The style of painting is not derived from the antique but is obviously inspired by miniatures and manuscripts. Movement and expression are its most striking qualities.

St Peter receiving the keys of the Kingdom of Heaven. Ninth-century fresco. Apse of the church at Müstair (Tyrol). In 1947 some Carolingian frescoes were discovered in this church and a complete ninth-century painted interior was revealed. Some scenes had been repainted in the twelfth century. The early parts and the whole effect are marked by powerful design and background architectural motifs; the style is transitional between classical and Byzantine influence and the painting of the Ottonian period.

been more recently painted with liturgical and eucharistic themes: the back wall represents the blood of the Saviour being collected in a vase, while opposite the altar is a procession of male and female saints carrying palms, and also a crucifixion. Another building whose paintings have been preserved is the *solarium* of the abbey of Lorsch – a room with architectural decorations, painted columns supporting a richly moulded architrave and a white ceiling; the whole creates a *trompe-l'oeil* of a portico open to the sky, in the Roman tradition.

Illuminated manuscripts

Besides these few remains, from which a vague idea of Carolingian murals can be gained, we still possess a number of illuminated manuscripts, the best of which are among the treasures of our libraries. Taken as a whole, they enable us to follow the development of this splendid art. Before Charlemagne's day, miniature painting was dominated by the Irish and Anglo-Saxon style, with its emphasis on decoration and the marvellous richness of its borders and capital letters. These designs were generally copied from stuffs or gold and silver objects: some of the animals look as if they were cut out of metal and stuck on to the page. In spite of their brilliant colours, the design is flat without attempt to create an effect of depth, the patterns are linear and the objects stylised. This great, though limited, form of art was only practised in Columban monasteries; manuscripts from other studios were much more primitive, and any human figures were awkwardly painted and in hieratic attitudes. In Charlemagne's reign, a fresh impetus was given to this form of art by the double influence of work from the British Isles and the Mediterranean; the inspiration of mosaics and murals is also very visible. This was the time when manuscripts were entirely written in gold or silver lettering on purple-dyed parchment, a sumptuous but rather barbarous form of decoration which flourished in the workshops of the palace of Aix-la-Chapelle. A typical example is Godescalc's Evangeliary. Large figures were beginning to appear against backgrounds sprinkled with little decorative motifs, and there was an attempt to create depth, a third dimension, as for example in the London Evangeliary. Gold played an important part in these amazingly rich decorations, but the design remained fairly stylised. The 'Ada' Evangeliary, and manuscripts of a similar sort, reveal a style – or perhaps a whole school – of splendid illumination. Soon after this date, every studio seems to have developed a style of its own, although each produced a few especially rich examples which had an influence on the work of the others, making it difficult to be sure

Crucifixion. Miniature from the Epistles of St Paul, late eighth century. Würzburg, Universitätsbibliothek, ms. p. th.69, fol. 7. This miniature is in the pre-Carolingian style, showing Irish influence, and was probably executed in the region of Würzburg. The design betrays a certain awkwardness, for instance in the scale-like folds of Christ's tunic. Symbolic birds perch on the cross. Below are the crosses of the two thieves. At the bottom, the Virgin and Apostles.

St Mark. Miniature from the 'Ada' Evangeliary, about 800. Trèves, Stadtbibliothek, cod. 22, fol. 59v. This manuscript has an annotation, evidently made at a later date, saying that it was copied for a lady called Ada, whom some have supposed to be Charlemagne's sister. The style is reminiscent of Godescalc's Evangeliary, but with a stronger sense of depth in the background. The 'Ada' school spread the art of illumination eastwards and southwards, particularly in Bavaria.

The four Evangelists with their emblems.
Manuscript from Charlemagne's palace school, early
ninth century. Aix-la-Chapelle, the Cathedral treasure.
The page reproduced here clearly shows the
influence of antiquity. The world appears
to be divided into four parts.

of the place of origin of manuscripts. The characteristic feature of
the development of illumination is the influence of Byzantine
painting; it is impossible to say exactly when this began, but it
probably had some connection with the improved relations between
the courts of Charlemagne and Constantinople in 812. The Rheims
school of illumination shows this influence more than any other.
We possess several manuscripts from this workshop: for example
Ebbo's Evangeliary, remarkable for the full-page figures of the
Evangelists, dressed in luminous white cloaks. They are given an
intense feeling of movement by the fact that the usual thick continuous outlines were replaced by little vibrant touches, creating an
almost ethereal, spiral effect, expressive of the evangelists' inspiration. This was the beginning of a new mode of expression, seen later
in some Romanesque painting and sculpture. The same qualities
and treatment, but more remarkable still, are to be seen in the
Utrecht Psalter, where hundreds of figures have been drawn with a
nervous, rapid and astonishingly lively pen and left uncoloured;
a striking three-dimensional effect of light and shade has been given
by cross-hatching. Such was the art that developed from the fusion
of Anglo-Saxon, Irish and Frankish techniques, added to remarkable originality of thought and execution. These sources of
inspiration were soon abandoned, and illuminators began once
more illustrating manuscript copies of Terence, Prudentius and
Aratus, with imitations of fourth-century work. Drogo, natural
son of Charlemagne and papal deputy for the Empire in 842,
inspired the Metz school; this became the court school under
Lothar, who kept going the tradition of the palace school of
Aix-la-Chapelle, and went on producing books with gold lettering,
sometimes on a purple background. The most magnificent volume
from this studio was Drogo's Sacramentary; the strapwork initials
still showed an Irish and Anglo-Saxon inspiration, but it was
decorated also with scrolls, acanthus leaves and figures in a way
that was entirely original though showing a classical influence. At
the abbey of St Martin of Tours, where the habit of copying
manuscripts had never been lost, Alcuin's guidance, and the

FINCIT EVANGELIVM

SECUNDUM MARCUM

NITIVm

EVANGELII IHV XPI
FILII DI SICVT SCP
TVM EST IN ESAIA
PROPHETA
ECCE MITTO ANGE
LVM MEVM QVI
PRAEPARABIT VI
AM TVAM

St Luke. Miniature from Ebbo's Evangeliary, before 835. Épernay, Bibliothèque Municipale, ms. I, fol. 90v. Ebbo, Archbishop of Rheims, attempted a conversion of the Danes and presided over the assembly at Soissons in 833 when Louis the Pious was compelled to abdicate. As a result, he was deposed in 835, but was reinstated by Lothar in 840. This sumptuous manuscript is typical of the Rheims school. The floating draperies suggest figures set in motion by God's breath.

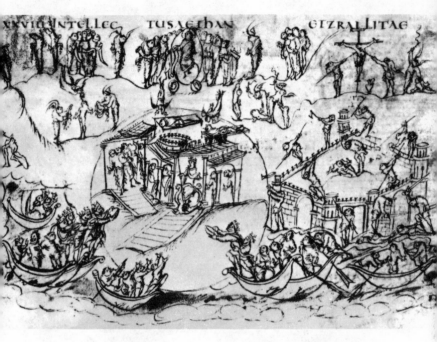

proximity of the educational centre he had created, developed a school of art from which came some of the purest masterpieces of Carolingian miniature. It is known that in the ninth century this abbey possessed a bible executed in Rome in 440, shortly after the Manichaean heresy had been denounced. This may have been the copy used by Alcuin for his revision of the Bible, some time before 800, but it was certainly taken as a model of illumination and imitated until the middle of the ninth century. Its influence can be seen in the Grandval Bible, executed at Tours about 836 and now in the British Museum, and also in Charles the Bald's Bible, presented to him by Count Vivian, Abbot of St Martin, and illuminated with a great many miniatures in 846.

Christ in majesty, surrounded by the four great Prophets and the
four Evangelists. Miniature from Charles the Bald's Bible, about 846.
Paris, Bibliothèque Nationale, ms. lat. 1, fol. 329v. A magnificent page;
remarkable both for its composition and for its sense of movement.
The continuity of the Revelation is shown by the association
of the Prophets of the Old Testament with the Evangelists.

These two books, produced at a ten years' interval by the same
workshop, show marked differences in technique. The Grandval
Bible uses perspective imitated from Byzantine work to give an
illusion of depth; in Charles the Bald's Bible perspective is conveyed by a series of planes, as in all medieval painting. A few years
later the workshop of the abbey of Tours produced its finest
illuminated manuscript: another Evangeliary, that of Lothar. The
serenity, majesty and rich colouring, the vitality emanating from
some of the figures such as the portrait of Lothar seated on his
throne surrounded by his guard, make this one of the masterpieces
of art of all time. Not long afterwards, in 853, Tours was destroyed
by the Normans and its artistic output came to an end. The
Rheims school was revived and became the head of the artistic
movement under Hincmar. The most important volumes that can
be attributed to this period and this studio are the Evangeliary from
the Crawford collection in the J. P. Morgan Library, and the Bible
of St Paul-Hors-les-Murs, executed for a sovereign called Charles,
most probably Charles the Bald. A school grew up attached to the
court of Charles the Bald, although its exact situation is not known;
it produced some very fine works like Charles the Bald's Book of
Hours, Psalter and coronation Sacramentary; these are remarkable
for the decorated initial letters, the borders and figures, all of them
very similar to the art of the Rheims school, but with an original
flavour of their own, and a lavish splendour never surpassed in the
Carolingian epoch. We can also distinguish the Franco-Saxon
school, whose centre was probably at the abbey of St Amand (the
second Bible of Charles the Bald and the Stockholm Sacramentary
came from it), and the Swiss school, with similar methods of
decoration, well-known from the St Gall manuscripts, which have
fortunately never left that place.

The whole splendid flowering of art during the ninth century was
brought to a halt by the Norman invasions and the anarchy of the
tenth century. Some abbeys survived these disasters: Trèves,
Reichenau, St Gall, St Aubin at Angers, Bobbio and Monte
Cassino in Italy, and many others. But the great artistic impulse of

CAN I INQVO IIII

MATH   MAR   LVC   IOH

FINIT   CAN I   INQUO   IIII
MATH   MAR   LVC   IOH

Table of Canons. Second Bible of Charles the Bald, 871–7. Paris, Bibliothèque Nationale, ms. lat. 2, fol. 351v. This is a manuscript from the so-called 'Franco-Saxon' school, centred around the abbey of St Amand (France, Nord). It was executed for Charles the Bald, who bequeathed it to the abbey of St Denis. The sober design and the strapwork ornaments illustrate to perfection the Anglo-Saxon decorative style treated with the revived classicism of the second Carolingian Renaissance.

the middle of the ninth century was shattered: gold and silverwork, architecture, sculpture and painting were not exactly in a decline, but the output was much smaller, and it was not even possible to replace masterpieces that had been destroyed. Moreover, those interchanges between studios, so vital to progress, had come to an end. This state of stagnation lasted until the eleventh century, when there was a revival in Germany with the Ottonian style, and in France with Romanesque. But from the artistic point of view, as in the case of literature and learning, the Carolingian period remains the blossoming period of many exceptional minds and talents, whose contribution to civilisation was to have a profound influence on times to come.

9 Rapid evolution and decadence

The last attempt to preserve unity

The extraordinary outburst of cultural, artistic and intellectual activity during the ninth century could never have happened without the impulse given it by Charlemagne and the stable society created under his rule. Charles Martel and Pepin the Short had prepared the ground for Charlemagne's achievement – the realisation of a united Empire. There were no wars except at the frontiers. Inside the realm, obedience to the Emperor's orders everywhere assured that great benefit desired by the Church, whose preservation was held to be the sovereign's essential duty – peace, and its indispensable corollary, order. Peace sprang from unity: the whole population of the Frankish empire, all of whom were Christians, were governed by a single prince, whose duty was to lead them to safety, making decisions concerning temporal matters himself, and entrusting spiritual guidance to the highest authority in the Church, the pope.

But by 800 this ideal realised by the Frankish Emperor had already become an anachronism. It was a return to Constantine's theories, but it took no account of new developments, and could only last under the rule of an exceptional man, with sufficient breadth of vision to govern such a vast territory alone, and enough intelligence and commonsense to avoid being encumbered with theories, and to adopt a pragmatic line of conduct. After his death, latent forces made themselves felt; Charlemagne's concessions seemed inadequate; the nobles, avid for power and wealth, formed themselves into local clans with special interests; theorists among the clergy undermined the king's power; the episcopate took the upper hand, and very soon armed revolt got the better of the divided and irresolute government. Within ten years, the promised peace gave way to a general state of anarchy, increased by the threat of invasion, by devastation, pillage and the necessity of finding local protectors to make up for the impotence of the central authority. This revolution was facilitated by the structure Charlemagne himself had imposed on society; it had presented no dangers under his rule, but it now ended in the breaking up of the Empire and the spontaneous creation of a new regime.

Louis the Pious succeeded his father in 814 and died in 840; the last attempt at unity took place early in his reign. But imperial authority was soon nothing but a fiction in the hands of this honest but feeble prince. From now on, the only thing that counted was the personal attachment of the nobles to their overlord, the bond of individual fidelity.

At the beginning of the reign a complete change of political orientation took place. The little group of Charlemagne's intimate advisers, his first cousins Adalard, Wala and their sister Gundrada, Bernier and his sister Theotrade, were all dispersed. Louis the Pious gathered round him men he had known in his kingdom of Aquitaine: Helisachar, Fredugis, Count William of Toulouse, St Benedict of Aniane, Agobard. A secret battle for power began between their clans, and particularly between the policies of the influential Wala and his enemies. Wala was convinced that the unity of the Empire must be preserved at all costs. His adversaries were in favour of reforms to remove the Church from the Emperor's absolute control, and were probably not averse to some division of territory between the princes of the house of Charlemagne. Louis the Pious began by renouncing all control over papal elections; he also guaranteed the integrity of the States of the Church on the basis fixed in 774, and promised not to interfere in their administration. This was the first step in reducing the Emperor's domains. But what was to become of the Empire after his death? This problem agitated Louis the Pious and his circle. Until 806, even Charlemagne himself had not been worried by this question, and had made no disposition concerning the succession. He seemed to consider that the *regnum Francorum*, like the Germanic kingdoms, was the property of the reigning monarch, and must be shared among his heirs when he died. As for the Empire, it was above all the Roman imperial dignity – *auctoritas* and *potestas* attached to a man, without definite territorial foundation. He probably did not fully understand the Roman concept of Empire, although he set great store by it; in about 801 or 802 he tried to revive it for a short while, but abandoned the attempt as soon as he met with difficulties. As early as 781, the necessities of government had compelled him to give certain territories special status, not of course independence, but autonomy. In regions such as Italy and Aquitaine, where consciousness of race and memories of independence were solidly rooted, he had in this way created kingdoms and entrusted them to two of his sons, Pepin and Louis, whom he treated as viceroys subject to his orders; but their presence gave the population the illusion of independence under their own prince. He made no legal disposition as to the duration of these empirical solutions. On 2 February 806, Charlemagne decided to issue a decree to settle the question of the succession and the fate of the Empire: this was the *Divisio regni*, which confirmed the measures previously adopted on behalf of the two vassal kingdoms, and assured the rights of their rulers, while adding that *Francia* and Aix-la-Chapelle were to belong to Charles, his eldest son. The boundaries of the three parts of the *regnum* were laid down. This act did not take effect because Charles and Pepin died before their father, in 811 and 812. But it is interesting to notice its implications: there was no mention of succession to the Empire, and in article 20 Charlemagne merely declared that during his lifetime 'kingship and the Empire' would remain in his hands. The net result was that for the rest of his life Charlemagne would go on treating his sons as viceroys, that his territories were to be divided after his death according to the Germanic custom, and that nothing was settled about the succession to the Empire and the dignity of Emperor. Must one conclude that he had given up the idea that the Empire would survive for ever, or that he had shrunk from the task of trying to find a solution for handing on his authority? Neither of these can have been true, for Charlemagne was a typical man of action, accustomed to look ahead and give orders, and he set too much store by the renaissance of the Empire to let it disappear with him. Yet this document expressed for the first time the principle of 'confraternity', or friendly agreement between the heirs to the different kingdoms, and gave no predominance to the eldest son, except that his share was more important than that of his brothers and included the capital, Aix-la-Chapelle. If he did not mention the Empire it was because it was replaced by the idea of the *regnum Francorum*, indivisible although shared among the brothers; also it must be remembered that in 806 Charlemagne made many efforts to get the Eastern court at Byzantium to recognise him as equal in importance to the 'Basileus', without offending the latter. It was therefore an unfortunate moment for a successor to the Empire to be named, and yet he could not defer the division of his territories, and wished to leave his sons' position clear in the event of his death. The provisional character of the division is clearly shown in a clause announcing that a further act was to follow – an act which was never drafted, because the deaths of two of his sons made it useless.

In 813 the Western Empire was officially recognised by Byzantium. Immediately after this event, Charlemagne solemnly declared his son Louis heir to the whole State, although Pepin's son Bernard was at this time King of Italy. The deaths of Charles and Pepin having put an end to any possible dispute, we shall never know what Charlemagne envisaged for the imperial succession when there were still several claimants; however there is reason to think that he would have insisted on some sort of territorial partition, though he would probably have given one of his sons the title of Emperor, pre-eminence over the others and greater power. But the results of Charlemagne's silence began to be felt in the ninth century.

It was in fact over the problem of the succession (which an accident might make urgent at any moment) that political theorists came into conflict with one another, and at first it was the views of Wala and his friends that triumphed. He it was who inspired Louis the Pious to issue his solemn act, *Ordinatio imperii*, in 817. Louis the Pious had three sons: Lothar, born in 795; Pepin, born in 800; and Louis, born in 804. But the terms of partition provided by this act were quite different from those of 806: the younger sons received very unimportant shares, and almost all the territory came to Lothar; Pepin and Louis had to be content with small kingdoms –

Seals of Carolingian emperors: (a) Seal of Louis the Pious, height 1½ inches. Paris, Archives Nationales, K 8, no. 10. The Emperor is wearing a laurel wreath in imitation of the Roman emperors. The inscription is: CHRISTE PROTEGE HLUDOWICUM IMPERATOREM. (b) Lothar's seal, height 1¼ inches, same collection, K 10, no. 6. Here too the bust of the Emperor is crowned with the laurel. The inscription is: 'CHRISTE ADJUVA HLOTARIUM'. (c) Seal of Charles the Bald,

Pepin with Aquitaine, the marches of Toulouse and parts of Burgundy, Louis with Bavaria and the eastern marches. Bernard, son of Charlemagne's dead son Pepin, kept Italy, his father's kingdom. As soon as this division was announced, Lothar acquired imperial rank and his brothers became completely dependent on him. What was new in this act was that it conceived of the Empire both as a sovereignty and a suzerainty: the eldest of the reigning house enjoyed a power superior to his brothers', who had to report to him every year, pay him taxes, and agree never to go to war or make a treaty without his consent. The emperor had the right to reprimand them and even depose them should they prove intractable. An important clause dealt with the succession: when a king died his kingdom must not be divided, but must pass to his eldest son, whose relation to the emperor would remain the same as his father's; should there be no male heir, the emperor would inherit. The act of 817 was thus not only a division of the realm but also a new political constitution: Lothar ruled over practically the entire *regnum Francorum*, while his brothers only possessed marches; he was sole sovereign, his brothers were vassals or height 1½ inches, same collection, K 14, no. 12. The Emperor wears a moustache as in the miniature from his psalter. The inscription is: 'KAROLUS MISERICORDIA DEI IMPERATOR AUGUSTUS'. (d) Seal of Charles the Fat, height 1½ inches. Colmar, Archives du Haut–Rhin, Douët d'Arcq, no. 10879. These four seals ratified the acts of the sovereigns, each of whom was emperor at the time they were affixed by the chancellory.

viceroys subject to recall. The title of *rex* merely implied a hereditary viceroyalty. The unitarian party had triumphed. There was no violent departure from the acts of 806 and 813, but Wala and his supporters had brought about modifications of them. The 817 system marked a transition between the old Germanic custom of equal shares and patrimonial inheritance, and a unitarian regime founded on the rights of the first-born and inspired by Roman traditions. It was aimed at the constitutional defect in the Frankish monarchy by which equal shares at every succession threatened to go on breaking up the Empire indefinitely. This act was submitted to the assembly of 817, to whom Louis the Pious declared that he could not admit that 'a partition made by man, out of tenderness or consideration for one of his sons, could break the unity of the Empire created by God'. This religious argument shows that learned clerics had had a share in drafting the *Ordinatio imperii*; it reveals the influence of the intellectuals of Charlemagne's reign. The act marks a very definite stage in historical evolution: the idea of Empire first takes practical shape in it, having hitherto been principally an abstraction. But its consequences were of short

202

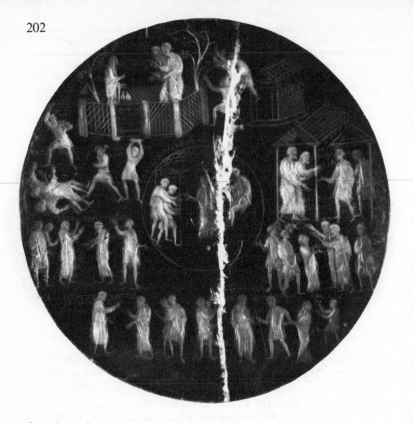

duration, for it came up against the inveterate traditionalism, spirit of dissension, desire for independence and thirst for power of the kings, all of which tendencies had a free rein as a result of the weakness of Louis the Pious. And the birth of another son to the Emperor – the future Charles the Bald – in 825 inevitably raised the question of partition and the settlement made by Louis the Pious, all over again. In 833, Agobard, a theologian of outstanding speculative intelligence and an expert in Roman law, blamed the Emperor for abandoning the notion of a united Empire. However, the little group of intellectuals who had evolved the system were too much in advance of their times to be understood. The majority of those in power, particularly laymen, could only conceive of royalty in the same terms as their ancestors had done, and the old Germanic notion of patrimonial monarchy was bound to triumph.

The act of 817 was the last attempt to preserve unity and establish
a powerful State.

After the birth of Charles the Bald, Louis the Pious, who was
dominated by his wife the Empress Judith, tried various means to
diminish Lothar's authority, and reduce the shares of his other
sons to the advantage of the young Charles. Then came the armed
rebellion of the Emperor's sons and their supporters. Abandoned
by the nobility and dignitaries of the Church, Louis the Pious was
forced to abdicate in 833; later came his restoration to power by
the followers of Pepin and Louis, and Lothar's disgrace and official
submission. All these events were confused by every sort of political
intrigue, as well as by wars, summary executions and bloodthirsty
revenge. This chaos finally destroyed the monarchy, and helped the
rise of certain aristocratic families, whose influence effaced or
limited the authority of the princes. This was the chief social
phenomenon of the second quarter of the ninth century. It was
connected with the personal fidelity of the leaders to certain princes
of the imperial blood, the establishment of clans in various regions,
and finally with the revival of racial consciousness in the territories
under Frankish rule.

Particularism

Charlemagne had set himself to put an end to national duchies and
dispossess the autochthonous dynasties governing them. He therefore passed a series of resolutions suppressing the autonomy of
Thuringia, Alemannia and Bavaria. Bavaria still preserved its own
powerful traditions however, and the Emperor had been obliged
to recognise the fact to some extent, even after Tassilo had been
dispossessed. But in the case of Italy and Aquitaine, he had solved
his difficulties, and given them moral satisfaction, by making them
into kingdoms and bestowing them on his sons Pepin and Louis.
This measure not only respected ethnic particularism, but satisfied
several requirements of the contemporary outlook: it gave each
of his sons a throne, even though they were merely viceroyalties not

affecting the unity of the Empire; it created large governments allowing for more flexible administration; and lastly it assured the defence of the Empire's nerve-centres on the frontiers of the *regnum*, which were exposed to danger from without. This was not a new idea; it arose from Frankish conquests of territories inhabited by foreigners. Already in the seventh century, at the request of the local aristocracy, Austrasia had three times been promoted to the status of a kingdom under a theoretically autonomous prince, though attached to the *regnum Francorum*. In Italy a state of considerable anarchy prevailed in the eighth century. When in 774 Charlemagne seized the crown of Lombardy, he set himself up as the successor of the kings of Pavia, who had found it extremely difficult to control the Lombard dukes. The duchies of Spoleto and Benevento had never formally accepted dependence, and in practice evaded the Frankish king's authority, as their predecessors had done that of the Lombard kings; the territory surrounding Venice, and Sicily, Naples, Calabria and Apulia in the south, were still in the hands of the Byzantines; the Papal States, consisting of the exarchate of Ravénna, Pentapolis and Emilia, were also in theory independent. As King of the Lombards, Charlemagne set himself to organise the interior administration of the realm, leaving Lombard officials (the *gastaldi*) in their posts, and merely putting them under the supervision of Frankish counts. He also extended his control over the duchies. Although in 781 he gave the Lombards his three-year-old son Pepin for their king, he kept the government of Italy in his own hands all his life, and never stopped using the title of *Rex Langobardorum* on official documents. At this time the States of the Church were directly dependent on the *regnum Francorum*, and the duchy of Spoleto, governed by Hildebrand, recognised the royal authority. Yet Charlemagne never succeeded in definitely subduing the duchy of Benevento, and in spite of the formal concessions agreed to by Dukes Arichis and Grimoald, in spite of several inspections by the *missi* at a time when Charlemagne's power must have given these princes pause, the situation in the south of Italy was still very confused in 814. Italy was like a

Cross of Desiderius, latter half of the
eighth century. Brescia, Museo Cristiano.
A very pure and simple example of the
goldsmith's art, encrusted with
precious stones and glass cabochons,
probably made in Italy.

newly conquered territory, whose submission to the Franks had only been obtained by uniting the kingdoms under Charlemagne's personal authority.

It was the same with Aquitaine. The conquest of this region had only been completed in 768, by Pepin the Short, after a stubborn and bloody resistance. In 778 Charlemagne gave the Aquitainians his son Louis for their king. But whereas in the case of Italy the remoteness, the difficulty of communications, the theoretical preservation of the monarchy by simply exchanging the dynasty of Desiderius for that of Charlemagne, and the relative passivity of the nobles, had made it possible to preserve the fiction of autonomy and still keep control over the northern regions at least – in Aquitaine the nobles were more reluctant to put up with Frankish rule, and their ethnic and traditional hatred of the conquerors and their recent violent outrages, made this country ripe for rebellion. Aquitaine was in contact with the Gascons (an indomitable ethnic group) and also exposed to attacks by the Moors, while her neighbours to the north-west were the unconquered Bretons. Charlemagne realised the danger of a revolt in Aquitaine as soon as he returned from his expedition to Spain in 778; at the same time he was threatened by conspiracies, a general rebellion in Saxony and the uncertain attitude of the Bavarians. The Frankish element had not established itself successfully in Aquitaine, and national feelings had developed there ever since the eviction of the dukes. He therefore installed a form of government by the nobility under the nominal authority of an autonomous king, who would not prevent his orders being carried out. That this was Charlemagne's intention was shown by his choice of Frankish counts and abbots for this region. He also did his best to gain the devotion of the bishops who were already there, and sent *vassi dominici* to keep firm control over the country. In spite of these measures, no real racial fusion took place, and separatist aspirations were far from disappearing. While Louis the Pious was King of Aquitaine, the country was constantly in danger from the Saracens and Gascons, and threatened with a rebellion of the nobles. After the death of Charlemagne things became much worse, and all the outlying territories that had been absorbed into the Empire began to develop national feelings destructive of unity. When Louis the Pious succeeded to the imperial throne he had to leave Aquitaine and make arrangements for the succession; after two years in which the region to have been re-attached to the Empire, it was found necessary to return to Charlemagne's solution. The *Ordinatio imperii* re-established the kingdom of Aquitaine under one of Louis's sons, Pepin; Bernard, who had ruled in Italy since his father's death, was now recognised as its king; and Louis the German, second son of Louis the Pious, was given Bavaria, indicating that here too particularist feelings were still very much alive and had to be satisfied. An even more ominous fact was that in all the territories of the Empire and the vassal kingdoms, especially the marches, groups of counties were being formed under the command of energetic and powerful men: one of these was the group of counties in the south, entrusted to Bernard of Septimania, son of St William, whose talents and ambition later aroused jealousy and alarm among the friends of Lothar, culminating in the anarchy of 833. At the end of Louis the Pious's reign Bernard was still a power to be reckoned with; during the ferocious struggles among the Emperor's sons, and even after the Treaty of Verdun, he tried to arbitrate between the princes.

Break-up of the Empire, government by the nobles

The Treaty of Verdun in 843 officially marked the end of a unity that had been in grave jeopardy for the last ten years. After this date events moved swiftly, and in another forty years Charlemagne's State was no more. A small class of influential men had come to power; supported by their clans and their vast domains, they had gained control over immense regions, and crystallised around their persons the particularist feelings of the local nobility. They now began gradually building up huge principalities in the very heart of the factitious kingdoms created by the Treaty of

Verdun, until fragmentation was complete, and all semblance of the state the kings had tried to establish was finally destroyed.

Nor did the efforts of the Church to keep some sort of common government going, by appealing to family feeling among the royal brothers, meet with any success. Each of the kings thought of nothing but despoiling his brothers, and every kingdom developed along its own line of least resistance.

The Treaty of Verdun divided the Empire into more or less equal parts: Lothar was to keep the title and dignity of Emperor and a more important share than his brothers, including Aix-la-Chapelle, capital of the Empire, and Rome, capital of Christianity, and reaching from the North Sea to the Adriatic. This was called Lotharingia. Louis received *Francia Orientalis*, east of the Rhine and the Alps; Charles, *Francia Occidentalis*, west of the Meuse, Saône and Rhône. Before his death, Louis the Pious had taken away Aquitaine from Pepin I and given it to Charles. Pepin's son, Pepin II, and his followers energetically defended his rights as autochthonous King of the Aquitainians; but he was sacrificed by his uncles, and his kingdom given to Charles the Bald. However, the young prince refused to be evicted and put up a stubborn defence. Throughout Charles the Bald's reign the question of Aquitaine remained a source of division, hatred and sometimes bloody war, destroying the unity of the kingdom of France and resulting at the end of the ninth century in the creation of a practically autonomous duchy.

The regroupment of territories into huge principalities seems to have been an unavoidable phenomenon, which the kings had to accept in the interests of organisation and control. It is known that Charles the Bald created a march of Burgundy. Before 843 this region had been situated at the heart of the Empire, and was in no need of a frontier organisation; but after the partition it was on the frontier between *Francia Occidentalis* and Lothar's realm, and could always be invaded from the Lyonnais, which belonged to the Emperor. Lothar now organised the Lyonnais as a march. In 853, Count Girard, whose legend was later immortalised in a verse

The *Divisio regni* of 806. For two years after his Coronation in 800, Charlemagne was probably preoccupied with the idea of empire, but he soon returned to the Frankish notion of a purely territorial *regnum Francorum* and the old rule of equal partition among the heirs. The act of 806 provided for his sons to receive kingdoms bringing in more or less equal revenues, and the question of imperial status was passed by in silence.

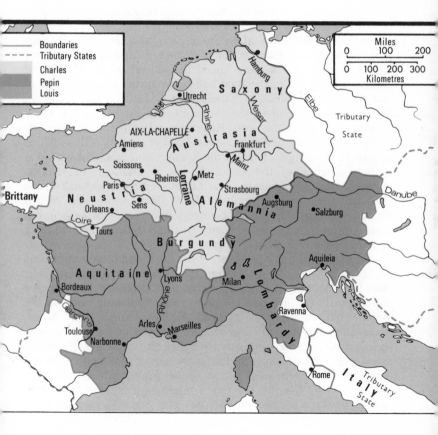

chronicle, was given the title of *marchio*, while in *Francia* Count Isembard was placed at the head of five counties; two other groups, one of two counties, the other of nine, were entrusted to two other counts. This organisation was still flexible: the counts could be recalled or transferred at the king's desire, and territories could be reshaped. But now came a definite change: after 868 a single march territory was formed under one responsible administrator, instead of a host of counts each directly responsible to the king; a vast military area was gradually being formed, which embraced the whole of Burgundy after Charles the Bald's reign. It was the same in Aquitaine: Pepin II, son of Pepin I of Aquitaine, constantly at war with his uncle, was forced to take refuge in Quercy and Agenais, and Charles the Bald had to group the other counties of Aquitaine in large blocs, each under a strong leader. Thus Bordelais, Berry, Auvergne and its dependencies, and the bloc made up of Limousin, Toulousain and Rouergue virtually became principalities. Raymond of Toulouse was head of a regular State, which at one time reached as far as the Spanish marches, and was as it were a satellite of the kingdom; but it disintegrated rapidly, perhaps for ethnic reasons. The Limousin became detached, but was recovered by the family of St William, which also owned Poitou. The Gascons parted company, not only with *Francia* but also with Aquitaine, and became virtually independent under a national duke of Frankish origin.

Although the territories north of the Loire had been occupied by the Franks a very long time ago they shared the same fate. The march of Brittany had been created as a defensive base against the Bretons – an independent race, given to making raids on the realm: the counties of Nantes, Rennes, Angers, Le Mans, Avranches, Bayeux and Lisieux were grouped under two or three counts with superior authority over the rest. Two clans descended from two counts living at the beginning of the ninth century, Lambert of Nantes and Rorgo of Le Mans, gradually gained power. During Charles the Bald's reign these families were decimated in wars against the Bretons and Scandinavians, and in bloody conflicts among themselves, but though they had lost some of the importance of their ancestors, they were still firmly established in these regions; in spite of executions, disgrace and confiscations, they succeeded in holding on to their inherited lands and forming the ruling class in that part of the country. In 852 the King appointed Robert the Strong, an able and energetic man, to be head of these counties, and entrusted him with the task of organising the defence of the population against the Breton invaders and the bands of Normans who came up the rivers and plundered the land. Head of the counties of Angers and Tours, and probably also of Le Mans, Chartres and Orleans, lay Abbot of St Aubin of Angers, St Martin of Tours and Marmoutier, Robert the Strong was killed in battle in 866, leaving two young sons, Odo and Robert. At this time it was still possible for Charles the Bald to disregard the tradition of inheritance, now fast becoming customary. Ignoring Robert's heirs, therefore, who were too young to serve him as their father had done, he gave Robert's honours to Abbot Hugh, a member of the Welf family. A large group of territories further north became the county of Flanders.

The kingdom was disintegrating on every side – separating into territories under great noblemen immune from the king's authority. The causes of these changes were both social and political. Since the end of the eighth century, the hereditary nobility had filled high offices, maintained family solidarity, and owned vast estates, allodiums and benefices (the most valuable of which were abbeys); they now felt called upon to play an important part – especially because since early youth they had been engaged in war and diplomacy, and because those who were energetic and gifted found wide scope for their activities in perpetual fighting and political unrest. Those who made their mark were supported by their whole clan and all their dependants. The problem they had to solve was the same as that of the kings: how best to distribute land so as to gain a following. Counts, especially those who were at the head of several counties, gave away land in which they in fact only had a life interest, and tried to become the seigneurs of

The partition of 843. The death of Louis the Pious was followed by two years of conflict after which Lothar had to renounce his dream of keeping the Empire for himself, as foreseen by the *Ordinatio imperii* of 817, and agree to a territorial partition giving him the title of Emperor and a little more important share than his brothers, including Aix-la-Chapelle and Rome. His brothers were legally his equals. His nephew Pepin II, who fought with him at Fontenoy-en-Puisaye, was overlooked and his kingdom became in theory part of *Francia Occidentalis*, which fell to the share of Charles the Bald. The Treaty of Verdun was drawn up by a commission of nobles, who travelled through the *regnum*, assessing the revenues of domains, towns and abbeys, so as to make the partition equal, in accordance with the principles of the Merovingian epoch.

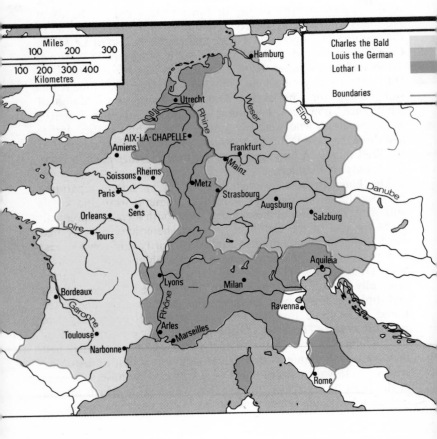

The partition of 870. Lothar II, son of Lothar I and
King of Lorraine, died in 869 leaving no children except by his
concubine Waldrade. Charles the Bald therefore seized his lands
whose riches enabled him to gain new followers, and had
himself crowned King of Lorraine. But his brother Louis the German
opposed him violently, and at the Treaty of Meerssen in 870,
Charles was obliged to consent to the partition of their
nephew's kingdom between them. This was another partition in the
Frankish manner, based solely on the revenues and personal property
of the sovereigns. The boundaries now fixed for *Francia Occidentalis*
remained practically unchanged for several centuries.

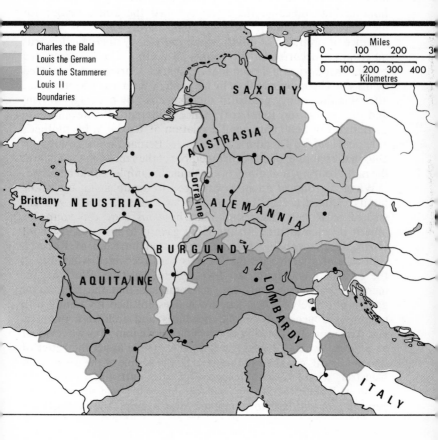

the *vassi dominici*, who were in theory direct tenants of the king. At the end of his reign, Charles the Bald endorsed this abuse by officially making the *vassi dominici* dependent on the counts.

Another factor was that the hereditary principle was gaining ground at every level of society. Though still not legally admitted, it was increasingly accepted in practice. In theory the king gave *honores* to anyone he liked; in practice, when a great nobleman holding high office in the State solicited the king's favour for members of his family, the king could hardly refuse. A striking instance of reversion of office, which was merely one stage towards inheritance, occurred in the county of Autun. The first recorded count, Theodoric I, a descendant of Charles Martel, was succeeded by his son Theoduin and then by his nephew Bernard of Septimania; after this the county passed to their kinsman by marriage, Warin, and then to his son Isembard; thence to Bernard Plantevelue, son of Bernard of Septimania and a relation of Warin on his mother's side; and lastly to Theodoric, a relation of Bernard's. The county was thus in the hands of one or other member of the same clan throughout the ninth century, and many other similar examples could be found.

When a group of counties belonged to a nobleman, his whole family claimed a right to it. As we have seen, Neustria was entrusted to Robert the Strong, but his sons were too young to inherit it when he died, so the King gave it to his cousin, Abbot Hugh. Hugh probably became the second husband of Robert's widow, and after his death Robert's sons recovered what was in the eyes of contemporaries their rightful heritage. We must remember that it was only by such practices that the king could govern effectively. When a count had established his family in a region, and acquired *allodia*, benefices and followers there, it was dangerous for the king to try and remove him: this was evident at Bourges, where Charles the Bald was unable to get the better of Count Girard, who had the support of the people of the town, or in Neustria, where he was unsuccessful in his attempt to quell the revolt of Robert the Strong, replace him by his own son and compensate him with territory in some other region. The necessity for such concessions was shown by the existence of the marches: ever since the beginning of the dynasty these frontier regions had been entrusted to men who could mobilise all available forces for the defence of the kingdom, and who thus became formidable potentates. It was the same in the kingdoms ruled over by Lothar and Louis the German; when Italy was threatened with invasion by the Moors, for example, the provincial nobles of the south rebelled against Lothar and organised their country in three principalities: Salerno, Benevento and Capua. If on the whole Lothar's rule was a peaceful one, it was because he had the rich country that had once been *Francia* at his disposal, and could satisfy his faithful followers with abbeys and revenues.

The nobles realised their own power during the reign of Louis the Pious. They attached themselves to those who made them rich; they leagued together; they were always ready to rebel and choose their own seigneur. Thus the whole kingdom gradually became organised on the same plan as the marches: when Charles the Bald came to the throne he found several of these military commands in existence, and was obliged to create even more. He held on to the right to transfer or dispossess these great noblemen as long as he could, tried to treat them merely as his officers, and gave away the last lands in his kingdom to bind them to him. When he died, his feeble and impotent successor had to accept the new situation and the inheritance of offices. Charles the Bald had preserved the sovereignty, in theory at least. Under his successors it became mere suzerainty.

The Empire in 880 and the invasions of the ninth century. After Boso had been elected King of Provence in 876, the Empire existed in name only. On the death of Louis the Young in 882, Germany was united under Arnulf, bastard son of Carloman. After 888 the Empire and the throne of France ceased to belong to the Carolingian dynasty. The sovereigns of *Francia Occidentalis* had two dangers to face: the Norman invasions, which began under Louis the Pious and increased in severity under Charles the Bald, and the Moorish invasions from the south. The Moors also threatened Italy, and the Emperor gained glory by checking them and delivering Bari.

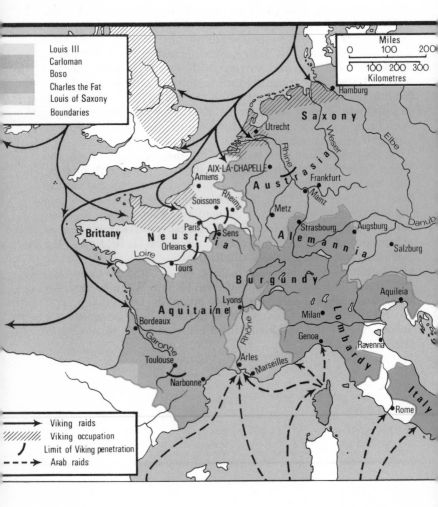

10 A one-way trend: the end of unity

The invasions

During the reigns of Charles the Bald and his brothers, the wide-spread peace that the Empire had enjoyed under Charlemagne became a mere memory. All the western kingdoms were ravaged by continual wars. Not only did the ambitious rivalry of princes and nobles degenerate into conflicts and private wars, each laying waste his enemy's land so as to deprive him of means of support, but the frontiers were no longer safe from enemies outside the Empire. A new period of invasions was beginning to set the whole of the West in ferment.

In the south, the Saracens of Spain and north Africa conquered Sicily, attacked Naples, Apulia and Calabria, made inroads as far as Rome, occupied Bari, thrust the Franks out of the Spanish marches and scoured the coasts of Languedoc and Provence. In the east, the Slavs sent expeditions into the kingdom of Louis the German, who had a hard struggle to repulse them. In the north and west, bands of Scandinavians, who had begun to be known as Normans, hurled themselves against all three kingdoms. They raided and plundered, and even got a foothold at the mouths of rivers whence they could spread into the interior. And lastly, the western frontier of *Francia Occidentalis* was constantly threatened and overrun by the Bretons. But the most disastrous and widespread raids, amounting to veritable invasions, were those of the Normans.

Over a period of sixty years, their repeated inroads became a permanent phenomenon and plunged the population into confusion and terror. These Normans came of various races; some of the raiders were Danes, others Swedes or Norwegians. The first Danish State was formed in the seventh century; the Danes took the place of the Jutes who had emigrated to England or settled on the shores of the Baltic and North Sea, between the Eider and the Elbe, next to the region occupied by the Saxons. In about 835 the existence of a Dano-Norwegian kingdom, the activity of gang-leaders, and dynastic quarrels, led to piratical expeditions setting sail and

Soldiers on horseback. Miniature from the Golden Psalter, late ninth century. St Gall, Stiftsbibliothek, ms. 22, fol. 140. Each soldier wears a simple helmet without a nasal, a tunic of cloth or leather covered with imbricated metal scales, reaching to the thighs, and over it a short cloak, leaving the right arm free. Each is armed with a spear, a long sword and a round shield. The cavalry developed as an arm of war under Charles Martel and became the pick of the army under his

successors. Its changed role was connected with
the development in horses' harness. Supported
by a saddle with very high pommels and cantle,
and with his weight on the stirrups, the rider
was united with his mount and could rely on his
firm seat, speed, and effect of shock.

pillaging Frisia, while on land the Danes were the Franks' most
relentless enemies. Their new and rapidly-developing civilisation
encouraged agriculture and commerce, and above all voyages to
distant lands. They had in fact invented a special technique of
ship-building, as has been shown by the different forms of boat
discovered in the last few decades. Their sea-going vessels were
masterpieces of naval carpentry: the fact that wooden pins and
vegetable fastenings were often used instead of metal to assemble the
pieces made it possible to build light, strong and resilient hulls,
while their manageability and size fitted them to face tremendous
seas. In the middle of the ninth century the Scandinavians were
launching maritime expeditions in two directions: towards the
Atlantic coasts, and towards Frisia and northern France. By 800,
people were beginning to dread these invasions, and Charlemagne
took steps to stop them, by stationing flotillas at the mouths of
rivers and fortifying ports like Boulogne. However in 819 the
Normans had already rounded the most westerly point of Brittany
and appeared on the coast of Aquitaine. From 830, raids became
more frequent, though they were sometimes repulsed, and the
monks of Noirmoutier had to abandon their island and go inland.
When quarrels among the Frankish princes diverted the armed
forces from defending their country, the Normans grew bolder;
in 844 they took Toulouse, in 853 Nantes and Tours; in 840 they
occupied part of Frisia, and Lothar was obliged to hand over the
port of Duurstede and the island of Walcheren to them, whence
they could defend the country against other bands of raiders. From
850 to 892 they attacked the regions round the mouths of the
Scheldt and Meuse more frequently still.

At the same time they altered their tactics. Instead of sending
small bands to make surprise attacks on various parts of the coast,
they collected large armies, which went into winter quarters at the
mouths of rivers, and thence opened a regular campaign of conquest and occupation. The Franks had to adapt their methods of
defence to these new conditions. Between 862 and 864 the country
was in a perpetual state of war; the sovereigns concentrated on

Charlemagne's talisman, early ninth century. Rheims,
the Cathedral treasure. This medallion contained
relics and was probably found in Charlemagne's
tomb when it was opened by the Emperor Otto III,
about the year 1000. It is a sort of phial,
mounted in gold and set with precious stones.

defence, built *castra* and bridges, and higher ramparts round
towns and fortresses. The result was almost immediate: invasions
became fewer, and pillage and devastation less common. Between
879 and 887 on the contrary, when the Normans heard that dynastic
quarrels and civil war had broken out once more in the ancient
Frankish Empire, and it was torn and weakened by dissension,
they again returned to the attack, and more than once invaded
and ravaged the region between the Seine and the Rhine. We know
that the Norman invasions of France were stemmed with tremendous difficulty at the end of the ninth century, and the
Scandinavians finally settled in Normandy. This region was now
occupied by both Gallo-Frankish and Nordic elements, fusing
together to form a civilisation that was especially original in its
feudal and legal organisation. Nevertheless the scourge of war and
the invasions of the second half of the ninth century profoundly
influenced social development and the physiognomy of western
Europe: populations were regrouped under local chiefs, castles
were built, the military command organised – all these were the
first steps towards feudal civilisation.

The supremacy of local chiefs

The general insecurity, the importance of entrusting every responsible man with several functions in a district where he could
carry them out in person, and the fragmentation and regrouping of
territories to facilitate this, were all factors as essential to the
development of events as were the ambitions of the royal princes
and the traditions of inherited royalty. The old Empire began to
break up more rapidly during the latter part of the Carolingian
period. Lothar died in 855 and his realm was divided among his
three sons: the eldest, Louis II, succeeded him as Emperor, but
actually ruled only over Italy; Lothar II received Lorraine, and
Charles Provence, both with the title of King. When Charles died
in 863, the kingdom of Provence ceased to exist and was divided
between Louis II and Lothar II; Charles the Bald failed in his

attempt to annex part of it. After the death of Lothar II in 869, however, he seized his nephew's kingdom and had himself crowned King of Lorraine at Metz. It was a fleeting triumph, for his brother Louis the German also had designs on their nephew's inheritance, and successfully claimed the richest portion at Mierssen in 870. When Louis died in 875, his kingdom too was divided, and his three sons, Carloman, Louis the Young and Charles the Fat were all given slices of *Francia Orientalis*. Charles the Bald also had three sons: Louis the Stammerer, Charles the Child (who was created King of Aquitaine, but died in 866) and lastly Carloman, who distinguished himself only by his misdeeds, and was finally blinded by his father to prevent him doing any more harm.

The only capable man in this whole generation of princes, the Emperor Louis II, after reconquering southern Italy from the Saracens and restoring the glory of the empire, died in 875, leaving an only daughter, Ermengarde, married to Boso, Count of Vienne. The imperial throne was once more vacant, and the Pope, anxious for a return to a Christian government such as Charlemagne's, offered the crown to Charles the Bald, in return for his agreeing to protect Rome against any renewed offensive by the Saracens. When he died two years later in 877, the only direct descendants of Charlemagne still surviving were the three sons of Louis the German (Carloman, King of Bavaria and Pannonia; Louis the Young, King of Franconia, Saxony and Thuringia; and Charles the Fat, King of Swabia). Apart from them there was only Ermengarde. These genealogical factors were extremely important to contemporaries, who still thought of the *regnum Francorum* as the patrimony of the house of Charlemagne, and subsequent events were the result of the struggles between these cousins. Meanwhile the dynasty was dying out and its surviving members were becoming so degenerate that it was impossible to find any reputable men among them, so that the kingdoms passed one by one into the hands of princes who were not descended from Charlemagne, or whose relationship was more or less remote. Nor did there any longer exist a reality corresponding to the notion of the Empire. The popes still set store by it as the only institution which could save the unity of the Christian world, and Pope John VIII proclaimed as an unshakeable principle that emperors must be nominated and chosen by the pope, a doctrine that was maintained throughout the Middle Ages; but even the candidates to the imperial crown had no belief in this unity, nor in the reality of their mission.

So ended the ephemeral attempts of Louis II and Charles the Bald to resurrect the Empire. Aspirants to royal status and kingdoms now sought the support of the nobles, and thrones were gained by election. The principle of inheritance in the royal line was forgotten, and kings were now created by the assembly of nobles. In 877, Louis the Stammerer could only obtain the throne of France by means of territorial concessions which finally ruined the monarchy; and in 879 Boso got himself elected King of Provence by the assembly of nobles at Mantaille.

By the end of the ninth century the real power had passed in this way from the king's hands to those of the nobles. The most influential of them only remained faithful to the king insofar as he endorsed their claims and officially recognised their usurpations. Thus, when Abbot Hugh died in 878, the immense principality he had founded north of the Loire became the property of Odo, son of Robert the Strong, who was probably his relative, while in the south, Bernard Plantevelue, Count of Auvergne, by claiming to be a faithful follower of Louis the Stammerer, succeeded in ousting his rival, Bernard of Gothland (who was a rebel against the King) from what was left of the kingdom of Aquitaine, and building up a huge duchy, which became independent during the tenth century. On the death of Louis the Stammerer in 879, the nobles took advantage of the confusion caused by the fact that the King had three sons born of two marriages, whose legitimacy was open to question. The situation was taken in hand by the chamberlain Theodoric; he received the royal insignia from the dying King, ignored his wish that his eldest son should be named his successor, and summoned an assembly at Meaux to consider who should receive the crown – a hitherto unheard-of procedure. While one party of nobles offered it to Louis the Young, King of Germania, another succeeded in having Louis III and Carloman, the two eldest sons of the dead king, consecrated. Thus the nobles disposed of both crown and kingdom. When Carloman died in 888, the only heir of the royal blood was the young Charles the Simple; but two great seigneurs, neither of them connected with the dynasty – Lambert, Marquis of Spoleto and Odo, son of Robert the Strong – became candidates for the throne of France. The nobles decided in favour of Odo.

The events of the period between 877 and 888 thus show the political evolution of the West: first, the end of the Empire, then the disintegration of the ancient *regnum Francorum*, lastly the greatly increased part played by important laymen, both in the government of the State and the disposal of the crown, so that the power of the aristocracy took the place of that of the king. These political developments were accompanied by no less important changes in the social structure.

The seigneurial regime

Under Charlemagne, the social structure of the whole Empire was based on ties between man and man, fidelity, the granting of benefices for life, and the services of followers to their seigneur. It was noticeable that this system affected all levels of society, but the chief characteristic of the period was the very firm hold on the whole organisation maintained by the sovereign. He alone was responsible for the administration of justice, minting of money, and war; he distributed benefices as he liked, without regard to inheritance. In fact he was the sovereign lord of all free men, and whatever bonds they might contract between themselves were invalid against him: any man who took his seigneur's part in a revolt against the king was a rebel and liable to punishment. If we cast a glance over the social and juridical state of Europe in the twelfth century, when the feudal system was at its height, we shall find that the ties between man and man were so essential to the structure of society that a vassal was subject to no other jurisdiction than that of his seigneur, whom he was absolutely bound to support, even against suzerain or king: this bond was emphasised by a formal oath of homage, given in exchange for the exactly defined benefits the vassal received from his seigneur. His personal

Reliquary presented by Pepin II, King of Aquitaine, middle of the ninth century. Treasure of the Abbey of Conques. Relics were put in precious containers, mostly of wrought gold or silver: metal and stones were mounted on a wooden framework. When his father died, Pepin II was disinherited by his grandfather, who allotted Aquitaine to Charles the Bald. He joined forces with his uncle Lothar against Louis and Charles in 841, and in 845, by the Treaty of St Benoît-sur-Loire, succeeded in getting Charles to recognise him as King. Fighting soon broke out again. Taken prisoner in 852, he escaped, and although on the run, without resources and a drunkard, he kept up guerilla warfare for some time with the help of a few nobles from the centre of Aquitaine and some bands of Normans. His death soon settled the problem of Aquitaine, which had for ten years caused continuous trouble to Charles the Bald.

dependence had become a concrete reality. Also, when a vassal died, his seigneur could not refuse to give the tenancy to his son or heir, if he duly paid homage and carried out the services required. This was the final stage of development, but the main features of the system were already fixed by the tenth century, and had begun to take shape at the end of the ninth.

Even earlier, in the latter part of the eighth century, although fidelity and benefices were legally distinct, they were often combined in the person of a vassal, and expressed in ceremonies anticipating those of homage. When Tassilo, duke of Bavaria, acknowledged Pepin the Short as his master in 757, he 'commended himself as his vassal with his hands', as the *Royal Annals* put it; when in 814 Harold the Dane submitted to Louis the Pious, Ermold the Black relates that 'with clasped hands, he surrendered himself and the kingdom that was his by right to the King', and that the Emperor took his hands in his – a gesture that symbolised the essential nature of homage. This 'commendation' created the tie, but it was used in quite different cases – for instance when a poor, unarmed man sought protection, or a great nobleman received land as a benefice; in the same way the duties and services owed to the seigneur were susceptible of infinite variation. In the eighth and ninth centuries these formalities began to be associated with a vow, the oath of allegiance: God was called upon to witness the agreement, and some sacred object such as the Gospels or a relic was touched, this physical contact being an essential element of the oath. The bond thus created was purely personal; it was a reciprocal agreement involving no exchange of property. However this was the period that saw the development of the *beneficium*, or tenure granted a vassal to enable him to serve his master, although this was still a purely optional obligation at this time. There was no legal connection between commendation and benefice. But since the commendation implied the seigneur's duty to help support his vassal, and the benefice was a means of doing so, a class of vassals holding property given them by their seigneur soon began to appear. The vassals of the head of the State – or *vassi dominici* – had to serve as mounted soldiers like other vassals and were an essential part of the Carolingian army. After about 830, vassals who had sworn allegiance to their seigneur in return for money and land, used even to follow him against the king. This enabled Lothar and his brothers to recruit an army against Louis the Pious, and each of the Emperor's sons to have an army at his disposal in 841. But things were moving fast: when the princes' armies were engaged at the battle of Fontenoy-en-Puisaye, Bernard of Septimania and his followers awaited the outcome at a distance, before deciding which side they should join and choose for their seigneur. This illustrates the point of no return in the transformation of society: the great seigneurs could now call upon armed forces and were therefore so powerful as to be virtually independent.

Another quite different sort of development was taking place. A vassal at every grade of the structure of vassalage was motivated by the same desires: to acquire benefices and increase his fortune, to make the benefice heritable by joining it to his allodium, and thus to absorb not only the benefices but also the duties and revenues that belonged to it into his patrimony. These tendencies were absolutely contrary to the very notion of vassalage, namely that it was personal, that it automatically came to an end on the death of either contracting party, and that the seigneur's right over

Tassilo's chalice, about 770. Kremsmünster (Austria), the abbey treasure. One of the most magnificent chalices of the eighth century. As the inscription shows, it was presented to the abbey by Tassilo, duke of Bavaria, who tried to preserve his autonomy but was defeated by Charlemagne. The style of the workmanship is Anglo-Saxon; it probably came from Northumberland. Saxon goldsmiths achieved perfection at a very early date, as the Sutton Hoo treasure proves. Note the fine images of Christ, the Evangelists and the saints, and the decoration of the empty spaces. This is a work of startling originality – it is the first time that figures appear on a chalice before the twelfth century.

the property conceded was paramount; yet they were natural and universal, and had a profound effect on the structure of society. Only a strong central authority could stem them and maintain the principles of vassalage, and of Charlemagne's successors, Charles the Bald was the last to try. By the middle of the ninth century inheritance of benefices was becoming habitual though not legally accepted. Bernard of Septimania, heir to his uncle Theodoric, was reluctant to let his estate return to the imperial domains when he died, and in 843 he tried to regain them by procuring Pepin of Aquitaine's submission to Charles the Bald. When Charles insisted on his right to take away Robert the Strong's benefices in the region of the Loire, Robert refused to accept the land in Burgundy offered him in compensation, and the King's authoritative action resulted in the rebellion of his noble vassal, who remained in a state of open revolt against him for several years. The move towards inheritance was so marked that at the end of his reign, in 877, Charles tried to check it by publishing the capitulary of Quierzy, in which he insisted on his right to nominate whom he chose to vacant *honores*, and also reserved the rights of succession of a deceased count to his sons, subject to the sovereign's approval; however he admitted that a count's office could be inherited if he took religious vows. Article 9 declared that the same rules should apply to benefices as to offices. It is a document of the first importance in the history of social development, for it shows a gradual slide towards the inheritance of offices and benefices; the Emperor declared his right to oppose this custom, and stated that inheritance of offices was not legal, but the precautions taken, the measures decreed, and the respect shown to custom, all combine to show that it did exist already in fact. As for the restrictions he tried to impose, they had been completely forgotten a year later.

The state of affairs recorded rather than decreed by the capitulary of Quierzy developed very rapidly in the next ten years. In 877, when Louis the Stammerer succeeded his father and claimed the right to distribute *honores* as he chose, he was confronted by a general revolt of the nobility, and had no choice but to abandon his pretensions and accept the protection – but also the tutelage – of Hincmar. Thenceforth the counties remained in the hands of dynasties, and sons usually succeeded their fathers: in Vermandois, there was the family of Herbert, descendants of Bernard, King of Italy, and through him, of Charlemagne; in Flanders, the house of Baldwin; that of Bernard and William in Auvergne; of Vougrin in the region of Angoulême, Périgueux and Agen. Thenceforth counts were no longer officers of the king, but hereditary seigneurs who had appropriated the estates and regalian rights of the county – to administer justice at first, and later on also to mint money. In Burgundy, for instance, a count still presided over a tribunal with the ancient title of *mallus* in the tenth century, but in his own name instead of the king's. Power passed into the hands of local potentates of greater or lesser importance, but whether dukes or counts they always held it on a hereditary basis, even though they were still in theory pledged to fidelity to the king.

A more important social change was the increasing frequency with which benefice and service were combined. The movement begun in Charlemagne's reign had developed throughout the ninth century and military service was now the most important element in vassalage. In 892 an account of the dispute between the canons of St Martin of Tours and Patericus, vassal of Count Robert, brother of King Odo, shows that a seigneur's consideration for his vassal was a function of the number of men he furnished for his army. The same document informs us of another phenomenon that appeared at this time: plurality of allegiance. In the third quarter of the ninth century, very great noblemen like Girard of Vienne, Boso or Abbot Hugh owned benefices in several kingdoms and were therefore vassals of several kings simultaneously. The Tours document shows us that at a humbler level the vassal Patericus was the vassal of the Count of Le Mans and Count Robert at the same time. It was certainly an advantage for a vassal to have several ties of dependence, but it undermined the contract of vassalage, for it meant that the seigneur could no longer count on his man in all circumstances. Charlemagne disliked this practice and forbade it, but by the end of the ninth century it seems to have been widespread, and so troublesome that in the eleventh century, when society was making a general effort to put an end to anarchy, measures were taken to limit its effects: liege homage was introduced, binding vassals more strictly than simple homage had done.

A few decades later, medieval Europe had acquired its distinctive features – tenancies had almost everywhere replaced allodiums, the whole of society was founded on personal dependence, tenure and especially service, which became the essential element of the regime and determined the hierarchy of land-ownership: this was feudal society.

These developments were not complete until the eleventh century. They were determined by the old Germanic notion of a personal bond, and achieved as a result of the impetus given by the Carolingian kings, the greatest of whom – Charlemagne – believed that he would strengthen his power by insisting on an oath of fidelity. If they all tried to use the ties of vassalage as a means of government, it was because of the feebleness and inefficiency of the administrative structure: the lack of a regular army when there was a need of fighting men, especially cavalry, led to the institution of benefices; the weakness of a State incapable of keeping the peace within its frontiers obliged the kings to extend the oath of allegiance to all freemen; the inadequacy of government officials resulted in the practice of using the king's followers to dispense justice and administer the realm; the lack of effective supervision made privilege more widespread. The system of vassalage was designed to serve the interests of the monarchy, and the whole kingdom was conceived of as a hierarchy of vassals – already in 837 Louis the Pious declared that his sons were his vassals. All this combined to create confusion between public and private law, inherited property and tenure, life-interest and heritable interest, and the exercise of public and private authority (the seigneur's right of *bannus* over his men). It was from such confusions as these, from such progressive usurpation, from the replacement of public power by personal ties, that the feudal system was born. The end of the ninth century was a period of general anarchy and administrative impotence, but it witnessed the beginnings of a system which was to be preserved for several centuries.

11 The legacy of Charlemagne

The Carolingian period came to an end in the tenth century with the gradual extinction of the race which gave it its name, and above all with the decline of its prestige. By the end of the ninth century the control of all the kingdoms and the Empire itself gradually slipped from the hands of the descendants of St Arnulf and Pepin of Landen. The dynasty that came to power in 717 with Charles Martel was dispossessed during the hundred years between 888 and 987. After Charles the Bald, the Empire passed to two sons of Louis the German in succession: Carloman, who reigned for two years, and then Charles the Fat, who died disliked by everyone in 888. Only one of the princes seemed to have the necessary qualities to rule; this was Carloman's bastard son Arnulf. King of Germania in 888, Emperor in 896, he died in 899, leaving Italy torn between various claimants who wore the imperial crown by turns: Guy of Spoleto, Louis of Provence (son of Boso and grandson of Louis II), Berengar of Friuli. A few years later the throne of Germania was definitely lost to the Carolingians. Fragmentation increased: the kingdom of Provence and the recently-formed Burgundy were short-lived. In France, after the death of Carloman, Louis the Stammerer's son, in 888, the nobles elected Odo in preference to his rival Guy of Spoleto. The legitimists wanted to restore the dynasty in the person of Louis the Stammerer's third son, the youthful Charles the Simple, who ended his life dismally as a prisoner of his distant cousin Herbert of Vermandois, having been supplanted by Robert the Strong's sons and their brother-in-law, Raoul of Burgundy. A somewhat more permanent restoration brought Louis IV, Lothar and Louis V to the throne. When the latter died as the result of an accident, after only a year on the throne, the nobles again chose a descendant of Robert's, Hugh Capet, as King of France. From now on no descendant of Charlemagne's occupied the French throne, nor those of Germania and the Empire.

The reign of the Carolingian dynasty was therefore comparatively brief. It began brilliantly and ended ingloriously. Taken as a whole it must be rated a defeat.

Yet the reign of this house undeniably coincided with one of the

232

most dazzling periods in history, and its members made great contributions to a new form of civilisation which left its mark on the whole world, and traces of whose influence can still be felt.

Besides, it is not for the historian to judge. It is too easy a task, once events have taken their course. As Ferdinand Lot wrote, we are in the position of gods towards the men of past ages, because we know what their future was to be. The historian must trace developments, describe successes and failures, establish the causes and consequences of events – in a word, he must try to understand.

If we take a look at the civilisation that developed under the Carolingians, partly as the spontaneous result of economic and social influences, partly under the inspiration and direction of men who spread these influences over a vast area of the world, we shall get some idea of the contribution made by this period in those spheres on which every civilisation depends – administration, law, social structure – and be in a position to try and distinguish and evaluate its chief trends.

In the domain of administration and the theory of the State, the Carolingian period made few innovations, though it established certain fundamentals. There was an immense effort at organisation. Most institutions and the administrative structure had been inherited from the Merovingians, and came from two sources – Germanic customs and Roman ideas – upon which the influence of the Church was grafted. These origins left their imprint on the form taken by central and local authority and ecclesiastical institutions. We have seen that the central power was essentially in the hands of the king, who exercised it with the help of councillors, court and assemblies, and under the supervision of the *missi dominici*, at least until the middle of the ninth century. We have also seen that the monarchy was limited, and that a king or emperor was not an all-powerful figure clothed in *auctoritas* and *potestas*, like the Roman emperor, but had in theory to be ruled by the *consensus* of his subjects and the intervention of the bishops. In spite of the strong government instituted by Charlemagne, it was the aristocratic current that triumphed in the end, and took over the power of the monarchy. As for the organs of power, making up the *palatium* of the Carolingian kings, they were an indication of the private and patrimonial nature of the government.

These two features, the part played by the nobles in politics and the patrimonial character of the monarchy, survived for many generations and were to reappear in France not only in the Middle Ages but also during the Ancien Régime, and up to the eve of the Revolution. When, at the beginning of the fifteenth century, intelligent men tried to separate the finances of the State from the king's privy purse, they came up against customs inherited from the Merovingians and Carolingians, and their efforts ended in failure; the last Valois kings and even the Bourbons still considered themselves as the fount of all justice: as Ferdinand Lot has shown, the assassinations of the Duc de Guise and Concini were both executions carried out as a result of the king's judgment. They were relics of the Germanic idea that the leader's authority was limited only by ancestral custom – a notion preserved by the Carolingians and handed on to their successors.

Yet there were new elements at work in their day which had a restraining influence on their personal power: the ascendancy of the Church and memories of Roman law. The Christian ideal of royal duty was very different from the Stoic theory of Marcus Aurelius, and had different repercussions. And it was the first time that any attempt had been made to realise the idea of a single centralised government, through legislation by capitularies and the supervision of the *missi dominici*, since the Roman Empire; even the notion of a public decree was transformed by chancellory practices and the increased use made of writing. Of course this was swept aside and to some extent abolished with the decline of the king's power and the renewed ascendancy of the aristocracy. We must not forget, however, that the Carolingians, or at least the greatest of them, had a clear idea of what a State should be, and that the same measures were revived later, when it was possible to emerge from chaos and decadence. The ordinances of the Valois kings, the commissioners of St Louis, and the advanced organisation

of the chancellory under the Capets, were all derived from the institutions of Charlemagne's reign. The idea of local government was not an entirely new one. The institution of counts had been taken from the Merovingians and improved by stricter control from the central government, but Charlemagne's great achievement was to create the administrative machinery which resulted in a complete though short-lived transformation, for the appropriation of offices soon brought an end to the central administrative structure and entirely changed the concept of local government.

The development of ecclesiastical institutions, directed by the sovereign, was more definite and durable. In place of the somewhat anarchic Church of the Merovingian period, the Carolingian kings constructed a hierarchy and defined the part the episcopate were to play in the administration of the State; they created a national Church so solidly built and powerful that they lost all control over it and were forced to submit to its tutelage. However, it was through the Church that the idea of a united State survived; it was the Church that proclaimed the pre-eminence of the monarchy, gave a permanent lustre to the emperors' glory, and helped restore the French monarchy and some degree of internal peace within the state. Again, the Carolingian kings were responsible for the revival of monasticism, which benefited the civilisation of the whole world. The period that witnessed all these transformations deserves an honoured place in history.

From the social point of view the Carolingian epoch was no less important. Of course we shall never know enough about the way

Reliquary of Charlemagne. Wooden casket covered in plaques of copper, silver-gilt and *champlevé* enamel, about 1165, Paris, Louvre. When Charlemagne was canonised in 1165, one of his arms was placed in this reliquary by order of Frederick Barbarossa. The figures on the lid show that at this time Charlemagne was venerated at Aix-la-Chapelle alongside the Virgin. This was the first object associated with the veneration of Charlemagne as a saint.

of life of a population that was still very primitive and sparsely scattered. The contribution of the previous period – the fusion of races that took place under the Merovingians – bore fruit. Although the Frankish nobility ruled society, the *regnum Francorum* was now inhabited by a single population, and Franks, Aquitainians, Bavarians, Alemanni, even Saxons, in spite of still lively separatist leanings, intermarried and adopted each other's customs. The Frankish nobility contracted alliances with the nobility of other parts of the Empire. Modern nations are the result of this fusion. Society was purely rural in character, and life centred round the village church and was ruled over by the owner of the great domain. The revival of order and hierarchy, backed by the government, strengthened the ties of dependence, and created those local centres under the leadership of a master which later were to become seigneurial domains. The power of these local leaders was deliberately fostered by Charlemagne; under his weak successors it got out of control and took the place of the old administrative structure of the hundred, *vicaria* and county. The protection these leaders gave their vassals, and their possession of châteaux, increased their hold over the population. The West had moved from government by the king to the regime of the seigneurs and their domains; it was an imperfect method of keeping order – and order soon crumbled – but it acted as a palliative of disorder. Here again we see the Carolingian period as a transitional phase, as the basis of a society in which personal ties and tenure replaced the Roman notions of the State, property and civic duty, but which compared to the anarchy of the late Merovingian period was a very complete construction and the beginning of a new order.

However, the primary importance of the Carolingian period was in the sphere of culture. Scientific and literary culture was mainly intended as part of the education of clerics, and orientated towards the Church. But as we have seen, laymen also benefited, and there was a revival of secular education as a basis for religious culture.

After the bottomless barbarism of the seventh century, there was a genuine revival of Latin language and literature, and a return to the nobility and breadth of scope of ancient and humanist thought. The multiplication of books, and the creation of schools, modest results of the first Carolingian Renaissance, led in the ninth century to a flowering that astonished contemporaries and appears to us today as one of the rare moments of intense intellectual activity history has to show. But even more than any results in the sphere of thought or creative art, it was the methods, attitudes of mind and thirst for learning of the contemporaries of Louis the Pious and his sons which immortalised this movement and reverberated through the centuries to come. This renaissance rescued the remains of classical culture from destruction, and provided nourishment for the whole of the Middle Ages, and through them for the modern era. It is impossible to overpraise the man who set it in motion – Charlemagne.

The Carolingian epoch left behind few works of art: its architecture and sculpture produced hardly anything that was not imitative; but it rediscovered and perfected techniques in the ninth century which gave rise to such original currents as Ottonian and Romanesque art. The only original art, born of the fusion of different elements, was the painting and decoration of manuscripts, and the Carolingian style has been accepted throughout Europe as a permanent manifestation of genius. It was not seriously modified until the twelfth century, and even then the essentials of the tradition were preserved. In the eleventh and twelfth centuries, an apocalyptic scene at St Sever, a decorated manuscript at St Martial of Limoges, or an ornamental letter in the Souvigny Bible, still bear witness to the persistence of traditions and techniques inspired by the magnificent artists of the reigns of Louis the Pious, Lothar and Charles the Bald.

It is because of its culture that Carolingian civilisation still lives today; but some of the institutions and social features of the period also left their mark on succeeding ages. It was a significant moment in the history of humanity, and for the medievalist a study of it is the key to many problems. How can one understand the ties between man and man, the concept of monarchy, the spirit of unwritten law, the role of the Church, the mentality of clerics and scholars in the different kingdoms of the Middle Ages, unless one first makes a close study of the period in which the outlines of medieval society were first sketched in, unless one looks back to that short period of about fifty years during which all the different European countries were under the sway of one mind and common institutions, without losing their own individuality? What does it matter that Charlemagne's dream ended in failure – and so soon? The unity, realised for a few decades, turned out to be utopian. But it left behind not only the idea of unity, never lost even when particularist feelings were rife, but a way of thinking common to all the peoples of western Europe, derived both from their Roman inheritance and Carolingian civilisation. The Carolingian period was only a brief stage in the evolution of history, and yet it was of paramount importance, not so much for what it achieved at the time, as because of its consequences for the history of the world.

Chronology

714–5	Death of Pepin of Heristal. Efforts of Plectrude, his widow, to preserve the union between Neustria and Austrasia.
716–9	Charles Martel conquers the Neustrians. The two kingdoms are united under his rule. His campaign against the Saxons.
720	Charles Martel subdues Aquitaine.
728–30	He conquers the Bavarians and Alemanni.
732–3	The Moors advance on Tours. Victory of Charles Martel between Tours and Poitiers.
733–4	Conquest of Frisia.
735	New campaign in Aquitaine.
737	Death of the Merovingian king Theodoric IV. Charles Martel refuses to accept any successor to him.
738	Campaign in Provence.
741	Death of Charles Martel. The *regnum Francorum* is shared between his two sons, Pepin and Carloman, who succeed him as mayors of the palace.
742	Pepin and Carloman put down rebellions of the Aquitainians and Alemanni. At Vieux-Poitiers they swear a treaty dividing the *regnum Francorum* according to their father's wish.
742–3	Beginning of ecclesiastical reforms undertaken in Austrasia by Carloman, inspired by St Boniface. Council of Estinnes.
743	Accession of Merovingian Childeric III.
744	Pepin the Short, won over to ecclesiastical reform, convokes the council of Soissons.
747	Carloman abdicates and retires to Monte Cassino. Pepin the Short sole mayor of the palace.
750–1	Negotiations between Pope Zacharias, threatened by the Lombards, and Pepin the Short. The Pope in favour of a change of dynasty. Pepin deposes Childeric III, and has himself elected King by the nobles and consecrated by St Boniface at Soissons.
	Pepin undertakes the conquest of Septimania.
753	Pope Stephen II, still in difficulty with the Lombards, visits Gaul. Interview at Ponthion.
754	Pepin founds the States of the Church by the donation of Quierzy. Stephen II consecrates him and his sons Carloman and Charles at St Denis, and forbids the Franks to choose a king from any other dynasty. Pepin goes to Italy and launches

	an expedition against the Lombards. Martyrdom of St Boniface.
759	Pepin reconquers Lower Languedoc from the Moors.
760–8	Successive campaigns in Aquitaine. Death of Duke Waifar. Final submission of the duchy.
768	Death of Pepin the Short. The *regnum Francorum* is shared between his sons Carloman and Charles. Continuation of the *Chronicle* 'of Fredegarius' inspired by Childebrand and Nibelung, kinsmen of Pepin.
771	Death of Carloman. Charles ousts his brother's son and becomes sole King.
772	Beginning of the Saxon wars.
773–4	Charlemagne's campaigns against the Lombards to help the States of the Church. He takes Pavia, dethrones King Desiderius and has himself proclaimed King of the Lombards.
777–8	Spanish campaign. Disaster overtakes Charlemagne's army when crossing the Pyrenees. Death of Count Roland.
778	Widukind leads the Saxons to rebellion.
781	Charlemagne makes Aquitaine a kingdom under his son Louis and Italy under his son Pepin. Theodulf the Goth summoned to court.
782	Final annexation of Saxony. Alcuin arrives in Gaul.
782–7	Paul the Deacon in Gaul.
784	Birth of Raban Maur, the writer.
785	The king insists on an oath of fidelity from all free men. Pope Hadrian I condemns adoptionism.
786	Theodulf nominated Bishop of Orleans.
787	Second council of Nicaea and return to the veneration of images.
788	The Avars attack Bavaria. Duke Tassilo deposed.
791–2	Charlemagne takes part in theological controversies and publishes the *Libri Carolini*.
794	Council of Frankfurt. Paulinus of Aquileia publishes his *Libellus sacrosyllabus* against the adoptionists.
796	Defeat of the Avars. Alcuin made Abbot of St Martin of Tours.
796–805	Royal Chapel at Aix built.
Before 799	Death of Peter of Pisa.
799	Defeat of the Nordalbingians.
800	25 December. Charlemagne crowned Emperor by Pope Leo III.
801	Alcuin settles at St Martin of Tours.

804	Death of Alcuin.
805–6	Conquest of Bohemia.
806	Charlemagne publishes the *Divisio regni*, providing for the equal division of the Empire among his sons after his death.
807	Ambassadors from Harun ar-Raschid received at Aix.
809	Council of Aix-la-Chapelle decides the controversy about the Procession of the Holy Ghost, restores *Filioque* to the *Credo*.
812	Agreement between Charlemagne and the Byzantine court, recognising him as Emperor of the West. Death of Pepin in Italy; he is succeeded by his son Bernard.
814	January. Death of Charlemagne. His son Louis the Pious succeeds him.
After 814	Einhard writes his *Vita Karoli*.
816	Agobard nominated Archbishop of Lyons.
816–7	Ecclesiastical reforms inspired by St Benedict of Aniane. The Emperor gives up his claim to control the elections of popes.
817	The *Ordinatio imperii* affirms the principle of a united Empire: Lothar, eldest son of Louis the Pious, is to succeed him, and his brothers will receive small kingdoms only and be dependent on him; after their death, their kingdoms are not to be shared; the status of Italy is unchanged. Rebellion of Bernard of Italy.
818	Bernard of Italy surrenders. His trial, blinding and death.
819	After the death of the Empress Ermengarde, Louis the Pious marries Judith, daughter of Count Welf.
821	Death of Theodulf.
822	Penitence of Attigny. Italy is given to Lothar.
823	Birth of Charles the Bald. Amalarius writes *De ecclesiasticis officiis*, concerning the dogma of the eucharist.
824	Lothar publishes the *Constitutio Romana*, giving the Emperor effective power over the Pope and the administration of the States of the Church.
829	Council of Paris. The bishops are consulted about the duties of the king. Endowment of Charles the Bald. Growing influence of the Empress Judith and Bernard of Septimania. Discontent of the nobles and of the 'imperialist' party led by Wala.
830	Rebellion of the sons of Louis the Pious. Assembly of Nimeguen. Failure of the rebellion.
831	Assembly of Aix-la-Chapelle. Louis the Pious regains power.

Lothar is relegated to Italy; the rest of the Empire divided between Louis, Pepin and Charles; the *Ordinatio imperii* is abolished. Jonas of Orleans publishes *De institutione regia*. Beginning of the Norman invasions.

831–3   Second rebellion of the Emperor's sons. Abandoned by his followers at Lügenfeld, Louis has to surrender to his sons; he is tried at St Médard of Soissons, and abdicates.

834   Restoration of Louis the Pious. Lothar retires to Italy.

835   Louis the Pious crowned at Metz and Thionville. Important addition to Charles's share. At St Denis, Hilduin undertakes a series of hagiographic works.

836   Death of Wala.

837   Rebellion of Louis the German.

838   Death of Pepin I of Aquitaine. His son Pepin II is disinherited by Louis the Pious, who gives Aquitaine to Charles. Resistance of Pepin II.

839   Reconciliation between Louis the Pious and Lothar. The Empire is shared between Lothar and Charles, except for Bavaria which is left to Louis the German. The notion of the Emperor's supreme authority definitely comes to an end.

840   20 June. Death of Louis the Pious. Lothar claims the whole Empire and supreme power. Alliance between Louis and Charles.

841   Lothar and his nephew Pepin II conquered by Louis and Charles at the battle of Fontenoy-en-Puisaye. Equivocal part played by Bernard of Septimania.

842   Oaths of Strasbourg, confirming the alliance between Louis and Charles (the earliest memorial of the Romance language). The two brothers occupy Aix-la-Chapelle, and have Lothar deposed by the assembly of bishops.

843   Treaty of Verdun, by which the Empire is divided between the three brothers, Lothar retaining the imperial throne, theoretical pre-eminence and a larger share of territory. Assembly of Coulaines, in which Charles the Bald recognises the nobles' share in the government.

843–5   Nithard writes the *History of the Sons of Louis the Pious*.

844–51   Attempt at political union, the 'Confraternal Government'.

844   Bernard of Septimania, ally of Pepin II, taken prisoner and executed by order of Charles the Bald.

845	The Normans, who have been scouring the shores of the North Sea, the English Channel and the Atlantic ever since 830, advance as far as Paris and exact payment to withdraw. Charles at war with Pepin II in Aquitaine. Pepin wins a battle in which Nithard the historian is killed. Treaty of St Benoît-sur-Loire between Charles and Pepin.
846–55	Louis the German's campaigns in Bohemia.
846	Saracen raid on Rome, occupying a quarter of the city.
847	Louis II, son of Lothar, drives the Saracens out of Benevento. Ramparts of the 'Leonine City' built at Rome.
848	Charles the Bald declared King of Aquitaine at Orleans. Gottschalk begins to spread his doctrine of predestination. He is condemned by the council of Mainz.
850	Lothar shares the Imperial throne with Louis II. The Normans settle at the mouths of the Loire and Seine. Charles the Bald defeated by the Bretons.
851	Charles the Bald forced to recognise the Breton Erispoë as King and ruler over the march of Brittany.
851 9	Ratramn of Corbie writing.
855	Death of Lothar. His realm is divided: Louis II is emperor and keeps Italy; Lothar II receives the kingdom of Lorraine, and Charles the kingdom of Provence. Charles the Bald nominates his son Charles the Child King of Aquitaine.
856–61	The Saracens raid Naples, and the Normans Neustria.
857–60	Lothar II attempts to divorce Queen Theutberga.
858	Invasion of *Francia Occidentalis* by Louis the German.
858–67	Reign of Pope Nicholas I, who re-establishes the prestige of the papacy and tries to impose the theory of papal supremacy.
859	Defeat of Louis the German. Council of Savonnières, at which Charles the Bald explicitly acknowledges the supremacy of the episcopate over royalty.
861	Robert the Strong is given command of the region between the Seine and the Loire.
862–6	John Scotus Erigena writes *De divisione naturae*.
863	Treaty of Entrammes: Solomon, King of Brittany, gains the country between Mayenne and Sarthe. Death of Charles of Provence; Charles the Bald tries in vain to annex his kingdom, which is divided between Louis II and Lothar II.

864   Assembly of Pîtres: reform of the currency and defensive measures against the Normans. Capture and death of Pepin II.

865   Louis the German provides for the division of his kingdom between his three sons, Carloman, Louis the Young and Charles the Fat.

866   Robert the Strong is killed fighting against the Normans at Brissarthe; his 'honours' are given to Abbot Hugh, first cousin of Charles the Bald.

866–7   Louis II drives the Saracens out of Italy, leaving them in occupation of Bari alone. Revival of the notion of Empire.

869   Death of Lothar II. Charles the Bald is crowned King of Lorraine by Hincmar at Metz, but has to give in to the threats of Louis the German and share Lorraine with him.

871   Louis II retakes Bari, the stronghold of the Saracens.

875   Death of Louis II, leaving only a daughter, married to Count Boso. Charles the Bald crowned Emperor, at the request of Pope John III.

877   Charles the Bald prepares campaign to help the Pope in Italy, and publishes the capitulary of Quierzy. On his way home, he dies; his son Louis the Stammerer succeds him as King.

878   Carloman, son of Louis the German, receives the kingdom of Italy. In France, rebellion of the nobles against Louis the Stammerer, who is obliged to come to terms with them.

879   Death of Louis the Stammerer. The nobles offer the crown to his sons Louis III and Carloman. At the assembly of Mantaille, near Arles, the nobles elect Count Boso, son-in-law of the Emperor Louis II, King of Provence.

881   Charles the Fat, third son of Louis the German, is crowned.

882   Death of Louis III, King of France.

884   Death of Carloman, King of France. Emperor Charles the Fat elected King by the nobles; virtual restoration of the Empire.

885   Paris besieged by the Normans; its defence directed by Odo, son of Robert the Strong, and Bishop Gauzlin.

887   Assembly of Tribur. Abdication of Charles the Fat. Arnulf, bastard son of his brother Carloman, becomes King of Germania.

888   Death of Charles the Fat. Odo elected King of France.

896   Arnulf crowned Emperor.

Bibliography

General works

A general survey of the history of Europe from 717 to 888 is given in several important and easily available text-books: *Cambridge Medieval History*, vols. 1, 2 and 3, Cambridge and New York, 1911–22, with extremely useful collections of maps, still valuable in spite of its date of publication; L. Halphen, *Les Barbares* (Collection 'Peuples et civilisations'), 4th edition, Paris, 1940; F. Lot, C. Pfister and F. L. Ganshof, *Les Destinées de l'Empire en Occident de 395 à 888*, forming the first volume of the *Histoire du moyen âge* of the *Histoire générale* edited by G. Glotz, 2nd edition, Paris, 1940–1. These two works are fundamental for the history of the period. See also: J. M. Wallace Hadrill, *The Barbarian West 400–1000*, London, 1952. R. Latouche, 'La Gaule Mérovingienne' and J. Devisse, 'La France Carolingienne' in *Histoire de France*, edited by M. Reinhardt and N. Dufourcq, Paris, 1954; D. A. Bullough, *The Age of Charlemagne*, London and New York, 1965; A. E. Thompson, *The Early Germans*, Oxford, 1965, H. A. Lamb, *Charlemagne*, London, 1962. The chronology is set out by J. F. Böhmer, *Regesta imperii*, 2 vols. in a new edition, Weimar, 1956–7. Besides these general works there are two collections of articles by the best specialists on every aspect of Carolingian civilisation: *Karl der Grosse, Lebenswerke und Nachleben*, 4 vols. Düsseldorf, 1965–6, and *Das erste Tausendjahre*, 3 vols., Düsseldorf, 1960. On the history of certain special regions of the Carolingian Empire, the reader may consult: E. Lavisse, *Histoire de France*, vol. 2, part 1, Paris, 1903; L. M. Hartmann, *Geschichte Italiens*, vols. 3 and 4, Leipzig, 1897–1915; E. Lévi-Provençal, *Histoire de l'Espagne musulmane*, vol. 1, Paris, 1944. The historical sources for this period are listed in A. Molinier, *Les sources de l'histoire de France des origines aux guerres d'Italie*, vol. 1, Paris, 1901; W. Wattenbach and W. Levison, *Deutschlands Geschichtquellen im Mittealter. Vorzeit und Karolinger*, 5 parts, Weimar, 1933–7.

Origins

On society during the Merovingian period, the reader may consult Sir Samuel Dill, *Roman Society in Gaul in the Merovingian Age*, London and New York, 1926; on institutions, J. Tardif, *Études sur les institutions de la France. Période mérovingienne*, Paris, 1881; on the Frankish kings, the article by R. Büchner, 'Das Merowingische Königtum', in the collection *Das Königtum*, Lindau and Constance, 1956; J. M. Wallace-Hadrill, *The Long Haired Kings*, London, 1962; on customs and archaeology, F. Salin, *La civilisation mérovingienne*, 4 vols., Paris 1950–60; on the change of dynasty see P. Muntz, *The Origin of the Carolingian Empire*, Oxford and New York, 1960 and L. Levillain, 'L'avènement de la dynastie carolingienne et les origines de l'État pontifical', in *Bibliothèque de l'École des chartes*, 1934, pp. 225–95.

The reconstruction of western Europe

On the monarchy, see the collection *Das Königtum*, quoted above. On the Empire itself, L. Halphen, *Charlemagne et l'Empire Carolingien*, Paris, 1947; H. Fichtenau, *Das Karolingische Imperium*, Zurich, 1949 (English translation by P. Muntz, *The Carolingian Empire*, London and New York, 1954); R. Folz, *Le couronnement impérial de Charlemagne*, Paris, 1964. On institutions, a remarkable synthesis by F. L. Ganshof, 'Charlemagne et les institutions de la monarchie franque' and 'Charlemagne et l'administration de la justice', in *Karl der Grosse*, referred to above, vol. 1, pp. 369–419. On legal history, H. Brunner, *Deutsche Rechtsgeschichte*, 2nd edition by Von Schwerin, Leipzig, 1927, and H. Conrad, *Deutsche Rechtsgeschichte*, Karlsruhe, 1954. On the *missi dominici* the most valuable work is still V. Krause, 'Geschichte des Instituts der Missi dominici' in *Mittheilungen des Instituts fur Oesterreichische Geschichtsforschung*, vol. 11, Vienna, 1890, p. 193 sqq. On central institutions, J. Fleckenstein, *Die Hofkapelle der Deutschen Könige*, Stuttgart, 1959.

The social structure

A great many books published in the last few years have contributed to our knowledge about the nobility: *Studien und Vorarbeiten zur Geschichte des Gross-fränkischen und Frühdeutschen Adels*, edited by G. Tellenbach, Fribourg-in-Brisgau, 1957; this work illuminates and explains the facts set out in P. Guilhiermoz, *Essai sur les origines de la noblesse*, Paris, 1902, and R. Poupardin, 'Les grandes familles comtales à l'époque carolingienne' in *Revue historique*, vol. 72, revised and corrected in *Le royaume de Bourgogne*, Paris, 1907, and adding the results of later research of every sort. It is also necessary to read G. Tellenbach, *Königtum und Stämme in der Wiederzeit des Deutschen Reiches*, Weimar, 1939; F. Rousseau, 'La Meuse et le pays mosan en Belgique', in *Annales de la Société archéologique de Namur*, vol. 39, Namur, 1930.

The economy and the sources of wealth

Very little is really known about the economy of this period, owing to the fragmentary and sporadic nature of our sources. A great many works have been devoted to the subject, without reaching anything more than an approximate view of it. The first important book to attempt to explain it is: H. Pirenne, *Mahomet et Charlemagne*, Paris-Brussels, 1937 (English translation *Muhammed and Charlemagne*, by Bernard Miall, London and New York, 1939) a sparkling work but one that must be read with extreme caution; by the same author, *Histoire économique et sociale du moyen âge*, revised edition, Paris, 1963 (English translation, *Economic and Social History of Medieval Europe*, by I. E. Clegg, London and New York, 1936). Pirenne's thesis aroused the curiosity of all historians of the period and led to numerous publications: M. Lombard, 'Les bases monétaires de la suprématie économique. L'or musulman', in *Annales*, 1947; F. Himly, 'Y-a-t-il emprise musulmane sur l'économie des États européens du VIIIe au Xe siècle?', in *Revue suisse d'Histoire*, 1955; J. Duplessy, 'La circulation des monnaies arabes en Europe occidentale du VIIe au XIIIe siècle', in *Revue numismatique*, 1956. On agriculture: G. Duby, *L'économie rurale et la vie des campagnes dans l'Occident médiéval*, vol. 1, Paris, 1962; in spite of the existence of this synthesis, it will be useful to read: F. L. Ganshof, 'Manorial Organisation in the Low Countries', in *Transactions of the Royal Historical Society*, 1949. General surveys of the subject have been made in R. Lopez, *Naissance de l'Europe*, Paris, 1962, and above all in the wide but detailed synthesis of R. Latouche, *Les origines de l'économie occidentale*, (Collection 'L'Évolution de l'Humanité') Paris, 1956 (English translation *The Birth of the Western Economy: Economic Aspects of the Dark Ages*, by E. M. Wilkinson, London and New York, 1961); one should add to these: F. L. Ganshof, 'Note sur le "Praeceptum Negotiatorum" de Louis le Pieux', in *Studi in onore di A. Sapori*, vol. 1, Milan, 1957. A general review of the problems is given in *Cambridge Economic History*, vol. 1, Cambridge and New York, 1942 and vol. 2, Cambridge and New York, 1952.

The foundations of government

There is no study of the whole subject. For detailed studies the reader may refer to *Karl der Grosse*, quoted above, and articles and chapters in general works. On the subject of benefices and vassalage, besides M. Bloch, *La société féodale* (Collection 'L'Évolution de l'Humanité') 2 vols., Paris, 1939–40 (English translation, *Feudal Society*, by L. A. Manyon, London and Chicago, 1961), F. L. Ganshof, *Qu'est-ce-que la féodalité?*, 3rd edition revised, Brussels, 1957 (English translation *Feudalism*, by P. Grierson, from 2nd French edition, London, 1952), and R. Boutruche, *Seigneurie et féodalité*, Paris, 1959, suggestive points of view will be found in F. L. Ganshof, 'Benefice and Vassalage in the Age of Charlemagne', in the *Cambridge Historical Journal*, 1939; by the same author, 'L'origine des rapports féodo-vassaliques', in *Settimane di studio sull'alto medio evo*, Spoleto, 1954, and 'Les relations féodo-vassaliques aux temps post-carolingiens', in the same collection, 1955; C. E. Odegaard, *Vassi and fideles in the Carolingian Empire*, Cambridge, Mass., 1945. On immunity, M. Kroell, *L'immunité franque*, Paris, 1910; this should be supplemented by F. L. Ganshof, 'L'immunité dans la monarchie franque', in *Recueils de la Société Jean Bodin*, vol. 1, 2nd edition, Brussels, 1958. Certain aspects of society and distribution of power in the Carolingian Empire are analysed in O. Bertolini, *Roma di fronte a Bisanzio e ai Longobardi*, Bologna, 1941, and C. Violante, *La società Milanese nell'età precommunale*, Bari, 1953. Finally, the impoverishment of landed property under the Carolingians may be traced in J. Thompson, *The dissolution of the Carolingian fisc in the ninth century*, Cambridge, 1935, and J. Dhondt, *Études sur la naissance des principautés territoriales en France*, Bruges, 1948.

The Church

The essential work is A. Fliche and V. Martin, *Histoire de l'Église*, vol. 5, by L. Bréhier and R. Aigrain and vol. 6, by E. Amnan. Paris, 1934. On particular points Mgr. E. Lesne, *Histoire de la proprieté ecclésiastique*, Lille, 1910; Dom Patrice Cousin, *Précis d'histoire monastique*, Paris, 1956; Mgr. E. Lesne, *La hiérarchie épiscopale depuis la réforme de Saint Boniface jusqu'à la mort d'Hincmar*, Lille, 1905; *Karl der Grosse*, quoted above, vol. 2, *Das geistige Leben*; E. de Moreau, *Histoire de l'Église en Belgique*, Brussels, 1945; C. J. Hefele and H. Leclercq, *Histoire des conciles*, vols. 3 and 4, Paris, 1907.

The renaissance of literature

For a general survey of literature and the great Carolingian Renaissance, refer to J. de Ghellinck, *Littérature latine du moyen âge*, vol. 1, Paris, 1932. For more detail, M. Manitius, *Geschichte der lateinischen Literatur des*

248

Mittelalters, 3 vols., Munich, 1911–31. For the literature of the period immediately preceding the Carolingian Renaissance, P. Riché, *Éducation et culture dans L'Occident barbare, VIe–VIIIe siècles*, Paris, 1962. See also M. L. W. Laistner, *The Intellectual Heritage of the Early Middle Ages*, Oxford and New York, 1957; E. Patzelt, *Die Karolingische Renaissance*, Vienna, 1924, reprinted 1965 with additions by Cyrille Vogel. On theological controversies, see the appropriate articles in J. M. A. Vacant, *Dictionnaire de théologie catholique*, Paris, 1890–1950. On the political aspect of canonical theory, J. Reviron, *Jonas d'Orléans*, Paris, 1930; Mgr. Arquillière, *L'Augustinisme politique*, Paris, 1934; Mgr. Bressolles, *Doctrine et action politique d'Agobard*, Paris, 1949; J. Devisse, *Hincmar et la loi*, Dakar, 1962.

The renaissance of the visual arts

It is still useful to consult A. Michel, *Histoire de l'art*, Paris, 1905–29, but this book should be supplemented by more recent works: J. Hubert, *L'art pré-roman*, Paris, 1938; C. Heitz, *Recherches sur les rapports entre architecture et liturgie à l'époque carolingienne*, Paris, 1963; G. Plat, *L'art de bâtir des Romains à l'an 1100*, Paris, 1939; *Karl der Grosse*, quoted above, vol. 3, *Karolingische Kunst*; K. J. Conant, *Carolingian and Romanesque architecture*, Harmondsworth, 1959 (*Pelican History of Art*); R. P. Hinks, *Carolingian Art*, Ann Arbor, Michigan, 1962. On painting and illumination of manuscripts: A Grabar and C. Nordenfalk, *Les grands siècles de la peinture. Le haut moyen âge*, Paris, 1957 (English translation, *Early Medieval Painting: from the Fourth to the Eleventh Century*, by Stuart Gilbert, Geneva and New York, 1957). On sculpture, E. Mâle, 'La décoration sculptée à l'époque carolingienne', in *Mercure de France*, 1957.

Rapid evolution and decadence

On the events of this period, besides the books on its general history quoted above, an account of the Treaty of Verdun and its results will be found in J. Calmette, *La diplomatie carolingienne du Traité de Verdun à la mort de Charles le Chauve (843–77)*, Paris, 1902; interesting details in R. Folz, *Le couronnement impérial*, quoted above. On the particularist movements and the life in those regions that freed themselves from the Empire: L. Auzias, *L'Aquitaine carolingienne*, Paris and Toulouse, 1937; R. Poupardin, *Études sur les institutions politiques et administratives des principautés lombardes de l'Italie méridionale*, Paris, 1909; by the same author: *Le royaume de Bourgogne*, quoted above, and *Le royaume de Provence sous les Carolingiens*, Paris, 1901; R. Parisot, *Le royaume de Lorraine sous les Carolingiens*, Paris, 1899; F. L. Ganshof, *La Belgique carolingienne*, Brussels, 1958; R. d'Abadal y de Vignals, *Catalunya Carolingia*, 2 vols., Barcelona, 1926–52; J. Dhondt, *op. cit.*

A one-way trend: the end of unity

On the invasions, especially by the Scandinavians and other northern races, see L. Musset, *Les peuples scandinaves*, Paris, 1951, and *Les invasions* (Collection 'La Nouvelle Clio'), 2 vols., Paris, 1965. On the Moors and their relations with western Europe, the best guide is the work by Lévi-Provençal, quoted above. For the establishment of feudalism, the books already referred to by F. Lot, L. Halphen and F. L. Ganshof are indispensable. See also H. Mitteis, *Lehnrecht und Staatsgewalt*, Weimar, 1933; *Recueils de la Société Jean Bodin*. 1. *Les liens de vassalité et les immunités*, Brussels, 1936; *Settimane di studio sull'alto medio evo*, Spoleto, 1954, and by the suggestive article by J. F. Lemarignier, 'La dislocation du "pagus" et le problème des "consuetudines" (X^e–XIe siècles)', in *Mélanges dédiés à la mémoire de Louis Halphen*, Paris, 1950.

Acknowledgments

I have based my point of view on the critical work devoted to this period by many eminent specialists in learned books and scholarly periodicals. There is not space here to list all those that have been useful to me. I will only say that among many others the most indispensable have been books and articles by Ferdinand Lot and Louis Halphen, who taught me, and by the modern scholar who knows the period best, Professor F.L.Ganshof. The short bibliography gives only a very feeble indication of my debt to these writers, as well as to many others who have made this attempt at a synthesis possible.

I would like to thank Surrey Art Designs, who drew the maps, Miss Naomi Narod and Miss Diana Souhami, who collected the illustrations, and the following sources (the number refers to the page on which the illustration appears): Frontispiece, 11, 14, 15, 33, 67, 94, 104, 162, 163, 170 (bottom), 177, 178, 179, 186, 187, 189, 221, 234–5 Ann Münchow, Aachen; 17, 19, 20, 22, 62, 113, 114, 125, 135, 137, 192, 194 Bibliothèque Nationale, Paris; 27, 167, 224 Giraudon, Paris; 48, 87, 90, 200 (left and right), 201 (left) Archives Nationales, Paris; 58 Hachette, Paris; 59, 101, 158, 218 Stiftsbibliothek, St Gall; 82, 111, 168, 182, 183 André Held, Écublens; 93 Rheinisches Bildarchiv, Cologne; 140 Archives Photographiques, Paris; 146 Réunion des Musées Nationaux, Versailles; 149 Österreichische Nationalbibliothek, Vienna; 159 Schmölz and Ullrich, Cologne; 165 Pierre Artaud and Co., Nantes; 170 (top) Elisabeth Oberrauch, Rome; 171 (top) Fotostampa Sciarri, Cortona; 171 (bottom) Vorarlberger Landesmuseum, Bregenz; 173 (left) Kunsthistorisches Museum, Vienna; 173 (right) Schatzkammer der Residenz, Munich; 174 Germanisches Nationalmuseum, Nuremberg; 175 Pierpont Morgan Library, New York; 185 Hirmer Fotoarchiv, Munich; 190 Universiteits Bibliothek, Utrecht; 191 Bibliothèque Municipale, Épernay; 201 (right) Archives du Haut-Rhin, Colmar; 202 British Museum; 205 Museo Cristiano, Brescia; 227 Stift Kremsmünster.

World University Library

Books published or in preparation

Economics and Social Studies

The World Cities
Peter Hall, *London*

The Economics of Underdeveloped Countries
Jagdish Bhagwati, *MIT*

Development Planning
Jan Tinbergen, *Rotterdam*

Human Communication
J. L. Aranguren, *Madrid*

Education in the Modern World
John Vaizey, *London*

Decisive Forces in World Economics
J. L. Sampedro, *Madrid*

Money
Roger Opie, *Oxford*

Key Issues in Criminology
Roger Hood, *Durham*

Society and Population
E. A. Wrigley, *Cambridge*

History

The Emergence of Greek Democracy
W. G. Forrest, *Oxford*

The Roman Empire
J. P. V. D. Balsdon, *Oxford*

The Scientific Revolution 1500–1700
Hugh Kearney, *Sussex*

Muhammad and the Conquests of Islam
Francesco Gabrieli, *Rome*

The Civilisation of Charlemagne
Jacques Boussard, *Poitiers*

The Crusades
Geo Widengren, *Uppsala*

The Ottoman Empire
Halil Inalcik, *Ankara*

Humanism in the Renaissance
S. Dresden, *Leyden*

The Rise of Toleration
Henry Kamen, *Warwick*

The Dutch Republic
Charles Wilson, *Cambridge*

The Left in Europe
David Caute, *Oxford*

The Rise of the Working Class
Jürgen Kuczynski, *Berlin*

Chinese Communism
Robert C. North, *Stanford*

The Medieval Italian Republics
Daniel Waley, *London*

The Culture of Japan
Mifune Okumura, *Kyoto*

The History of Persia
Jean Aubin, *Paris*

Language and Literature

French Literature
Raymond Picard, *Paris*

Russian Writers and Society
Ronald Hingley, *Oxford*

Satire
Matthew Hodgart, *Sussex*

The Romantic Century
Robert Baldick, *Oxford*

The Arts

The Language of Modern Art
Ulf Linde, *Stockholm*

DUE